W9-AQL-095

Twayne's United States Authors Series

EDITOR OF THIS VOLUME

Warren French

Indiana University

Philip Roth

TUSAS 318

PHILIP ROTH

By BERNARD F. RODGERS, JR.

Chicago City-Wide College
City Colleges of Chicago

TWAYNE PUBLISHERS
A DIVISION OF G. K. HALL & CO., BOSTON

12/1978
Am. Lit. Cont

Copyright © 1978 by G. K. Hall & Co.

Published in 1978 by Twayne Publishers,
A Division of G. K. Hall & Co.
All Rights Reserved

Printed on permanent/durable acid-free paper and bound
in the United States of America

First Printing

Frontispiece photo of Philip Roth copyright Nancy Crampton

PS
3568
0855
Z88

Library of Congress Cataloging in Publication Data

Rodgers, Bernard F   1947-
Philip Roth.

(Twayne's United States authors series; TUSAS 318)
Bibliography: p. 181-87
Includes index.
1.   Roth, Philip—Criticism and interpretation.
PS3568.0855Z88   813'.5'4   78-17105
ISBN 0-8057-7249-9

Contents

About the Author

Bernard F. Rodgers, Jr., was born in Pennsylvania and raised in Dunellen, New Jersey. A graduate of Mount Saint Mary's College (Md.) and the University of Bridgeport, he received his Ph.D. from the University of Chicago in 1975. Since then, he has taught English and humanities with the Chicago City-Wide College, one of the City Colleges of Chicago. He has also lectured on American literature with the University of Chicago's Extension Division and the Chicago Public Library's Writing in Chicago Program, and served as producer of the University of Chicago's daily television program, *Perspectives.*

He is the author of *Philip Roth: A Bibliography* (1974) and of essays and reviews on modern American literature which have appeared in the *Chicago Tribune, Chicago Review, Critique: Studies in Modern Fiction*, and *The Fitzgerald/Hemingway Annual.* He is currently editing *Contemporaries: An Anthology of Chicago Fiction.*

Preface

The giants of the first half of this century are dead. In their places the critic of contemporary American fiction finds a bewildering plethora of highly individual artists employing widely varying techniques with equally varying success. One measure of the critic's dilemma is that though most of us would have little difficulty drawing up a laundry list of twenty living American fictionists "worthy" of serious study, few of us could reach agreement on a shorter list of the four or five "best." Virtually every month, it seems, a new book is published which forces us to conclude that the reports of the death of the novel, like those of Mark Twain's premature demise, have been greatly exaggerated. At the same time, increasingly vocal and vehement demands for racial, ethnic, and sexual identity have exposed the stew in the American melting pot and wrought havoc on the once-fixed canon of American literature.

Faced with this combination of diversity and militancy, the overwhelmed critic's response is, all too often, to classify writers with vaguely similar concerns, techniques, or backgrounds into broad categories, and then to gloss over the differences within those categories. American fiction dissolves into Jewish-American, Afro-American, Native-American, Chicano, Feminist, and Gay fiction—hyphenation replaces investigation.

Philip Roth has been both a beneficiary and a victim of this critical tendency. The vogue of the Jewish-American writer in the late Fifties certainly contributed to the initial reception of *Goodbye, Columbus* (1959). And, almost overnight, on the basis of this slim volume of five stories and a novella he found himself lionized and categorized as the third term in what quickly became a popular critical entity: Bellow-Malamud-Roth.

He has been paying ever since for that early fame.

For so much of the commentary on his fiction has continued to be preoccupied with determining the nature and extent of his relationship to Jewish-American religious and literary traditions that other elements in his work, which are just as important, have been consistently ignored or obscured. This ethnic emphasis has combined with a continuing critical bias which views humor—especially in its coarse-grained, "native American" manifestations—as somehow "subliterary" to make extensive examination of the bulk of his fiction incredibly scarce. Not only has most Roth criticism focused on *Goodbye, Columbus, Letting Go* (1962), and *Portnoy's Complaint* (1969)—at least partially because these are the novels most amenable to such an ethnic approach—but even analyses of *these* books seldom go far beyond discussions of their Jewish dimensions. The remainder of Roth's work—the larger part which includes *When She Was Good* (1967), *Our Gang* (1971), *The Breast* (1972), *The Great American Novel* (1973), *My Life as a Man* (1974), and his most recent novel, *The Professor of Desire* (1977)—is frequently dismissed, when it is discussed at all, as either repetitive or as a series of artistic aberrations, regrettable self-indulgences distinguished solely by their author's enormous inventive talent.

When his fiction is viewed from such an ethnic perspective, it is almost inevitable that the critic will conclude with Wilfred Sheed that Roth must be faulted for his "vagrant choice of subjects." For the implication behind Sheed's judgment—a common one in Roth criticism—is that only when Roth writes fiction which is definably "Jewish" is he *not* vagrant in his choice of materials. But since Irving Howe seems to be right in observing (in *World of Our Fathers*) that "among the more consequential American Jewish writers" Roth is the "first for whom the Jewish tradition [yields] little...sustenance," the effect of this common opinion is to squeeze Roth between a rock and a very hard place: he is damned when he does treat "Jewish" subjects *and* damned—worse, ignored—when he doesn't.

Though Roth's work has most certainly varied in quality and importance, it seems to me that any critical approach which forces us to dismiss fully half of his work out of hand must be suspect. And the ethnic approach to Roth's fiction seems especially inadequate for several other reasons as well.

From the start, Roth has been more adamant than most of his fellows in his rejection of the limitations imposed by the label "Jewish writer." "I do not write Jewish books," he told an Israeli audience in 1963; "I am not a Jewish writer; I am a writer who is a Jew. The biggest concern and passion in my life is to write fiction, not to be a Jew."[1] While there is much that may be classified as

"Jewish" in his fiction, there is also much—more—that is not. And overemphasis on the ethnic dimensions of some of his characters and themes has effectively precluded thorough examination of the artistic roots which better explain the logic of his fictional development since *Goodbye, Columbus*. Thus, though his ties to other Jewish-American writers have been studied *ad nauseam*, the connections between his fiction and that of F. Scott Fitzgerald, Henry James, Theodore Dreiser, the nineteenth-century native American humorists, and Franz Kafka have been left largely unexplored. Finally, the emphasis on Roth's Jewishness is unfortunate because it has worked to isolate him from his non-Jewish contemporaries. Whereas if he is viewed as an American realist who has attempted to expand and adapt the realistic mode to deal with his own concerns and the social and literary exigencies of contemporary culture, the evolution of his fiction can serve to illuminate the impulses behind the direction the writing of many others has taken during the last twenty years.

In the first critical study of Roth's work, *The Fiction of Philip Roth* (Haddonfield, N. J., 1974), John Nobel McDaniel documented the extent to which extraliterary emphases have dominated discussion of Roth's fiction, and then shifted the emphasis to Roth's art. He concluded that "we can best assess Roth's artistry by viewing him, rather broadly, as a writer whose artistic intentions are 'moral,' whose method is realistic, and whose subject is the self in society" (p. 202). His conclusion is my starting point.

My purpose has been to explore *how*, and perhaps more importantly *why*, Roth has constantly experimented with various fictional techniques within the realistic mode in his efforts to convey his perceptions of the moral consequences faced by men and women acting in contemporary American society. It seems to me, as it did to McDaniel, that *as an artist* Roth has placed his faith in Realism, not Judaism. And, that from the wider perspective available when the ethnic emphasis is set aside for a while, Roth's career is not marked by a vagrant choice of subjects but by a single-minded dedication to a significant goal: finding subjects and techniques which will reveal the effect of the interpenetration of reality and fantasy in the lives of his representative Americans. This concern is what makes an aesthetically coherent whole of his otherwise diverse fictions and supplies the developmental logic which his critics have so often failed to discern.

Of course, Roth has not been alone in his obsession with the reality/fantasy dichotomy. As Tony Tanner, Raymond Olderman, and many others have pointed out—usually by quoting Roth's "Writing American Fiction"—concern with this dichotomy has been an underlying theme and driving force behind much of the best contemporary American fiction. But every writer begins his artistic journey bearing the baggage of his own background and viewpoint; each must travel his own road. And though he may eventually converge with others on the same thematic plain, it is his particular journey, his own peculiar path from the fictions of yesterday to those of tomorrow, which makes a good writer interesting and worthy of critical examination. In the pages that follow, I have attempted to map Roth's artistic odyssey from his earliest college stories to *The Professor of Desire.*

He once commented that "the fantasy that the writer spins out attaches to the reality and one's fiction changes as the fantasy changes" (SD, p. 75). Without insisting on an over-schematization which would ignore the obvious fact that few writers progress in clearly separable or mutually exclusive steps, I submit that Roth's fiction has so far gone through three distinct phases in an attempt to keep pace with the reality its author has seen. These phases are roughly chronological and may be differentiated by their dominant technical strategies. The first phase, discussed in Chapters 1 through 5, encompasses *Goodbye, Columbus, Letting Go, When She Was Good,* and the short fiction published between 1959 and 1966 and is firmly grounded in the models, tenets, and restraints of traditional realism with a moral emphasis. In the books discussed in Chapters 6 through 9—*Portnoy's Complaint, Our Gang,* and *The Great American Novel*—Roth employed wilder comic techniques which echo the raucous and ribald qualities of nineteenth-century native American humor. Most recently, in *The Breast,* "Looking at Kafka," *My Life as a Man,* and *The Professor of Desire* (Chapters 10 through 13), he has attempted to synthesize the techniques of the earlier phases in Kafkaesque tales which vividly convey the confluence of the real and the fantastic in the quotidian.

Through studies of the matter and manner of the major novels and stories he has written during the last twenty years, through interpretation of the extensive comments he has made about his work and that of others, I have attempted to show that, in its progress through these three phases, Roth's path has been both consciously and conscientiously chosen.

BERNARD F. RODGERS, JR.

Acknowledgments

This study, like its companion *Philip Roth: A Bibliography*, was begun while I was a graduate student at the University of Chicago. While there, I had the good fortune to work with Walter Blair, Hamlin Hill, and James E. Miller, Jr.—a good fortune that can only be fully appreciated by those who have shared it. Like Bernard Kaliss, John Williams, and James Light before them, each of these teachers contributed to whatever is most worthwhile in what follows through his criticism, his encouragement, and his example.

Since 1973, Philip Roth has answered all of my inquiries and requests with a graciousness and good humor that far exceed anything I might reasonably have expected. I am grateful to him for his consideration, and for his permission to quote all of the material in the following pages to which he holds the copyrights. All parenthetical references to Roth's books are to the Houghton Mifflin edition of *Goodbye, Columbus* (1959); the Random House editions of *Letting Go* (1962), *When She Was Good* (1967), *Portnoy's Complaint* (1969) and *Our Gang* (1971); the Holt, Rinehart and Winston editions of *The Breast* (1972), *The Great American Novel* (1973), and *My Life as a Man* (1974); and the Farrar, Straus Giroux editions of *Reading Myself and Others* (1975) and *The Professor of Desire* (1977). Portions of this study have appeared in slightly different forms in *Chicago Review* and *Critique: Studies in Modern Fiction*.

The Department of English of the University of Chicago and the Ford Foundation provided grants which helped to finance my writing and research during the early stages; the Writing in Chicago Program, funded by the National Endowment for the Humanities and the Chicago Public Library, provided office space and other assistance during the preparation of the final draft.

My friend and colleague Gus Kolich, now of Pennsylvania State University, was a part of this project from the beginning. Almost everything included here benefited at one time or another from his patient, thoughtful, and sensitive comments over a number of years, and I am grateful.

This book is dedicated to my parents, Bernard and Anna Gulla Rodgers, for all they have given and continue to give; and to Patti, for all the rest.

Chronology

1933   Philip Roth born on March 19 to Herman and Bess (Finkel) Roth.

1946–
1950   Attends Weequahic High School, Newark.

1950–
1951   Attends Newark College, Rutgers University.

1951–
1954   Attends Bucknell University. B. A. in English, *magna cum laude*; Phi Beta Kappa. First story, "Philosophy, Or Something Like That," published in Bucknell literary magazine, *Et Cetera* (1952), which he helped found and edited.

1955   M. A. in English, University of Chicago. Enlists in the army; discharged within a year due to a back injury suffered in basic training.

1956–
1958   Ph.D. candidate (1956–1957) and Instructor, University of Chicago. "The Contest for Aaron Gold" chosen one of *The Best Short Stories of 1956*. Reviews TV and films for *New Republic*.

1959   Marries Margaret Martinson Williams, February 22. *Goodbye, Columbus* published. Houghton Mifflin Literary Fellowship; National Institute of Arts and Letters Grant; Guggenheim Fellowship. *Goodbye, Columbus* awarded the Jewish Book Council's Daroff Award; *Paris Review's* Aga Khan Award for "Epstein"; "The Conversion of the Jews" chosen one of *The Best Stories of 1959*.

1960   National Book Award for *Goodbye, Columbus*. "Defender of the Faith" included in both *The Best Short Stories of 1960* and *The O. Henry Prize Stories of 1960*. Joins the faculty of the Iowa Writers Workshop.

1961   "Writing American Fiction."

1962   *Letting Go*. Writer-in-residence, Princeton University. Ford Foundation grant in playwrighting.

1963   Legally separated from Margaret Martinson Roth, March 1.

1964   "Novotny's Pain" among *The O. Henry Prize Stories 1964*.

1965 Begins teaching one semester each year at the University of Pennsylvania.

1967 *When She Was Good*; "Jewish Patient Begins His Analysis" and "Whacking Off."

1968 Margaret Martinson Roth killed in an automobile accident in Central Park, May 19.

1969 *Portnoy's Complaint.* Paramount film of *Goodbye, Columbus.*

1970 Elected to the National Institute of Arts and Letters. "On the Air."

1971 *Our Gang.* A dramatic adaptation of "Epstein," "Defender of the Faith," and "Eli, the Fanatic" by Larry Arrick, titled *Unlikely Heroes*, opens in New York.

1972 *The Breast.* Visits Prague, Czechoslovakia, and Kafka's gravesite. Warner Brothers film of *Portnoy's Complaint.*

1973 *The Great American Novel* and " 'I Always Wanted You to Admire My Fasting'; or Looking at Kafka."

1974 *My Life as a Man.*

1975 *Reading Myself and Others.* General Editor of the "Writers from the Other Europe" series for Penguin Books.

1976 "In Search of Kafka and Other Answers."

1977 *The Professor of Desire.*

CHAPTER 1

The Feel of This Cockeyed World

A S the applause began to die out, the dark-haired young man in the conservative business suit adjusted his horn-rimmed glasses and prepared to address the crowded auditorium. His audience had gathered at the Stanford University campus on this foggy Friday night to attend the second session of *Esquire*'s 1960 symposium on "Writing in America Today." The previous evening they had heard John Cheever bemoan the "abrasive and faulty surface of the United States in the last twenty-five years"; at the third session James Baldwin would describe them as a part of an "incoherent people in an incoherent country."[1] Tonight they were here to learn what the much-publicized literary *wunderkind* who now stood before them would have to add to the gloomy portrait his compatriots were sketching.

A few of his listeners were aware of the details of his remarkably brief apprenticeship: that he had graduated from Bucknell University in 1954 after publishing his first fictions and satires in the college literary magazine, *Et Cetera*, which he had helped found and had edited; that a year later his story "The Contest for Aaron Gold" had appeared in *Epoch* and had then been chosen one of *The Best Short Stories of 1956*; that by his twenty-sixth birthday in March of 1959 his fiction, satire, and reviews had already appeared in *Paris Review*, *Chicago Review*, the *New Yorker*, the *New Republic*, *Commentary*, and *Esquire*; that by the end of that year he had received more accolades than most writers receive in a lifetime. Most of them knew that his first book had been both a critical and popular success and had, just six months before this October evening in Palo Alto, been chosen for the National Book Award for Fiction. As he began to speak it was quickly apparent to all of them that his talents as a monologist and critic were a match for his fictive precocity.

The address young Philip Roth delivered to that symposium was later published in *Commentary* as "Writing American Fiction" (1961), and in the interim it has become one of the staples of criticism of the contemporary American novel. While it is frequently quoted to help explain the fiction of his fellows, however, its centrality to the development of his own work from *Goodbye, Columbus* to *The Professor of Desire* is usually underestimated or misunderstood. Too many critics have simply echoed Stanley Edgar Hyman's early assessment of the article as an overpraised young upstart's willful attack on his literary elders and betters. But rereading the essay and Roth's reply to letters about it suggests a contrary view: although he did criticize some aspects of some of his elders' works, the tone of the piece was sympathetic, not condemnatory; *de*scriptive, not *pre*scriptive. His purpose was to describe the hurdles in the path of the serious contemporary American realist—to outline a cultural and artistic dilemma which he saw as both general and personal. In the process he provided an invaluable introduction to the premises which have prompted the technical experimentation which has marked the evolution of his own fiction.

The essay makes the personal nature of the problem quite clear. Roth cites Harvey Swados's description of the emergence of a new prose style among many Jewish writers—"a nervous muscular prose...a kind of prose-poetry that...is risky writing"—as an introduction to his own discussion of Bellow, Malamud, and Herbert Gold.[2] What Roth does not point out—and this is crucial to an understanding of the essay's personal element—is that Swados had singled out *Goodbye, Columbus* as one of the best examples of the prose style he was trying to define.[3] When Roth begins his analysis by saying that "it is in its very riskiness that we can discover some kind of explanation for" this writing, then, his explanation is as relevant to his own artistic problems as it is to Bellow's or Gold's. "The writer pushes before our eyes," he wrote, "it is in the very ordering of our sentences—personality in all its separateness and specialness." And his use of "our" and "the writer" was clearly meant to include himself.

He further underlined the personal ramifications of his critical judgments when he explained, in a letter replying to comments about the essay, that his purpose had been to "make some suggestions as to how and why it [dramatizing contemporary reality in credible fictions] is arduous today, and particularly so for the writer whose concerns are social and whose talent and instinct lead him to write in the mode of realism.... I intended to examine the relationship between our experience and our art, and perhaps to come up with some reasons to explain the discomfort many writers feel—myself included—with realism, and with satire too, where one ends up doing less than one intended."[5]

"Writing American Fiction" begins with an exemplary tale designed to suggest why it is so difficult to create credible fictions in the realistic mode out of contemporary American experience. A description of the actual disappearance and murder of two teenage sisters in Chicago, which focuses on both the grotesque events themselves and the grotesque media machinations that surrounded them, Roth's story of the Grimes girls is a classic illustration of the vision and techniques we have since come to ascribe to "black humor." The moral of his tale, he wrote in the essay's most frequently quoted passage, was that faced with real events like these, "the American writer in the middle of the 20th century has his hands full in trying to understand, describe, and then make *credible* much of American reality. It stupefies, it sickens, it infuriates, and finally it is even a kind of embarassment to one's own meagre imagination. The actuality is continually outdoing our talents, and the culture tosses up figures almost daily that are the envy of any novelist.... The daily newspapers fill us with wonder and awe (is it happening? is it possible?)" (RM, pp. 120–21). But, he went on, since it is "the tug of reality, its mystery and magnetism which leads one into the writing of fiction," how can the writer respond when reality no longer mystifies but stupefies, no longer draws but repels? When reality itself becomes unreal and actuality becomes *in*credible—when words alone seem incapable of expressing the full weight of the paradox—what will be the realist's subject? his landscape?

Surveying the recent writing of the best of his contemporaries to find the answers to his questions, Roth came to the conclusion that they seemed to have been driven to relinquishing the portrayal of contemporary reality to the writers of superficial palliative fiction, "the *amor-vincit-omnia* boys." They seemed to him to have retreated—into timeless worlds of fable (Malamud), into mysticism (Salinger), into politics and nonfiction (Mailer), into unearned affirmations (Bellow and Gold)—into strategies of ignoring social realities and celebrating or examining the self in isolation.

Roth's observations, however, were not a derogation of the artistic ability of writers whom he had always admired but a comment on the nature of an American reality which was capable of engendering such widespread avoidance reactions in its best artists. The most important aspect of the essay, in terms of Roth's work, is that it shows that while he was clearly committed to the goal of capturing contemporary social realities in his own fiction the recent work of his contemporaries made him feel that the odds against his succeeding in that mission within the conventions of realism were tremendous.

Several months after "Writing American Fiction" was published, he suggested just how he saw his task in an interview which appeared in *Mademoiselle.* His concern, he said then, was with "exploring the social being's private life. Our world is cockeyed; okay. Now what does it *feel* like to have it cockeyed? How human or inhuman does that cockeyedness make me?" (August 1961, p. 255). In other words, though he too would be concerned with exploring the self, he would also try to portray the effect of the fantastic nature of contemporary reality on that self's private life. Though the emphasis in his work has, as John Nobel McDaniel has pointed out, sometimes fallen on the private life and sometimes on the public, *both* have always been central to his fictive vision. In essence, Roth has sought from the outset of his career to write the kind of novel which Raymond Williams has described as characteristic of the best of the realistic tradition: "the kind of novel which creates and judges the quality of a whole way of life in terms of the qualities of persons. Neither element, neither the society nor the individual is there as a priority. The society is not a background against which the personal relationships are studied, nor are the individuals merely illustrations of aspects of the way of life. Every aspect of the personal life is radically affected by the quality of the general life, yet the general life is seen at its most important in completely personal terms."[6] In his best work—"Goodbye, Columbus," "Defender of the Faith," "Eli, the Fanatic," *Letting Go, When She Was Good, Portnoy's Complaint,* "Looking at Kafka," *My Life as a Man,* and *The Professor of Desire*—Roth has come very close to achieving this ideal balance. In fact, the revelation of a society and its individuals which Williams described in *Partisan Review* was spectacularly realized in Roth's first book, which appeared in the bookstores just as Williams's essay was published.

CHAPTER 2

People in Trouble (Five Stories)

I N *Goodbye, Columbus* (1959), a first book written according to
the dictum that the aspiring author should begin by writing
about the people and places he knows best, Roth is already preoccupied with the central conflicts in American life as they are experienced in the everyday lives of his Jewish characters. These conflicts
are economic, psychological, and generational, as well as religious,
and they repeatedly point to the underlying incongruity between
ethical ideals and material realities in American culture. Like
Portnoy's Complaint, Goodbye, Columbus is one of Roth's two
most popular, and most identifiably Jewish, books. It is important
to recognize, however, that even in this earliest work Jewishness is
used in the stories not to universalize, as in Malamud's fiction, but
to particularize: to make universal conflicts more specific—"of a
time, a place, a group of people, a situation"—and thus more
realistic.[1]

"The pressures of personal history and literary idealism that
cause a first book to be written are like none the writer is ever to
experience again," Roth has noted. "The example of the great
writers will never be stronger (for both good and bad) and, at the
same time, his own forest of memory, fantasy, and obsession will
never again be so vast or so virginal"(RM, p. 172).

A mix of memory and invention, these first stories drew upon the
Jewish milieu of his Newark boyhood for their content and the
realists he admired for their form.

His literary education at Bucknell (1951–54) and the University
of Chicago (1954–57) had encouraged him, he tells us, to judge
"fiction writing to be something like a religious calling, and literature a kind of sacrament." And he chose the realistic short story as
his form because, at the time that he was writing them on Drexel
Avenue in Chicago, he felt it was "the genre which constituted the

19

most thoroughgoing investigation of conscience available" (RM, p. 77). Like Peter Tarnopol, his fictional persona in *My Life as a Man,* young Roth was dedicated to creating "art of the earnest moral variety"; like Tarnopol's persona, Nathan Zuckerman, Roth sought to emulate the serious moral commitment of Henry James, Joseph Conrad, and the masters of European realism. The more immediate models for his first fictions, however, seem to have been provided by the writing of F. Scott Fitzgerald and the Jewish authors who had begun to achieve prominence at the time Roth began writing: J. D. Salinger, Bernard Malamud, and America's own European master, Saul Bellow.

Roth and his publisher were apparently aware that this early work varied widely in quality since they arranged the five stories in the collection so that earlier stories alternated with more mature ones, just as first-person narratives alternate with stories told in the third person. The most effective means of tracing Roth's rapid artistic maturation within the covers of this first book, therefore, is to look at the stories in the chronological order of their original publication (and probable composition), rather than in the order in which they appear in the book.[2]

Like most of the stories "Phil" Roth wrote for Bucknell University's *Et Cetera*—stories like "Philosophy, Or Something Like That," "The Box of Truths," "The Fence," "Armando and the Fraud"—the earliest stories in *Goodbye, Columbus,* "You Can't Tell a Man by the Song He Sings" and "The Conversion of the Jews," exhibit an obvious debt to the undergraduate literary hero of the Fifties, J. D. Salinger.[3] In spite of Roth's early objections to the comparison, all of these stories now seem Salingeresque in their use of sensitive adolescent protagonists who are forced to encounter the imperfectibility of the world, their self-consciously ironic narrative voices, their accurate transcription of adolescent dialogue, and their firm grasp of adolescent psychology.

"You Can't Tell a Man by the Song He Sings" is universally, and legitimately, regarded as the least significant story in the collection. One reviewer summarized the majority opinion by describing its inclusion as "unaccountable." Though it is a notch above the *Et Cetera* stories, which it resembles more than it does any of the other stories in *Goodbye, Columbus,* it is finally not so much a "story" as an anecdote with a politically fashionable anti-McCarthy moral. It does capture the feel of high-school life like some of John Updike's short fiction, especially in its portrait of one of those stereotypical "delinquents" who have been revived lately as the heroes of numerous nostalgic books, movies, and television shows. But its primary value to the reader who would study Roth's work is in the artistic distance it indicates Roth traveled in the very short time between its composition and that of the other stories in the collection.

"The Conversion of the Jews," on the other hand, rises above its considerable weaknesses—narrative coyness, straining for effect, rather superficial use of symbolic nomenclature and description—because it vividly depicts a fundamental clash of generations and values and metaphorically presents the attitudes which impelled the satire underlying the rest of the stories in the book.

Rabbi Binder's doctrinal explanations about the impossibility of an Immaculate Conception are not really the story's plot issue. His reaction to a student who would question those explanations is. Young Ozzie Freedman's crime—one for which he is humiliated and physically chastised by both his mother and his teacher—is, at least at first, simply that he questions the disparity he sees between what adults say and what they mean. Like Cynthia Reganhart's in *Letting Go,* Ozzie's child's sense of the literal meaning of words confuses and frustrates him when he must confront a world where those words have lost their meanings through equivocation. When Rabbi Binder announces that the floor of his Hebrew class is open to "free discussion," for example, Ozzie makes the mistake of thinking that the rabbi means *literally* "free" and acts accordingly." How can the Jews be "The Chosen People," he asks, when the Declaration of Independence proclaims that in America "all men are created equal"? Why do his relatives only seem to consider a plane crash a "tragedy" if there are Jews among its victims? If God could create everything from nothing in six days, then "why couldn't He let a woman have a baby without intercourse" if He wanted to? If he is supposed to be learning to "read" Hebrew, why won't Rabbi Binder allow him enough time to comprehend the meaning of the words?

The perversity of the young soon combines with the officious inflexibility of the old to escalate their confrontation according to an all-too-familiar pattern. Ozzie's initial questions are met with patient explanation; when the explanations do not satisfy him, Binder becomes impatient, falls back on his position of authority, and demands unthinking acquiescence; when Ozzie persists, Binder classifies him as a troublemaker whose aim is to disrupt and under-

mine the discipline of the class; finally the rabbi demands that
Ozzie *obey* out of respect even if he cannot understand, insists on
an apology, and humiliates Ozzie in front of his peers. Ozzie rebels.

The pattern is repeated in countless classrooms each minute of
every school day, and the conflict is only exacerbated by both the
gap in generations which places all of the power in the hands of the
insecure adult and the fact that, as a religious teacher, Rabbi
Binder interprets Ozzie's intractability as an attack on dogma.

It is not surprising, then, that when Rabbi Binder orders Ozzie to
descend from the synagogue roof to which the boy has fled in
panic, his commands are characterized as those of "a dictator, but
one—the eyes confessed it all—whose personal valet had spit neatly
in his face" (p. 148). Or that Ozzie, both confused and exhilarated
by the shouts of his peers and the power he feels over the adults on
the ground below, takes advantage of the situation *literally* to bring
his oppressors to their knees. Since this particular conflict occurs
within the context of religious instruction, rather than in a secular
classroom, Ozzie's choice of revenge—his "conversion of the
Jews" around him to a verbal expression of religious tolerance—is
a justifiable outgrowth of all that has come before, a farcical poetic
justice.

The story also functions as an effective metaphor for the pressures of the Jewish community which combined with the self-
righteousness of its young author to prompt the satiric thrust of
Goodbye, Columbus itself. Rabbi Binder, Mrs. Freedman, and
Yakov Blotnik personify all that Roth was determined to reject in
the attitudes of the Jewish environment which had surrounded him
for the first eighteen years of his life; and Ozzie Freedman's adolescent revolt against their xenophobia and closed-mindedness, their
constant concern for "what-is-good-for-the-Jews," reflects Roth's
own artistic revolt.

Though the story's denouement strains the reader's credulity, we
are forced to recognize that similar incidents, theoretically just as
"incredible," occur all the time. Only the slightest imaginative
pressure is required to push much of everyday reality into the realm
of farce, as Roth does here and as he has repeatedly done in his subsequent comic fiction. The strangeness Ozzie feels as he observes
himself, his friends, and the adults on the ground below him is one
which the daily newspapers and television news reports have indeed
made familiar to all of us; and one which paves the way for Roth's
comments in "Writing American Fiction." "Is it me? . . . Is it us?"

Ozzie asks (p. 156). And those questions, first posed by a frightened child on a synagogue roof, reverberate through all of Roth's work.

"My fiction is about people in trouble," he told an interviewer shortly after *Goodbye, Columbus* received the National Book Award.[4] "I seem to be interested," he said later, "in how—and why and when—a man acts counter to his 'best self,' or what others assume it to be, or would like it to be" (RM, p. 152). The crises of identity which such questions naturally precipitate link the three stories and the novella which round out his first collection and are fundamental to all his later work as well.

In contrast to the satiric vitriol which permeates the humor of "The Conversion of the Jews" and the other stories in *Goodbye, Columbus,* "Epstein" blends humor, pathos, and satire with an obviously warm affection for its central character and his plight. Duty, responsibility, guilt, hidden desires—all of the conflicting imperatives which form the characteristic tensions underlying Roth's fictions first appear in this early story. And here, for the first time, he seized upon sexual behavior as both a physical manifestation of his hero's psychological problems and a comic possibility.

Like Roth's comic novels, which it resembles in tone and texture, "Epstein" grew out of oral sources. Roth has described it as the story in his first book most strongly rooted in the vanishing world of his Newark boyhood, and has explained its genesis by recalling that "I wrote 'Epstein' when I was 24, 10 years after my father had recounted a similar tale of neighborhood adultery during dinner one night (mealtime being Scheherazade-time in our kitchen). At 14, I was delighted to hear that scandalous passion had broken out on our decent, law-abiding little street, but my special pleasure came from the blend of compassion and amusement which entered into the telling of the story. Ten years later, when I set out to transform delicious neighborhood gossip into fiction, I tried as best I could to be faithful to the point of view of the original narrator which seemed to me to be morally astute and in its unself-righteous gaiety endearing. In the writing, of course, I shifted the intestines around in order to get at what I took to be the vital organs, and then, too, tacked on a cardiac seizure to give my fiction the brutal edge that Mr. Reality, for some reason or other, had strangely neglected to impart in this particular instance..." (RM, p. 173).

The story is a tale of a middle-aged man's short-lived affair with the attractive widow across the street. One of the functions of fiction, Roth would say several years after he wrote it, is "to redeem the stereotype and give it its proper weight and balance in the world," and in "Epstein" we find the first of many examples of what he meant (SD, p. 75). Where most people would simply dismiss Lou Epstein as just another victim of "male menopause," in this variation on the legendary situation of the married man who suffers a heart attack *in flagrante delicto* with his mistress, Roth manages to make the cliché come alive.

In "Defender of the Faith" Roth again explores a Jewish hero's crisis of identity, but this time the exploration is quite a bit more serious. The most frequently anthologized of the stories in *Goodbye, Columbus,* it remains the most powerful and most controversial. Alfred Kazin accurately assessed its impact when he observed in *Bright Book of Life* that what distinguishes Roth from many other Jewish novelists is his "toughness": "the power of decision and ability to stand moral isolation that is the subject of his story 'Defender of the Faith' . . . the refusal of a merely sentimental Jewish solidarity."[5] Set in 1945, when the recently discovered details of the Holocaust made the pressures to accept such a solidarity greater than at any previous time in modern history, this story explores one man's refusal to capitulate to those pressures and his decision to follow his heart—a refusal which grows out of his heightened sense of his own human limitations.

The Nathan Marx who introduces himself in the story's opening paragraph is a war-weary veteran, emotionally drained by combat, who has been rotated back to the States after two years in the European theater. He thinks that he has been so hardened by his experiences that he is no longer susceptible to the old sentimental attachments. The story focuses on the external and internal conflicts which gradually force him to recognize that, in fact, he does not have the "infantryman's heart" he thinks he has developed at all, and probably never did.

The catalyst in the process of Marx's self-discovery is Private Sheldon Grossbart who, as his name suggests, crassly attempts to trade on their shared Jewishness in order to gain undeserved favors for himself and his two friends, Fishbein and Halpern. Through this relationship with Grossbart, Marx learns that he is not a man who can accept the merely sentimental Jewish solidarity Kazin describes.

As soon as Grossbart learns that his new sergeant's name is Marx—"Marx, you know, like Karl Marx. The Marx Brothers. Those guys are all—M-A-R-X, isn't that how you spell it, Sergeant?"—he sets out to manipulate him. (Grossbart and his partners often seem cast in the Marx Brothers mold themselves as the story develops.) It is important to note that, from their very first encounter on, Grossbart is repugnant to Marx in almost every way. The first time he meets the private he describes him as "fish-eyed," and he consistently presents Grossbart in the worst possible light; the private's wheedling tones and rhetorical techniques are as transparent to Marx as they are to the reader. Yet as soon as they meet, Marx's hard-boiled facade begins to crack and he finds himself thrust into a succession of new roles dictated by the emotions to which he had thought himself immune.

When Grossbart first appears at his door, Marx finds himself playing the part of a sarcastic non-com, "of Charlie McCarthy, with every top sergeant I had ever known as my Edgar Bergen." Before their first conversation has ended, however, Marx's composure has already been upset by feelings of anger and defensiveness, and he finds himself assigned the new role of fellow Jew by Grossbart. The next morning in Captain Barrett's office he is surprised to find that he has become a "defender of the faith" before his Gentile commanding officer.

Grossbart is able to manipulate Marx into acts of favoritism because, once he has penetrated the emotional walls the sergeant has erected in self-defense, Marx is vulnerable to the very sentimentality to which he had thought himself no longer susceptible. The full extent of Grossbart's success in capitalizing on these emotions (adding a dash of guilt for seasoning whenever necessary) is suggested through a minor grammatical variation with major significance. In their first meeting, Grossbart explains to Marx that he doesn't want to make trouble because "that's the first thing they throw up to you," using the pronoun "you" with its general, impersonal connotations. After he has maneuvered Marx into the role of his accomplice in the garnering of undeserved favors, however, Grossbart says that making trouble is the "first thing they toss up to us"—and by using "us" he implicates Marx personally.

Marx realizes that Grossbart is using him, but the pull of sentiment is so strong once unleashed—and Marx is so desperate for a new sense of identity—that he finds himself justifying his favoritism: "What was I that I had to *muster* generous feelings?

Who was I to have been so grudging, so tight-hearted? After all, I wasn't being asked to move the world. . . . Who was Nathan Marx to be such a pennypincher with kindness?''

But when Marx learns later that Grossbart has used the information he gave him to have his orders changed from an overseas assignment to an assignment in Monmouth, New Jersey—not Fishbein's, not Halpern's, just *his*—he retaliates by using his influence to see that Grossbart will be shipped to the Pacific as originally scheduled.

In doing so, Marx paradoxically becomes a "defender of the faith" again, not against the Gentiles now, but against another Jew. For the first time he comprehends that defending Grossbart's conduct and defending the faith are separate, even contradictory, tasks. "You owe me an explanation," Grossbart insists when he learns what Marx has done. Marx's response is that he did it for "all of *us*." "For all of us," because now Grossbart will continue to watch over Fishbein and Halpern. "For all of us," because Marx now sees that it is through Jews such as Grossbart, and through favoritism like that he himself has been guilty of, that the stereotypes which foster anti-Semitism are reinforced and perpetuated. "For all of us," because Marx has come to understand that though he does not have an infantryman's heart neither can he succumb in conscience to the purely sentimental Jewish solidarity which he has been all too willing to accept. Such an identity as a Jew is not an identity at all—to Marx or to Roth—but an escape from the necessary, and painfully lonely, search for one.

Much here recalls Saul Bellow's *The Victim,* a book for which Roth has repeatedly expressed his admiration. As Helen Weinberg says of Bellow's Asa Leventhal, Nathan Marx is "caught peremptorily and arbitrarily in an imprisoning situation that disrupts his routine life and forces him to re-examine his motives and goals."[6] Both Asa and Nathan have cut themselves off from other people when the action of their respective stories begins, and both are forced to become involved again because of their confrontation with oppressive antagonists. In both stories the central characters come to accept their own human limitations only after they have projected themselves into the thoughts and emotions of their "others." Both reach a crucial understanding of their own complicity, a realization that "I could do what he has done," and come away from the experience with a greater self-awareness and self-acceptance.[7] Both stories challenge stereotypes and clichéd responses to experience; both trace their protagonists' attempts to discover a viable sense of themselves as both men and Jews. It is characteristic of Roth's particular perspective, however, that in his story a Jew is persecuted and hounded for being a Jew not by a Gentile but *by another Jew.*

Like Lou Epstein, Eli, the Fanatic feels trapped by "normality" and suddenly seeks recourse in desperate action designed to give him a more vital sense of identity and purpose. While "Epstein" is a slice of life in which the central character's religious (as opposed to cultural) Judaism plays a relatively peripheral part, however, in Eli's story Judaism and what being a Jew does or should mean in contemporary America are central thematic elements.

Perhaps the single most important cultural phenomenon of the postwar era has been the suburbanization of America, and within the context of the internal conflicts and social pressures which that demographic shift has produced—both for those who left the cities and for those who were left behind—Roth examines the numbing secularism which he sees in contemporary American society. The story examines how this "cockeyed" world feels to Eli Peck, and, in the process, presents a graphic portrait of one suburban community and one of its more sensitive inhabitants.

"Assimilation" is the word inscribed on the invisible banner which hangs over Coach House Road in Woodenton, U.S.A., *circa* 1948—assimilation at any cost. Ethnic and religious identity is the threat which the appearance of a Yeshivah in their midst poses to Woodenton's Jews, and the hope it offers their spokesman, Eli Peck. The Jewish community's complaints and fears are expressed with ever-increasing insistence in the cacophony of voices which swirls about Eli's head throughout the story like Sartre's flies:

"A Yeshivah!" Artie Berg had said. "Eli, in Woodenton, a Yeshivah! If I want to live in Brownsville, Eli, I'll live in Brownsville."
"Eli," Harry Shaw speaking now.... "Eli, when I left the city, Eli, I didn't plan the city should come to me" (pp. 255–56).

These sentiments, however, are more than those of many suburbanites who oppose the introduction of racial busing to achieve integration in their schools, who oppose low-income housing or drug-rehabilitation centers in their communities; more than the second generation's embarrassment at the old ways, customs, and accents of their immigrant parents—although both these attitudes are certainly a part of those sentiments. Ted Heller, the most outspoken of Eli's friends, expresses the deeper fears which prompt the opposition of Woodenton's Jews to the Yeshivah in a passage which appears in the first published version of the story. " 'Look, Eli-pal,' " he says, " 'there's a good healthy relationship in this town because its modern Jews and Protestants. That's the point, isn't it, Eli? Let's not kid each other.... The way things are now are fine—like human beings. There's going to be no pogroms in Woodenton. Right? 'Cause there's no fanatics, no crazy people'—Eli winced—'just people who respect each other and leave each other be. Common sense is the ruling thing, Eli. I'm for common sense. Moderation.' "[8]

"Modern Jews," then, are those who are no different from their Protestant neighbors: "common sense," "moderation," "playing it safe," "fitting in," and "not rocking the boat" are the essence of their new Decalogue, the dogmas of their modern American religion. To Ted Heller and many of his Jewish neighbors, those religious principles seem more a matter of survival than choice after the Holocaust. In anonymity and assimilation, they think, there will be safety.

Eli Peck has attempted to accept the tenets of this modern religion, has tried to be such a modern Jew for quite a while, but not without debilitating effects. In a "wooden town" only wooden men like Ted Heller can be truly content, and Eli is not such a man. In a world supported by the twin pillars of normality and conformity—a world easily metamorphosed into the nightmarish fantasies of control and impotence we find in Ken Kesey's *One Flew Over the Cuckoo's Nest,* Joseph Heller's *Catch-22,* or any of Thomas Pynchon's novels—he remains a man forever tempted to go "beyond the last rope," to cross the thin, ever-shifting, socially defined line between "normalcy" and "neurosis."[9] Twice before the action of the story begins he had crossed that line and "found solace in what his neighbors forgivingly referred to as a 'nervous breakdown' " (p. 254).

In this shadow-world of control and balance inhabited by hollow men, the Yeshivah represents an alternative life totally committed to religious values in spite of derision, prejudice, sacrifice, and persecution. From the story's first pages it is evident that Eli will not be able to conduct dispassionate negotiations with Tzuref and the members of his Yeshivah, that he will be profoundly affected by his contact with those values. The story focuses on how—and why and when—this transformation which seems so inevitable will occur.

Just as "Defender of the Faith" invites comparison with *The Victim*, "Eli, the Fanatic" can be compared and contrasted with another book Roth admires, Bernard Malamud's *The Assistant.* Like *The Assistant*, "Eli, the Fanatic" traces the complex motives involved in its hero's conversion to a species of Judaism. We can as easily say of Malamud's novel, as Roth has of his own story, that it is concerned with "an attempt on the part of the hero to be heroic in a world in which passions, including his own, seem to be diminished; to attempt to be more than he once imagined himself to be." (SD, p. 70). Roth's story differs from Malamud's in its emphasis on the importance of the particular social circumstances within which its hero must act and its underlying pessimism about the efficacy or contemporary viability of its hero's conversion.

Both Frank Alpine and Eli Peck are drawn into relationships which will eventually bring about their conversions because of an emptiness they feel at the center of their lives. Both have a profound, though not totally recognized, need to discover a path to some kind of meaningful action. At first, both are outsiders whose motives are self-serving; both are unable to comprehend the spiritual values which are central to the worlds they enter. Eli can no more understand why the Hasidic Jew cannot afford to give up his old clothes, in spite of the pain and suffering they have brought him, than Frank can understand why Morris Bober cannot afford to give up the grocery store that is his prison. Both men's conversions are delayed by their romantic attachments; both are finally converted, however, and adopt physical signs of the tradition to which they are seeking to attach themselves—Frank, by his circumcision, and Eli, by donning the cast-off religious garments left on his doorstep by the Hasid.

Roth's vision of contemporary American reality makes his story both original and provocative in spite of its use of the conversion motif so common to Jewish fiction. Eli's conversion, unlike Frank Alpine's, is fundamentally no more than a gesture of rebellion comparable to Ozzie Freedman's mounting the synagogue roof. Eli and Ozzie are the first, but not the last, of Roth's "mad crusaders"—characters who flail against the absurdities around them through desperate actions. Eli's promenade down Coach House Road in the Hasid's garb is finally a rather pathetic religious act since clothes *do not* make the man, even if they are clothes with a tradition and a history. The pressures of conformity and con-science whose conflicting demands frustrate Eli's desire for genuine self-assertion *within* the community are never really resolved in the story. They cannot be. Instead they are temporarily assuaged, and Eli's *formal* effort to link himself to a religious tradition which he and his neighbors have long ago spiritually disavowed—like Mrs. Freedman's nostalgic ritualism and Yakov Blotnik's rote prayer—seems finally to be more an act of self-indulgence than self-assertion.

"Eliyousawhim," blurts Ted Heller as the Hasid parades through the neighborhood in the suit Eli has forced on him; and this particular contraction, combined with the insistent repetition of Eli's name throughout the story like an incantation, points to one of "Eli, the Fanatic" 's central ironies. Eli's name means "Lord" in Hebrew, but the details of the story encourage us to see it as a truncated or Americanized version of the Hebrew prophet Elijah's. For his character and actions are an ironic reflection of his biblical namesake's intended to show just how far the decline of heroic action which Roth mentioned in his discussion of the story has progressed in the contemporary world. Elijah's mission was to confront the Israelites when they had forsaken the true God for the secular god, Baal—to show them the true religion through his words and actions. "A fanatic" according to Ted Heller's definition of the term, he was wholly dedicated to the service of his God, and because of his dedication he emerges as one of the great heroes of the Old Testament. When asked to explain his mission by the voice of God on Mt. Horeb, he twice replies that he has come, "Because of my great zeal for the Lord God of Hosts. . . . The people of Israel have forsaken thy covenant, torn down thy altars and put thy prophets to death with the sword. I alone am left, and they seek to take my life" (I Kings, 19:10, 14). He departed from the earth in a chariot of fire, leaving his mantle and continuation of his work to his disciple Elisha.

Eli also feels that he is alone in his dissatisfaction with the con-temporary descendents of Baal, the false gods Mammon and Freud who have usurped the God of Israel's place in the hearts and minds of Woodenton's Jews. He too feels that "they" are trying to take his life away—that his friends, his wife, his psychiatrist are all con-spiring to make him "normal" in spite of his need for something more meaningful than their materialism and psychiatry. But in a world where expressions of religious conviction are condescendingly labeled fanaticism, Eli's attempt at religious witness is, at best, a pale reflection of Elijah's or the Hasid's. Elijah risked his life time and again for his faith; the Hasid also risked his, and lost almost everything—wife, family, homeland, genitals—for his religious convictions. Eli risks *nothing,* loses *nothing.* He is not *allowed* to because in Woodenton his desperate attempt at heroic action becomes a farce destined to be "understood" into meaninglessness.

Eli knows very well—and so should we—that his erratic behavior will simply be passed off as a "temporary setback" and excused by both his wife and his friends as just one more proof of his sensitive and compassionate soul. Dr. Eckman will see to it that he returns to "normal" after a few psychiatric sessions; one of his neighbors, probably Ted Heller, will see to it that the zoning laws are enforced and the Yeshivah is expelled. Unlike Elijah's, Eli's clothes will not be passed on to his disciple: they are ripped off his back and thrown away.

Just as Eli sees himself reflected in the eyes of the Hasidic Jew, the Jews in Woodenton are reflected in the members of the Yeshivah: though the suburbanites now have split-level houses with manicured lawns, they are as much displaced persons as the European interlopers, for their spiritual roots have been torn up and cast aside in their scramble for acceptance. To Roth, Woodenton's Jews are contemporary grotesques who are doomed to spend their lives seeking an identity that will "fit in," continually altering their beliefs to match the current fashions. In the end, like a suit altered too many times to keep up with the latest trends, their religious identity will become a patchwork—a pathetic affair of bits and pieces—religious motley.

Each of these five stories, then, is marked by common technical and thematic considerations. Each grows out of conflicts between conformity and individuality, ethnic solidarity and assimilation, public image and private desires, material success and spiritual failure which, in one way or another, also inform all of Roth's subsequent fiction. Each investigates a morally consequential action undertaken in a recognizable American society which is a redoubtable barrier to such action. In each story a sensitive protagonist attempts to discover and then to assert a valid identity which is at odds with the image both he and others have previously had of him; in each case social pressures make that search more complicated. In none of these stories does Roth examine the self in isolation; in each he manages to convey a sense of the intrusion of the absurd and fantastic into the realistic everyday lives of his characters.

Roth's original style and perspective bring a fresh approach to themes which earlier Jewish writers had already explored, and the essence of his originality lies in his willingness to disappoint the expectations which readers of Jewish fiction had been encouraged to associate with Jewish heroes. In a recent essay entitled "Imagining Jews," Roth attempted to account for the amazing popularity of *Portnoy's Complaint.* He might as easily have been speaking of his earlier heroes when he said that one of the primary things which apparently made Portnoy intriguing to both Jews and Gentiles was that "going wild in public is the last thing that a Jew is expected to do—by himself, by his family, by his fellow Jews, and by the larger community of Christians whose tolerance for him is often tenuous to begin with, and whose code of respectability he flaunts or violates at his own psychological risk, and perhaps at the risk of his fellow Jews' physical and social well-being" (RM, p. 222).

Instead of finding Jewish characters who "go wild" in public—like Ozzie, Epstein, and Eli—readers of Bellow and Malamud had been conditioned (before 1959) to expect that a connection would be made in Jewish fiction between "the Jew and conscience and the Gentile and appetite." According to Roth, they expected the Jewish writer to "associate the sympathetic Jewish hero with ethical Jewhood as opposed to sexual niggerhood, with victimization as opposed to vengeful aggression, with dignified survival rather than euphoric gloating triumph, with sanity and renunciation as opposed to excessive desire . . . except the excessive desire to be good and do good" (RM, p. 229). In Roth's first stories, as in his later fiction, no such simple dichotomies exist. His Jews are as capable of appetite as they are of conscience, capable of "sexual niggerhood," vengeful aggression, euphoric gloating, and other excessive desires *as well as* their opposites. And the struggle between these contradictory impulses is at the base of Roth's Jewish fictions.

While his approach to his characters may have been a radical departure from that of his contemporaries, however, his literary techniques in these early stories were quite traditional. All of the stories are clearly realistic. Though comedy and farce provide some of their brightest moments, the comic impulse is carefully controlled and subordinated to the stories' moral points. If we look closely at the manic scenes which threaten to cross the line between reality and fantasy, it is not very difficult to discern an exuberant and talented young author chafing at the bit but determined to be, above all else, *serious* in his art.

Perhaps too determined. Alfred Kazin, Irving Howe, and Leslie Fiedler all qualified their praises of *Goodbye, Columbus* by faulting its author for a tendency to press his moral points too hard, and they were certainly accurate in their observations. But precisely because some of the stories suffer from that flaw—notably "The Conversion of the Jews," "You Can't Tell a Man by the Song He Sings," and "Eli, the Fanatic"—they make Roth's initial concern with establishing his fiction as both serious and moral that much clearer.

Both the early and the later stories are narrated from the perspective of the hero. Whether the narrative point of view is formally first-person, as it is in "Defender of the Faith" and "You Can't Tell a Man by the Song He Sings," or third-person, as it is in the rest of the stories, makes little practical difference. In each of the stories we learn what reality feels like to the protagonist and are encouraged to see the world as he sees it. And this is an important point to recognize at the outset, since this identification of hero and narrator has been Roth's most characteristic fictive voice from the beginning of his career to the present.

The combination of these themes and techniques with Roth's eye for social style, his ear for the American vernacular, and his grasp of psychological complexities helped to establish what Irving Howe described as "a unique voice, a secure rhythm, a distinctive subject," which made the author of these stories stand out even before they were collected in *Goodbye, Columbus.*

CHAPTER 3

The Disapproving Moralist
and the Libidinous Slob
("Goodbye, Columbus")

I N "Goodbye, Columbus," the brilliant novella which furnished
the title for Roth's first collection, these themes are given their
fullest, most mature, early expression. Neil Klugman's self-
conscious verbal quest for understanding and self-definition
achieves a moral complexity unrivaled by any of the early stories
except "Defender of the Faith." The story's acute social observation, accurate dialogue, minor characterization, and satire have
been so universally lauded that they need not be reexamined here,
but there is no comparable consensus about Neil's character and
motivations.

In general, critics have identified Neil with Roth, assigned his
views and limitations to his creator. To many of them, Neil is an
almost unimpeachable source of moral judgments—an incor-
ruptible young hero who sees, satirizes, and rejects the vacuous phi-
listinism of the Patimkins; a free spirit and artist manqué who
refuses to sell out to their materialism in spite of his love for their
daughter. To others, chiefly Roth's detractors, Neil is a self-
serving, unprincipled hypocrite—a contemporary version of the re-
visionist's Ben Franklin whose rhetoric masks an opportunist's
search for the main chance; a modern Gulliver who casts a misan-
thrope's jaundiced eye on everything and everyone around him
while he pursues Brenda with the fervor of a prospector with a
terminal case of gold fever.

The real Neil would seem to stand somewhere between these
critical poles, and much of the novella's impact grows out of his at-

tempt, in what is essentially an extended monologue, to locate himself along the spectrum between them at any given moment. Part-Grossbart, part-Marx, Neil should not be confused with Philip Roth. Neil's awareness of his own motives, unlike Nathan Marx's, is never fully equal to his creator's, for the ingenuous questions he poses at the end of his narrative have already been carefully answered in the story itself. Completely accepting Neil's version of events, then, is misleading; instead we must read between the lines, noticing what he does not say as well as what he does in order to draw essential conclusions and implications.

Roth wrote in the *New York Review of Books* that the conflict in *Portnoy's Complaint*—another novel cast as an extended monologue—stems from the fact that in Portnoy "the disapproving moralist who says 'I am horrified' will not disappear when the libidinous slob shows up screaming 'I want!' " (RM, p. 243). The same contradiction lies at the heart, and can be heard in the narrative voice, of "Goodbye, Columbus." And this split in Neil's character would seem to be responsible, in large part, for the wide divergence of critical reaction to him and his story.

The libidinous and acquisitive part of Neil sees Brenda and the affluent suburban world she inhabits, transforms them into a Polynesian maiden dwelling in an exotic American Tahiti, camouflages itself under the guise of love, and cries, "I want!" At the same time the disapproving moralist in him sees a spoiled little rich girl, a family of Brobdingnags living in a world of conformity and expedience, and decorously protests, "I am horrified." This internal struggle—and Neil's hazy awareness that he has been more willing than he would like to admit to heed the acquisitive cry and ignore the horrified whisper—is what gives his retrospective narrative its bitter, misanthropic tone. Like Portnoy, he seeks revenge and vents his frustration through verbal abuse; unlike his liberated successor, however, he is denied the outlet of obscenity and must settle for a more restrained mode of satiric attack.

This conflict within Neil (and so within his story) is clearly apparent in the novella's opening pages, in three of its crucial incidents, and in its suggestive and multi-faceted title.

The story's first pages establish "Goodbye, Columbus" 's characters in a textbook display of modern narrative technique at its best. In the first paragraph alone, Roth suggests the social and psychological gulf which separates the lovers and dooms the summer romance whose beginnings it recounts, introduces the mirror/glass imagery so appropriate to a struggle for identity, and implies the bias of his storyteller. "The first time I saw Brenda," Neil begins,

she asked me to hold her glasses. Then she stepped out to the edge of the diving board and looked foggily into the pool; it could have been drained, myopic Brenda would never have known it. She dove beautifully, and a moment later she was swimming back to the side of the pool, her head of short-clipped auburn hair held up, straight ahead of her, as though it were a rose on a long stem. She glided to the edge and then was beside me. "Thank you," she said, her eyes watery though not from the water. She extended her hand for her glasses but did not put them on until she turned and headed away. I watched her move off. Her hands suddenly appeared behind her. She caught the bottom of her suit between the thumb and index finger and flicked what flesh had been showing back where it belonged. My blood jumped.

That night, before dinner, I called her (p. 3).

Both their personalities are intimated here: her self-assurance, vanity, controlled impulsiveness, and careless sensuality; his cautiousness, subservience, desire, and bitterness. Neil seems to be presenting a careful physical description of their first meeting here—in a style reminiscent of the romantic fiction in popular women's magazines—but Roth is doing much more. Their accidental meeting, and the service he renders to Brenda, lead us to expect that Neil's story will have a plot drawn from Horatio Alger. One in which a contemporary Jewish Ragged Dick will, through pluck and luck, eventually achieve his just desserts: the rich girl and all that comes with her. Those expectations are aroused only to be disappointed. Though the clause which closes the second sentence is ostensibly just a part of Neil's physical description, it—and especially the phrase "myopic Brenda"—seems as much epithet as description, as much expletive as adjective, a gratuitous slap which betrays the thinly veiled petulance of the disappointed suitor that will color the whole of Neil's narrative.

At the same time, these initial images of Brenda's weak eyesight provide an important clue to her character by suggesting that her vision and understanding of their relationship will be limited and lacking in foresight. The rose simile also does double duty, as both a description of her beauty of the kind we would expect to find in a romantic tale, and as an indication of the thorny dilemma she will pose for Neil. In a second reading of the story additional ironies become apparent in light of Neil's subsequent behavior. Though the story begins with the assertion that he "saw" Brenda, he does not really see her here at all. In fact, the outstanding feature of their relationship is his refusal to view her or his feelings about her honestly from the start. Thus while he has plenty of foresight himself—too much—he too displays evidence of a kind of myopia.

What Neil never fully acknowledges, although he realizes it momentarily in Saint Patrick's Cathedral, is that Brenda is both a person and a symbol to him. She has no life in the novella except as a projection of his desires and fears. Without being fully conscious of it—even in retrospect as he tries to sort out their affair—he sublimates his immediate dislike for her as a person in the interest of his quest for the American Dream of money, status, and Edenic satiety which she and her family personify. To capture that dream, he must capture the girl; losing her, he loses his piece of the dream. While Neil never appreciates the crucial distinction between loving and wanting Brenda and loving and wanting what she represents, Roth tries to make sure that the reader will.

Neil's first date with Brenda in Short Hills—an affluent New Jersey suburb which he describes as one hundred and eighty feet closer to heaven than his native Newark—is a rendezvous with both a girl and a ticket to affluence. He quickly loses sight of the difference in the first flush of his excitement and desire. They have not spoken ten sentences to one another when Neil perceives that "Brenda reminded me of the pug-nosed bastards from Montclair who come down to the library during vacations, and while I stamp out their books, they stand around tugging their elephantine scarves until they hang to their ankles, hinting all the while at 'Boston' and 'New Haven' " (p. 11).

He will be provided with abundant evidence as the summer progresses which should confirm this impression: Brenda *is* just like those girls. But he ignores this uncomfortable realization, both at this point and later, because when he holds her for the first time he feels a "faint fluttering" beneath her shoulder blades, "like the fluttering of wings, tiny wings no bigger than her breasts. The smallness of the wings did not bother me—it would not take an eagle to carry me up those lousy hundred and eighty feet that make summer nights so much cooler in Short Hills than they are in Newark" (p. 14).

From this point on he devotes himself to wooing and winning her and programmatically refuses to see either the flaws in her character or the ambiguities in his own motives until he is in too deep, until he has convinced himself that Brenda is different from those other girls—that he loves *her* and not the opportunities she can provide for him. He creates a fiction of love with her encouragement and complicity, and then mistakes it for reality. He forgets his own early observation that "actually we did not have the feelings we said we had until we spoke them—at least I didn't; to phrase them was to invent them and own them. We whipped our strangeness into a froth that resembled love, and we dared not play too long with it, talk too much of it, or it would flatten and fizzle away" (p. 29).

In his headlong rush to satisfy the "I want!" within, Neil ignores numerous warnings posted along his path, just as Epstein did before him. He knows now that "right from the start Brenda was a practical girl." Too practical to sacrifice her comfort and security for a penniless librarian should she ever have to choose between them; but also practical enough to use him as a weapon in her Oedipal war of nerves with her mother. Though two weeks pass before she asks him anything about himself, and then she is only interested in his "prospects," he overlooks her selfishness too. Roth even provides Neil (and the reader) with Julie—"just like her sister," a miniature Brenda without her older sister's sexual appeal and social veneer—but Neil does not draw the inevitable conclusions about the weaknesses in Brenda's spoiled character which will never allow her to love him completely.

Neil's visit to a suburban deer park offers an effective paradigm of his behavior throughout the novella. Thinking about the women who have brought their children there to play, some of them high-school classmates of his turned housewives, Neil sees their station wagons, their chic clothes and hair-styles, and imagines that "they were the goddesses, and if I were Paris I could not have been able to choose among them, so microscopic were the differences. Their fates had collapsed into one. Only Brenda shone. Money and comfort would not erase her singleness—they hadn't yet, or had they? What was I loving, I wondered, and since I am not one to stick scalpels into myself, I wiggled my hand in the fence and allowed a tiny-nosed buck to lick my thoughts away" (p. 96). He lets Brenda do the same thing. "Tiny-nosed" after her plastic surgery, nicknamed "Buck" by her father, he allows her to stop him from thinking clearly and honestly by accepting the sex and pleasure she proffers. If he did let himself think about what he was loving—not *who* but *what*—the disapproving moralist in him would indeed wield a scalpel and condemn him for his venality. That is exactly what happens in Saint Patrick's Cathedral.

Neil sees himself no more clearly than he sees Brenda. Apparently unaware of what the description tells us about the darker side of his motives, he characterizes making love to Brenda (after being denied victory over Julie at Ping-Pong) as "so sweet, as though I'd finally scored the twenty-first point" (p. 46). Like Portnoy, his penis can conquer—at least temporarily—territories which he will never be allowed to occupy permanently. Looking back on his actions, Neil still doesn't fully comprehend that he too has been practical and pragmatic from the start. When he tells Brenda that "I'm—I'm not a planner . . . I'm a liver," he momentarily recognizes the duplicity implied by his hesitation, noting that "after all the truth I'd suddenly given her, I shouldn't have ruined it for myself with that final lie" (p. 61). But he suppresses that kind of recognition throughout much of his narrative. His cautiousness and practicality are constantly revealed nonetheless: in his qualms about taking a drink while "babysitting" for Julie; in his conversation with the Negro boy about the book of Gaugin prints; in the fact that, while trying to be what Brenda and her family want him to be, he retains his position at the library just in case things don't work out in Short Hills. And it is his subconscious recognition of this need to play it safe which is turned outward into his vehement attacks on both the Patimkins and his fellow employees. Unable completely to accept being a part of either group, unwilling to make a final choice, he keeps one foot in each camp and scoffs at both.

The conflicts introduced in the opening pages and elaborated through character descriptions like these are most forcefully dramatized in three crucial episodes: Neil's proposal that Brenda get a diaphragm, his reverie in Saint Patrick's Cathedral while she is picking it up at the doctor's office, and the novella's final scene.

Neil's demand that Brenda buy a diaphragm just before she returns to Radcliffe is probably the most significant expression of the dynamics of their relationship in the novella. Throughout the affair, Neil is painfully aware of the precariousness of his position, the tenuous hold he has on Brenda and all she represents. During their evening at the pool early in the story, for example, he thinks that he has lost her three separate times ("I was sure that when I left the water Brenda would be gone"; "I worried once again that if I stayed away too long she would not be there when I returned";

"it seemed as though she would never come back"). Like
Grossbart, Neil is not averse to using manipulative strategies and
sentiment to solidify his position. Brenda has said that, as far as
their future is concerned, "when you love me there'll be nothing to
worry about." So, worried that he will lose her, "when Brenda
finally returned to me I would not let her go.... 'That's it, Brenda.
Please no more games,' I said, and then when I spoke I held her so
tightly I almost dug my body into hers, 'I love you,' I said, 'I
do' "(p. 53).

Once we recognize his sense of insecurity, we should not be surprised at the panic which seizes him when the summer draws to a
close. With Brenda's departure only a few days away, he
desperately searches for a new strategy to bind her to him, just as at
the pool he had wished that he had taken her glasses so that she
could not leave without him. Since he is afraid that it may be too
soon to elicit a positive response to a proposal of marriage—he is a
young man afraid to open a bottle to get a drink—he proposes
instead that she buy a diaphragm. The prophylaxis he seeks is not
sexual, however, but emotional. He wants some kind of commitment, an admission of the long-term prospects of their relationship, a precaution against Brenda's forgetting him when she returns
to Boston—a tie that will not break in spite of distance and time. It
is exactly this kind of commitment, this assignment of serious consequences to their summer romances, that Brenda is reluctant to
acknowledge in the following exchange:

"I just don't feel *old* enough for all that equipment."
"What does age have to do with it?"
"I don't mean age. I just mean—well, *me*. I mean it's so conscious a
thing to do."
"Of course, it's conscious. That's exactly it. Don't you see? It wouldn't
change us."
"It would change me."
"Us. Together" (p. 82).

She eventually capitulates, and three days before Ron's wedding
(four before her return to school), they go to New York City to get
the diaphragm. While Brenda visits the doctor's office, Neil walks
into Saint Patrick's Cathedral and sees himself honestly, though
briefly, for the first time since their affair began. Leaning forward
against the pew in front of him, he recalls, "I began to make a little
speech to myself.... God, I said, I am twenty-three years old. I

want to make the best of things. Now the doctor is about to wed Brenda to me, and I am not entirely certain that this is all for the best. What is it I love, Lord? Why have I chosen? Who is Brenda? The race is to the swift. Should I have stopped to think?''

''I was getting no answers,'' he tells us, but he went on with his ''prayer'': ''If we meet You at all, God, it's that we're carnal, and acquisitive, and thereby partake of You. I am carnal, and I know that You approve, I just know it. But how carnal can you get? I am acquisitive. Where do I turn now in my acquisitiveness? Where do we meet? Which prize is You?'' Recognizing that ''it was an ingenious meditation,'' Neil felt ashamed and walked outside, where the noise of Fifth Avenue met him with an answer: ''Which prize do you think, schmuck? Gold dinnerware, sporting-goods trees, nectarines, garbage disposals, bumpless noses, Patimkin Sink, Bonwit Teller—But damn it, God, that *is* You!'' And ''God only laughed, that clown'' (p. 100).

His blasphemous and self-serving casuistry cannot hide his real motives. It embarrasses him instead, and he experiences the shock of recognition which he has been trying to avoid from the beginning of their relationship. When Brenda appears across the street, ''like a woman window-shopping,'' for a moment he is glad ''that in the end she had disobeyed my desire. As she crossed the street though, that little levity passed, and''—in an ironic echo of A. E. Housman's famous line—''I was myself again'' (p. 101). The acquisitive self lusting after the good life and willing to do almost anything to get it.

At the wedding two days later, he does not object when Leo Patimkin, Ben's unsuccessful brother, tells him that he has ''a good deal'' in Brenda. Or when he says that ''you'll go far. You're a smart boy, you'll play it safe. Don't louse things up'' (p. 117). Nor does he demur when Ben says that ''whatever my Buck wants is good enough for me. There's no business too big it can't use another head'' (p. 108). Neil's lack of narrative comment here is significant because his silence suggests that he has accepted his true desires to be those revealed to him on Fifth Avenue. When he first met Brenda, we remember, he felt that ''she had made a promise to me about the summer and, I hoped, beyond'' (p. 17). The family's treatment of him at the wedding leads him to believe that that promise will be kept. Later, as he bullies and blackmails his boss into granting him time off for Rosh Hashanah, he thinks that ''perhaps I was more of a businessman than I thought. Maybe I could learn to be a Patimkin with ease" (p. 120). Not a Leo Patimkin, however, who seems an unsuccessful reincarnation of Lou Epstein, but a Ben—or a Ron.

Shortly after Brenda returns to school in Boston, Neil calls her dormitory and learns that she is out and is not expected back until late that evening. (He suspects that she has a date.) Not long afterward, he is on a bus to Boston and Brenda, and, *as he arrives,* he decides that he has come to ask her to marry him. "It had been long enough," he thinks. "It was time to stop kidding around" (p. 126). Of course, Neil has *not* been kidding around; he has been serious about their affair from the beginning. Now he feels his hold on Brenda rapidly weakening and he is forced to take a chance and act decisively.

But it is too late.

Like Grossbart's, Neil's strategies have backfired. The diaphragm which he cajoled Brenda into buying—and which they only used together once, with less than satisfactory results—proves to be his nemesis, not his protector. Brenda left it at home. Her parents found it and realized the nature of the liaison between their daughter and their houseguest. When Neil perceives the inevitable dissolution of their affair which will follow that discovery, all of the insecurities and resentments which he has attempted to ignore flood to the surface in a stream of charges. His anger is not just directed at Brenda's carelessness; deep down he realizes that if agreeing to get the diaphragm was an expression of commitment on her part, leaving it at home was a rejection of that same commitment. Brenda sees the spite which has been an integral part of their affair and defends herself with countercharges. Forced to choose between Neil and her family, she makes the only choice her pampered nature allows her to make: she rejects him. He does *not,* as most critics suggest, reject her.

The text is really very clear on this point. Brenda *chooses* to go home for Thanksgiving without Neil because continuing their relationship would undermine her secure relations with her family. In trying to prove that the choice is Neil's, even as perceptive a reader as Dan Isaacs becomes trapped into twisting the meaning of these crucial scenes through a fascinating display of text-juggling and psychologizing. "Neil," he writes, "refuses to pay the price. He will not sacrifice his integrity for a comfortable position in the Patimkin household, even if it means losing Brenda ... twice he tells himself and the reader that he is on the verge of proposing marriage. But each time he substitutes a provocative act for what would have been a reassuring one."[1] But there is no evidence in the story to suggest that Neil *considers* asking Brenda to buy the diaphragm a provocative act—he considers it less provocative, safer than proposing marriage. In the hotel room things are *already* out of his control; there is absolutely nothing he could possibly do to erase her parents' hostility toward him—and that is exactly why he is so angry.

His hopes shattered, Neil passes Lamont Library and sees his reflection in the glass front of the building:

Suddenly, I wanted to set down my suitcase and pick up a rock and heave it through the glass, but of course I didn't. I simply looked at myself in the mirror the light made of the window. I was only that substance, I thought, those limbs, that face that I saw in front of me. I looked, but the outside of me gave up little information about the inside of me. I wished I could scoot around to the other side of the window, faster than light or sound or Herb Clark on Homecoming Day, to get behind that image and catch whatever it was that looked through those eyes. What was it inside of me that had turned pursuit and clutching into love, and then turned it inside out again? What was it that had turned winning into losing, and losing—who knows—into winning? I was sure I had loved Brenda, though standing there, I knew I couldn't any longer. And I knew that it would be a long while before I made love to anyone the way I had made love to her. With anyone else, could I summon up such passion? Whatever spawned my love for her, had that spawned such lust too? If she had only been slightly *not* Brenda . . . but then would I have loved her?" (pp. 135–36).

We have come full circle: from "the first time I saw Brenda" and images of her flawed vision, to intimations of the "first time I saw myself" and a hero confused by his reflection in the glass. Though Neil is too close, too emotionally involved to answer his own questions immediately, the answers lie in his narrative. We see that pursuit and clutching were turned into love by a conscience that would not allow him to chase wealth *per se;* that he *had* loved Brenda—wanted, needed, desired her—*first,* as a personification of his Dream, and *then* as a person. At the end of their affair he is still unable—perhaps unwilling—to accept that fact and what it implies.

His final ruminations remind us of Nick Carraway's observation about Jay Gatsby: "He talked a lot about the past, and I gathered that he wanted to recover something, some idea of himself perhaps, that had gone into loving Daisy. His life had been confused and disordered since then, but if he could return to a certain starting place and go over it all slowly, he could find out what that thing was. . . ."[2] Neil's narrative, begun at the "certain starting place" of the pool, seems an effort to make just this kind of sense out of his affair with Brenda. His life has been confused and disordered since—perhaps because he has been unable to face the fact that, like Gatsby, he had been willing to put himself in the "service of a vast, vulgar, and meretricious beauty."

It is probably inevitable that echoes of Fitzgerald's masterpiece should be heard in any tale about a poor boy's hopeless infatuation with both a woman and a Dream—especially when that infatuation is linked to an American epoch as it is in "Goodbye, Columbus." Brenda is Neil's Daisy, his "beautiful little fool." Just as Daisy inspired Gatsby's transcendent vision in Louisville, Brenda inspires Neil's vision of soaring over Newark to Short Hills and happiness; but by linking their dreams to Brenda and Daisy both Neil and Gatsby doom these dreams to destruction. This is so because, like Jordan Baker, Daisy, and Tom Buchanan, Brenda is one of the careless people who "smashed up things and creatures and then retreated back into their money or their vast carelessness . . . and let other people clean up the mess they made." Both Neil and Gatsby aspire to women who are above them and who are presented as *incapable* of sacrificing their comfortable lifestyles for their lovers because of their pampered natures. Like Gatsby, Neil expects his beautiful little fool to be better than she is.

Each of the dreamers brings about his own downfall by insisting that his lover make a choice. Neil insists that Brenda get the diaphragm as a form of commitment, just as Gatsby demands that Daisy deny her love for Tom at the Plaza Hotel. Both demands, intended to cement their respective relationships, cause them to crumble irreparably.

Yet important as these parallels are between the stories, the differences are more revealing about Roth's own voice and vision. He chooses to have Neil tell his own story, to be both the Nick Carraway and the James Gatz of his tale, both narrator and hero of his own romantic quest. The difference, of course, is crucial. For where Nick is "inclined to reserve all judgments," Neil is not. And in the place of Gatsby's "romantic readiness" and "extraordinary gift for hope," we find Neil's cautiousness.

By collapsing the separation Fitzgerald struggled to establish between his hero and his narrator, Roth freed himself to employ his characteristic means of introducing ambiguity and depth into his fiction: presenting the story from the perspective of the protagonist and thereby demanding that the reader participate in the narrator's confusion of fiction and reality.

The title of "Goodbye, Columbus" is open to a multiplicity of interpretations relating to both the novella and the collection as a whole. It has been viewed as indicative of a farewell to a past deeply rooted in ethnic culture, to the American Dream of equal opportunity, and to the infinite promise of an unspoiled continent; as representative of a nostalgic longing for a time and place of glory and conquest that is felt by both Neil and Ron, for the sexuality which made Neil a Columbus of the sensual, and as a foreshadowing of the story's ending where love becomes renunciation and loss; as a symbol of the effects of Americanization on second-generation immigrant families. To John Noble McDaniel, the combination of Neil's surname, which he interprets to mean "sadfellow" in Yiddish, and the refrain "Goodbye, Columbus," suggests the Jewish immigrant's curse on the unkept promises of the New World: *A klug zu Columbusn* ("Woe to Columbus").[3] While all these readings are suggestive, several more come to mind in light of our view of the novella.

Though McDaniel interprets Neil's last name to mean "sadfellow," for example, if the *u* in Klugman in pronounced long rather than short in Yiddish, it means "cleverfellow." Joseph Landis has used this ambiguity very effectively as a characterization of Roth's authorial perspective, but it also reflects the split in Neil's character as we have observed it: a split between the disapproving moralist and the acquisitive self.[4] The fundamental point about Neil's character is that, though he is saddened and repulsed by the flaws in the world around him, he is still clever enough to adopt roles and employ strategies designed to guarantee himself entry into its upper reaches.

The title also seems to imply a renunciation of self-deception, of Neil's image of himself as an altruistic explorer of a new world. Like the historical Columbus's—not the folkloric hero's but the actual man's—Neil's motives are split between idealism and materialism, between the search for a New Eden of love and abundance and the search for personal wealth and glory. While Columbus succeeded, discovered, and claimed his New World in October 1492, October brings the end of Neil's chance to find and settle his. He is left, instead, with a new, less heroic, less Columbian, vision of himself: a vision which first appeared in Saint Patrick's Cathedral, and which his questions at the end of the novella suggest he may soon be forced to understand and accept.

The title also reminds us of both the conclusion of Fitzgerald's novel—where the vision of the "fresh, green breast of a new world" gives way to waste and the dissolution of wonder; where we, like Nick, Gatsby, and Neil, are described as beating on "boats against the current, borne back ceaselessly into the past"—and of the contrasting ending of Saul Bellow's *The Adventures of Augie March*. Bellow's novel closes with Augie the yea-sayer grappling with life with both hands. "Look at me, going everywhere!" Augie declaims. "Why I am a sort of Columbus of those near-at-hand and believe you can come to them in this immediate *terra incognita* that spreads out in every gaze. I may well flop at this line of endeavor. Columbus too thought he was a flop, probably, when they sent him back in chains. Which didn't prove there was no America."[5]

But this kind of indefatigable optimism, this affirmation in the face of absurdity, is not possible for Neil. He cannot understand himself, much less the *terra incognita* which is Brenda. He does not have Augie's power to laugh at both himself and the world around him, nor does he have the strength of character which allows Bellow's hero to cut the ties that would bind him, to triumph over the temptations placed in his path to a "fate good enough" and a better world. Neil is no more Columbus than Eli Peck is Elijah. He does not continue to explore once he has failed in his first voyage out into the rough seas of the *terra incognita;* he retreats back into the reference section of the Newark Public Library, to a secure berth, and is "back in plenty of time for work." Unlike Augie unlike Columbus, Neil seems doomed to live the conventional life he loathes—one which will inevitably bring him increased frustration and bitterness—because he does not have the strength to break free and explore the unknown depths in himself and others, the strength to let go of his illusions.

CHAPTER 4

Serious in the Fifties (Letting Go)

IN "Imagining Jews" Roth wrote of Bellow's *The Victim* that: "To be Jewish in this novel is to be accessible, morbidly so, to claims made upon the conscience, and to take upon oneself, out of a kind of gruff human sympathy and responsiveness bordering at times on paranoia, responsibility for another man's pain and misfortune" (RM, pp. 224–25). Being human entails the same accessibilities in *Letting Go* (1962).

Roth's first full-length novel and its initial reception furnish a classic example of what is sometimes called the "second-book syndrome." In the author this phenomenon manifests itself in the impulse to top his earlier work, to write something which will be judged "more important" or "more serious" than its predecessor—an impulse which can easily lead to the straining for portentousness signaled by *Letting Go*'s three weighty epigraphs and 630 pages. In the reviewer it appears as a tendency to expect too much or to undervalue the highly touted author's second book in an effort to compensate for any excessive praise which may have been hastily lavished on the first—a tendency which amounts to a literary reflection of the more general media cycle of image-building and destruction. This combination often results in a dearth of serious analysis of the second book, *on its own terms,* until years after its initial publication when the overall shape of the writer's work has become clearer and the fires of literary politics have had time to cool. This phenomenon so clearly marked most of the reviews of *Letting Go* that, six months after it appeared in 1962, Richard Rand felt justified in observing in the *New Republic* that "the real issues in *Letting Go*—what literary effects has the author sought? what literary traditions is he working with? how richly does he realize their possibilities?—have yet to be seriously considered, which to my mind is unfortunate, because I found *Letting*

Go, next to *Pale Fire,* the most interesting novel of the year.''[1]

We can begin to answer Rand's first question if we recognize that Roth had almost completed *Letting Go* when he delivered the speech at Stanford that was to become the essay "Writing American Fiction.''[2] The novel may be viewed as an effort to grapple with the representational challenges he had outlined in his speech—an effort, that is, to capture the quality of contemporary American social reality and its effect on the individual in a credible fiction written in the realistic mode.

Like "Goodbye, Columbus,'' *Letting Go* is a novel of initiation and education. While it exhibits the same mastery of American vernacular, social detail, and characterization which his critics had admired in *Goodbye, Columbus,* however, Roth's novel is a much more difficult, much more complex work than his relatively slight collection. The tendency toward facile polarization of language and character which too frequently marred his early stories—a willingness to rely too heavily on sharp contrasts between the superior sensibilities of his struggling heroes and the inflexibility of the self-satisfied characters who surrounded them which inevitably pushed those stories into the realm of caricature and farce—is all but abandoned in *Letting Go.* Though social satire is still a prominent element in Roth's art, strict moral schematization is replaced in this novel by an acceptance of the centrality of accident and ambiguity to the realistic depiction of contemporary life. The novel, unlike the stories, is far too complex to allow the comforts of easily distilled moral judgments or clearly defined heroes and villains. Instead, it presents a world as cluttered by seemingly inconsequential action and trivial incident, as unpredictable and defiant of simple definition, as the real world it so accurately reflects; and peoples it with characters as caught up in the web of conflicting moral demands, as frustrated by their inability to make reality conform to their aspirations, as are many of its readers.

Roth titled the original manuscript he submitted to Random House "Debts and Sorrows,'' and he apparently considered that title so expressive of the book's central concerns that he retained it for the first section of the published version.[3] In fact, that title suggests the thematic foundations upon which he constructed his long, Jamesian analysis of conscience and illusion. "Debts'' conveys the nature of the troublesome moral choices, complicated by the conflict between duty and personal desires for self-satisfaction, which weigh heavily on the consciences of each of the novel's major characters. "Sorrows" suggests what the results of both attempting to pay *and* attempting to escape those debts will bring in this book. It also captures the outstanding quality of the lives of quiet and not-so-quiet desperation led by its characters—lives which, though no literary grammar would classify them as "Tragic" according to the Aristotelian rubrics, are nevertheless "tragic" in the more general sense of that term. To be trapped by one's own weaknesses and fears into a bad, mutually destructive marriage is, in this sense, "tragic"; to abdicate resonsibility for one's child in an effort to find personal happiness, and then to lose that child to accidental death is, in this sense, "tragic"; to waste one's life away in youth-ful romantic dreams of a miraculously better, nonexistent tomor-row is, in this sense, "tragic"; and in this sense of "tragedy" as a story of heroes and heroines who, as Richard Chase has argued, exhibit some "blindness to reality, a distortion of awareness, that puts [them]at the mercy of the perverse and self-destructive inner motives struggling in [them]for the upper hand," *Letting Go* is a contemporary tragedy.[4]

Alfred Kazin pointed to the root cause of most of the tragedy and sorrow in the book when he said in his review that Roth's primary concern in *Letting Go* "is with the pretentiousness, strain, and cruelty of people trying to live by unfulfillable notions of them-selves. The best things in this book invariably revolve around the fictions, the impossibly total satisfactions that people insist on, that people kill themselves to get. Human beings do not let go, they do not ride with the flow of existence; they try to plan and to corrupt and to scheme and to browbeat life into an order that is only a cry in their minds."[5]

The same concern is central to all of Roth's major work. Neil Klugman, Gabe Wallach, Paul and Libby Herz, Martha Reganhart, Lucy Nelson, Alex Portnoy, David Kepesh, Nathan Zuckerman, Peter Tarnopol—the names of his heroes and heroines form a neurotic honor roll of men and women trying to live by just such unfulfillable notions of themselves and others, just such useless fic-tions. In each of his novels Roth attempts to trace the sources of those personal fictions in the experiences of his characters, and in each he catalogues the toll in pain and heartache which those char-acters extract from themselves and those around them in their efforts to make their fictions real. The voices change, the central concerns remain the same.

The variation of this story that *Letting Go* tells focuses on four people—Gabe Wallach, Paul and Libby Herz, and Martha Reganhart—and on their relationships with one another, with their parents, and with their children. Central to each of these relationships are the character's personal fictions and illusions. The novel recounts the causes and consequences of those fictions, as well as the events which finally disabuse the characters of them and bring them to the "disillusioned and profoundly realistic perception about [themselves] and [their] situation" that Chase calls "tragic recognition."

Gabe, who narrates about half of the novel, is a rich young assimilated Jew from Manhattan, the son of a prosperous dentist, a graduate of the University of Iowa and professor of English at the University of Chicago. The central element in his character is an internal conflict which he attributes to the influence of the contrary personalities of his mother and father. He tells us early in his narrative that, as a child, "I was pulled and tugged between these two somewhat terrorized people—a woman who gripped at life with taste and reason and a powerful self-control, and a man who preferred the strange forces to grip him" (p. 45). Gabe is, to his and our chagrin, very much his mother's son. Like her, he tries to maintain his self-control in every situation, to remain aloof from the strange forces. Like her, though he thinks of himself as "Very Decent to People" he actually violates others constantly by both consciously and unconsciously manipulating them for his own purposes. While he is not alone in his manipulation of others—all of the characters are guilty of the same failing at times—we are most conscious of his transgressions because we are able to see his motives most clearly.

He begins by telling us that after reading his mother's deathbed confession to a lifetime of pushing and pulling others for her own ends, "I promised myself that I would do no violence to human life, not to another's, and not to my own" (p. 3). That is Gabe's fiction. By the end of the novel he has been emotionally bludgeoned into the shattering realization that, in spite of his promise, he has interfered in the lives of others time and again with consistently disastrous results.

Gabe is far from a sympathetic character; Joseph Heller's Bob Slocum aside, there are few *less* sympathetic narrators in contemporary fiction. He is self-centered, self-pitying, self-deceiving, self-important, sarcastic, and superior; and our appreciation of his weaknesses is intensified by the fact that we see into his thoughts and recognize the mixed nature of his motives. Roth wastes little time in making those weaknesses clear, and he structures the novel's incidents so that they are repeatedly highlighted. From the first pages of the book, almost every relationship Gabe begins, almost every action he takes, can be viewed as the result of ulterior or selfish motives, a product of his instinct for self-protection.

Fleeing his father's demands for love and comfort, for instance, he goes to graduate school in Iowa because "three weeks with a drowning roommate had been all that I could bear" (p. 19). Lonely in that alien environment, he makes overtures of friendship to Paul Herz, the most harried of his fellow students—and presses a copy of *The Portrait of a Lady* on him to cement the relationship—primarily because "I was about ready to find someone to complain to" (p. 4). Rebuffed in his attempts to gain Herz's friendship, he casually begins an affair with Marge Howells, a girl "in revolt against Kenosha, Wisconsin." Though he realizes from the outset that their liaison has no future, he allows the affair to continue because he is "as week in the face of loneliness as in the face of pleasure." When he does end the affair, he uses a visit to his father as an excuse to escape her demands, telling her to be out of his apartment when he returns. When he gets back and finds no trace of her, however, he fears that she has done something "foolish," so he rushes to the Herzes—ostensibly for information, actually for sympathy. In Paul's absence, he again indulges himself and casualy kisses Libby, thereby fueling her romantic dreams of escape from her predicament which will continue to undermine the stability of her marriage for years afterward.

Later, he is first attracted to Martha Reganhart, a Chicago divorcée with two children, because "I felt in her something solid to which I could anchor my wandering affections" (p. 169). She seems to offer a guarantee against his becoming involved with the Herzes again—with Libby—should they come to Chicago and the university. His relationship with Martha takes a serious turn when Gabe again goes to New York for Thanksgiving and learns of his father's plans to remarry. Upset by the news—Oedipus is as much a part of his narrative as Narcissus—he escapes to the hallway where he finds himself dialing Martha's number in Chicago on impulse. Then, again to escape the engagement party, he visits the elder Herzes. Both of these actions are prompted not by his concern for others, not by altruism or generosity, but by his desire to escape an uncomfortable situation. When he returns to Chicago, he toys with the idea of running away with Libby, and only after she throws him out of her university office in a fit of hysteria does he begin an affair with Martha instead.

When he and Martha have an argument, he walks out, goes to a faculty Christmas party, and callously flirts with vulnerable Peggy Moberly. He finally halfheartedly proposes marriage to Martha only after he recognizes his desire to seduce the pathetic waitress Theresa Haug, whom he is supposed to be trying to help, and fears what he may do if he does not place barriers around his emotions. When Martha asks him what she should do about her children—a crucial question which is meant to elicit the depth of the commitment he is offering her—he answers her question with another question and refuses to share responsibility for her decision. She lets the children go with her ex-husband, and her son, Markie, subsequently dies accidentally.

After Markie's death, for which Gabe refuses to accept any of the blame, and the consequent break-up of his affair with Martha, Gabe begins negotiations with a man named Bigoness (Theresa Haug's husband) aimed at securing the Herzes' right to a baby they are trying to adopt. (The baby is Theresa's.) But his motives are dominated here by a desire to redeem himself in Martha's eyes—and in his own—to compete with the responsibility and generosity displayed by Martha's other suitor, Sid Jaffe, not by a desire to help the Herzes. As soon as he thinks that he has arranged the adoption, he goes to Martha's new apartment, expecting that she will reward his diligence by going to bed with him again. Finally, as Bigoness again becomes adamant in his refusal to cooperate in the final adoption proceedings, Gabe desperately makes a complete commitment for the first time and follows his impulses. He goes to Bigoness with the Herz baby in the hope that he can settle the adoption problem once and for all; instead, he almost loses the Herzes' baby and breaks down emotionally in the middle of Bigoness's living room.

His breakdown is, in one sense at least, a positive sign—a momentary victory over his maternally inherited reserve and discretion, a Reichian destruction of the armor of the self. At the same time, it is but another example of his using others to satisfy needs in himself. It leaves him with a profound realization of the "selfishness of his own generosity," and allows him to begin to let go of his illusions—to accept, as Paul Engle has noted, that "there is nothing left for him to do but to let go, to get out of the lives of others and try to discover his own life."[6]

Paul, Libby, and Martha, like Gabe, find themselves involved in a variety of emotional relationships whose duties and responsibilities they must struggle to understand and accept. It is their collective misfortune that each of them comes into contact with Gabe at a time when they are especially susceptible to his appeals to their weaknesses. Paul's sense of martyrdom, Libby's romanticism, and Martha's longing for her stolen youth are each encouraged by his influence; and, as a result of the combination of their weaknesses and his, Engle adds, "to each of them he brings a certain grief." By the end of the novel, however, the three of them (Libby less certainly than the others) have learned painful lessons, have matured to the point where they can more fully accept both their own imperfections and the reality of their situations without recourse to the fictions and illusions that have previously ruled their lives. This is not to say that they find happiness, or that the novel ends optimistically, but that, having gained a fuller awareness of themselves and the world, there is at least a slim chance that their futures will be a little less painful than their pasts.

Paul Herz—whose last name means "heart" in Yiddish—is Gabe's opposite in most ways. The contrast between them, which Roth underlines by showing their different reactions in parallel situations and by his juxtaposition of scenes and centers of consciousness, is one of the novel's primary principles of coherence. Gabe is rich, Paul is poor; Gabe's father is a success who smothers his son with affection and money, Paul's father is a financial failure who leaves his son to his own devices as a child and disowns and exiles him as a man; Gabe breezes through the graduate program at the University of Iowa, Paul never completes the requirements for his degree; Gabe flees serious commitment and responsibility, Paul chooses to embrace it. Where Gabe can discard Marge Howells when he tires of her as easily as she throws away her empty bottles of Breck, and can dismiss her characterization of their affair as "love" without a second thought, once Paul has taken Libby's virginity he feels obligated not only to marry her but to view his feelings of obligation as love. Early in the story Gabe flees to New York and his father to escape his affair with Marge and keep himself free from attachments. When Paul goes home to the city it is to tell his parents that he has decided to accept a permanent attachment and marry Libby. When the conflicts within him seem insurmountable and cause him to have an emotional breakdown, Gabe cuts himself loose and flees to Europe to recuperate; though Paul travels East intending to cut himself loose from Libby and his family, his journey ends with his bonds strengthened and causes him to resign himself to returning to his wife and his commitments in spite of the frustrations he knows will persist.

Just as Gabe's psychological conflicts and behavior grow out of the tensions in his family, Paul's behavior and character are shaped by the tensions in his. His seriousness and desire for professional success are a direct response to his father's financial failures; his decision to marry young, a response to the lack of maturity and direction he sees in his Uncle Asher's life (and the attraction he realizes that life could have for him). The central irony of Paul's story is that in trying to be faithful to the spirit of the religious and familial values that permeated his home and shaped his conscience, he incurs his parents' wrath by marrying Libby, a Gentile. His high ideals are the source of much of his misery and suffering.

His decision to marry, he thinks, was not caused by "anything so simple, so unemotional as obligation," but by the desire to "place a constant demand upon his spirit, solidify his finest intentions by keeping beside him this mixture of frailty, gravity, spontaneity, and passion" (pp. 84–85). His ambition, that is, is to be a *mensch*. But he is innocent of how much such a relationship will sap his strength and oppress his spirit. His Uncle Asher tries to warn him, but his advice is couched in obscenities which alienate Paul and force him to defend the nature of his relationship with Libby. At the outset, Paul feels that "it all seemed so safe. Husband, wage earner, father—right on down the line, all the duties and offices laid out for him. From home to college to wife, no chances taken." Though he also realizes that "if marrying Libby was taking no risks, it was also taking every risk," he—like so many young American males before and after him—sees marriage as the necessary prelude to social confirmation of his coming of age. He is so well programmed that he is as psychologically incapable of accepting an unfettered single life as Gabe is of accepting a committed married one.

The marriage begins inauspiciously and quickly takes a turn for the worse. They are in desperate financial straits when Libby becomes pregnant; and Paul immediately begins to feel that he has lost control of the course of his life. His melancholy disposition leads him to conclude, as soon as they are faced with serious adversity, that his fate is being determined by accident—and that that is "life." After argument and reconciliation, conscience qualms and outside threats from their elderly neighbor, Libby finally has an abortion and their marriage sinks forever into a miasma of guilt and recrimination. Though Libby's health has always been frail, after the abortion she is constantly ill; while Paul knows that her illness is the result of a kidney ailment which predates their marriage, he, nevertheless, feels responsible. His guilt about the abortion combines with his fear of Libby's becoming pregnant again to rob him of his joy in their love-making and eventually he avoids making love to her at all. She feels frustrated, neglected; he feels put upon, trapped. The tension between them is constant. So when Gabe walks into their lives both Paul and Libby cast him in the role of a savior who will whisk Libby away to happiness, and give both of them a chance for a fresh start. But Gabe is unable to fulfill their expectations. Instead, their initial contact with him in Iowa yields only two tangible results, both of which complicate rather than simplify their lives: the kiss which fires Libby's romantic illusions, and Paul's seduction of Marge Howells, which only serves to intensify his guilts and bind him more firmly to Libby.

When Paul and Libby come to Chicago as a result of Gabe's intervention in their behalf their situation has in no way improved. Their problems and frustrations multiply until Paul finally travels East to New York City and decides to leave Libby before the adoption they are considering makes their marriage morally indissoluble to him; his resolution is short-lived, however, and he returns to her. They adopt the child, Rachel, who they hope will bring "joy to their middle years," and Paul turns to religion for solace. When the story ends, their marriage is limping along on the crutches of a shared past neither can escape and a shared sense of obligation to one another and their child that they hope will eventually bring some fulfillment.

Roth's story is clearly Dreiserian in its emphasis on the power of environmental determinism and chance; the atmosphere is claustrophobic, in spite of the fact that the action moves from Iowa to New York to Michigan to Chicago, and spans seven years. Underlying the novel's incidents is an overwhelming sense of entrapment, echoes of doors closing like Hurstwood's safe, never to be reopened. On one level the novel is a brilliantly imagined and documented brief against the false optimism—and its literary manifestations—apparent in a scene which occurs early in the book. Paul and his Uncle Asher stop in a seedy New York bar for a drink. "In the bar, a no man's land where Madison Avenue and the

Bowery met and embraced, a drunken youngster in a tight suit and tight hair had his arm draped around a seventy-year-old alchoholic—somebody's mother. 'Nothing in the world is irretrievable,' said the young man to the old woman, his head lolling down on his shirtfront. 'Nothing. If you'd just go back to County Cork and start all over you'd be amazed—' "(p. 83). *Letting Go* shows that an ordinary life is full of things that *are* irretrievable, that "starting all over again" is impossible—a fiction which can destroy any man or woman who is innocent enough to mistake it for reality. It shows us this by capturing the "felt life" of its characters, and by shaping that life into a profoundly pessimistic and moving vision of the limitations of personal freedom and the inevitability of debts and sorrows that can neither be escaped nor repaid.

The material for this novel grew out of Roth's own experience as a graduate student and instructor in English at the University of Chicago in the Fifties, and that experience was important to *Letting Go*'s Jamesian treatment and characters too. Theodore Solotaroff recalls, in a reminiscence about his friendship with Roth, that their relationship, which began at Chicago, grew out of a shared interest in Henry James and a shared background.[7] Just after *Letting Go* appeared, Roth named James and Tolstoy as writers he admired who had influenced him "a good deal" when he was writing his book because he found at the center of both men's work "a very strong moral concern" with which he identified (SD, p. 75). In his self-interview "Reading Myself" he restates his admiration for them both, and describes reading *The Wings of the Dove* in the University of Chicago Library—"transfixed by James's linguistic tact and moral scrupulosity"—as a kind of paradigm for the effect of his academic experience on his imagination during that period (RM, p. 82).

While traces of Tolstoy are evident in Roth's attention to the differences among classes and his obvious desire to encompass a whole world within his novel—the academic world and the graduate-student life on its fringes—it is the ghost of Henry James which haunts the pages of *Letting Go*. James, whose novels inevitably revolve around questions of manipulation, around what Richard Poirier has described in *The Comic Sense of Henry James* as the "central dilemma" of "who is exploiting the life of another human being"[8]; James whose *The Portrait of a Lady* is invoked in the novel's first pages. And Roth uses obvious and subtle, direct and indirect references to James and the characters and action of the greatest novel of the Master's first phase to establish an effective context for his own examination of the "fine amenities of brave decisions."

Gabe has been described as a "remarkable study in ambiguity," and the ambiguities of his character—and of our reaction to him—can be appreciated more fully if we recognize that he shares character traits associated in *The Portrait of a Lady* with Gilbert Osmond, Ralph Touchett, and Isabel Archer. The several critics who have discussed the relationship between *Letting Go* and James's novel have tended to oversimplify the connections: Paul is Roth's Osmond, they say, Gabe is his Ralph, Libby his Isabel—as if the characters in Roth's novel were merely reflections of those in James's. They are much more complex and original than that, and their complexity suggests the parameters of Roth's achievement.

Gabe is like Osmond in his manipulation of others and in his tendency to take advantage of their weaknesses. But he is also like Ralph in his role of observer of Libby's life and in his acts of generosity—offering his car, getting Paul the job at Chicago, helping the Herzes arrange the adoption—though his selfishness throughout demands that a simple parallel between them be rejected. Ralph is "the most admirably intelligent character" in James's novel, according to Poirier; that is not true of Gabe. Ralph's generosity, and that of his family, is "invariably indirect"; Gabe's generosity is invariably direct and always grows out of mixed motives.

Gabe also shares some of Isabel's less attractive qualities. We recall that Ralph warns Isabel that "you want to see, but not to feel," and the same weakness is fundamental to Gabe's character. He exhibits the same "cold, amoral aloofness, the possibly morbid passion for observing life at a distance" that Richard Chase has noted in Isabel. Like Isabel's, Gabe's life provides an object lesson in the "tragic implications of an idealism that in effect directs one to seek the rewards of the fully 'lived life' without descending from one's high pedestal into its actual conditions."[9] It is as true of Isabel as it is of Gabe that "toward those for whom I felt no strong sentiment, I gravitated; where sentiment existed, I ran" (LG, p. 30). One of Roth's central subjects, like James's in *The Portrait of a Lady,* is his characters' desperate struggles to retain their freedom as they are "gradually, tragically confronted by freedom's restrictions."[10]

If Libby and Gabe share character traits with Isabel Archer, so does Paul. His thoughtful night in Iowa (pp. 154–56) performs the same functions for *Letting Go* that Isabel's vigil in Chapter 42 of *The Portrait of a Lady* performs for that novel. Like Isabel, Paul is trapped into a disastrous marriage by his own ideals and innocence; like her, both Paul and Libby stay married out of a combination of a guilt, duty, fear, and principle.

Letting Go is also like *The Portrait of a Lady* in its use of the private lives of its characters to reflect the character of the society in which they are lived. One of the charges leveled against Roth's novel when it appeared was that it displayed the very flight from social reality which Roth had observed with dismay in the fiction of his contemporaries in "Writing American Fiction." But the frustrations Roth's characters experience are intimately bound up with the era in which they occur and the society which encouraged their false aspirations and illusions. Gabe, Paul, Libby, and Martha are, in a very real sense, representative of the American culture which produced them. All we need do is look around us to verify the accuracy of his insights about marriage, moral responsibilities, debts, and sorrows. In focusing on his characters' private lives, Roth was expressing a perception that is also apparent in *The Portrait of a Lady* and is essential to any attempt at psychological realism in the traditional Jamesian vein. That perception is of a basic fact of everyday existence, one which Joyce Carol Oates expressed in a recent interview by saying that, "One always thinks of a few other people, day after day; there's no escape. A father, a mother, a few beloved people—that is the extent of the universe emotionally. And if something has gone wrong inside this small universe, then nothing can ever be made right."[11]

In spite of its length, Roth's novel, like *The Portrait of a Lady* and James's later work, stands as a coherent whole through its masterful use of changing centers of consciousness and its carefully controlled juxtaposition of scenes. Alfred Kazin and Scott Donaldson have pointed to the principle of coherence in the book. According to Kazin, since Roth's "central subject varies from illusory human hope to the sheer absurdity of social pretense but somehow always presents the same image of a human being reaching for something that is not here, his book is full of different *kinds* of episodes illustrating the vanity of human wishes."[12] Donaldson makes a similar point. "There is too much surface detail here, the critics say, as they have said of American realists since Howells and Dreiser," he writes. "But it is unfair to damn a writer with the tag of superficiality if (1) his exploration of surface matters is not gratuitous but contributory to the progress of the novel, and (2) he doesn't neglect the depths beneath the surface. Almost nothing happens in *Letting Go* that does not work toward the author's goal, which is to explore in depth the kinds of letting go that may take place in the double interaction of self with self and self with society." [13]

If we combine the insights of Kazin's and Donaldson's statements, recognizing that the "progress" of the novel is at its core psychological rather than physical, it can indeed be argued that almost nothing happens in *Letting Go* which does not illuminate or advance the psychological journey of its central characters from innocence to experience and maturity. We forgive the first novelist his weaknesses—an occasionally embarrassing stab at portentousness, several arbitrary shifts in point of view, some excessive repetition, a few characters (like Mr. DeWitt) who are *used* rather than explored, a perceptible drop in interest in the last hundred pages or so—because his book is finally such an impressive achievement in the mode of Jamesian psychological realism in spite of them.

More importantly, we are willing to overlook these weaknesses in retrospect because, like the characters in the novel, we cannot help but conclude the experience of *Letting Go* with a deeper understanding of the uncomfortable truths expressed in those weighty epigraphs. Letting go of our guileless unrealism, our exaggerated expectations of one another, our illusions that we are completely free to shape our lives since "nothing is irretrievable" or irremediable, are not just literary themes—they are the painful experiences by which each of us must make the passage from the fictions of our youth to the realities of our disillusioned adulthood.

CHAPTER 5

In the Middle of America
(When She Was Good)

BY the time that *Letting Go* was published, Roth had already begun working on his next two novels. One he simply described at the time as his "book with no Jews" (SD, p. 61); the other was the Jewish novel which came very close to exhausting the possibilities inherent in that genre. In 1967 the book without Jews was published as *When She Was Good,* judged by many to be a rather self-conscious change of pace, generally found wanting, and consigned to the critical bookshelf reserved for minor works by major writers. The time has come to retrieve Roth's second full-length novel from the obscurity of that shelf, to dust it off and reconsider it in the context of the persistent struggle in his work to find the techniques most expressive of the tenor of contemporary American reality.

The five-year fictional silence which separated *Letting Go* and *When She Was Good*—the longest space between novels in Roth's prolific career—and the thousands of pages of the eight drafts of the latter under various titles which he labored over during those years, would seem to underline the acutely personal nature of the artistic dilemma he had outlined earlier in "Writing American Fiction." He expressed his dissatisfaction with both satire and realism as means to his ends in his reply to letters about that essay; and in both *When She Was Good* and *Portnoy's Complaint* he experimented with alternative forms and techniques which he apparently hoped would be more effective. During this same period, Roth made several statements about the purposes of his art which provide a revealing prelude to analysis of *When She Was Good*—his melodramatic fable of the American character driven mad by single-minded adherence to its own self-righteous fictions.

He spent the time between 1960 and 1962 in the American heartland as a member of the faculty of the Iowa Writers' Workshop; there he completed *Letting Go* and wrote the first draft of his next book, tentatively titled *Time Away.* In 1963 he traveled to Israel to participate in a symposium on Jewish writing sponsored by *Congress Bi-Weekly,* and, in the course of the dialogue, he expressed his views about the social function of fiction by observing that: "I do not think that literature, certainly not in my country and in my time, has direct social and political consequences. I think that it alters consciousness and I think that its goal is to alter consciousness.... Its task and its purpose is to create shifts in what one thinks is reality and what the reader does.... I do not think that literature is a call to action; it speaks to the consciousness" (SD, pp. 75–76). In the same discussion he said that to him part of the job of fiction is "to redeem the stereotype" to its proper weight and value in the world.

He elaborated on these observations in his essay "Writing About Jews," in which he defended himself against charges of anti-Semitism and self-hatred which had been leveled against his first two books by arguing that: "Fiction is not written to affirm the principles and beliefs that everybody seems to hold, nor does it seek to guarantee us of the appropriateness of our feelings. The world of fiction, in fact, frees us from the circumspections that the society places upon feeling ..." (RM, p. 151).

In these statements, as in all of his early essays and interviews, Roth emphasizes the ethical purposes and moral consequences which he saw as central to the artist's endeavor. Though the fictionist is neither social scientist nor political engineer, Roth argues, an author's work can and *should* have a social impact. To Roth that impact would appear to be a subversive one. Its subversiveness lies in the fact that, through fiction, a writer can touch the moral consciousness of his reader—can cause him to ask questions he might not otherwise ask or might not be willing to ask aloud—can alter his perception of the world around him and heighten his awareness of everyday reality.

Harry Levin argued, in a speech before the International Comparative Literature Association delivered in the same year that *When She Was Good* appeared, that a similar subversive intention has characterized the "realistic impetus" since the novel's beginnings. "The literary realist," he said, was destined from the start to be a "disillusioned idealist" whose method would "entail a systematic testing and unmasking of illusions. Like the rueful knight breaking up the illusory puppet show, every realistic novelist is a professional iconoclast, bent on shattering the false images of his day. His novels deal, in their own way, with a set of presuppositions which he demonstrates to be unreal, invoking as his touchstone the reader's sense of reality."[1] This iconoclastic impulse, this desire to alter the vision of his readers by exposing the popularly held illusions which surround them and inform their day-to-day existences, has been fundamental to Roth's art as well, from its earliest roots in the *Et Cetera* stories and "The Contest for Aaron Gold." And it has ramifications in both the form and content of *When She Was Good*.

Frank Kermode suggested the essence of the formal concomitant of this subversive impulse when he observed that novels "must always create a gap between their texts and narrative types, for otherwise they could not be new; all stories are banal and the redemption from banality must be, as Baudelaire remarked of *Madame Bovary,* and James in a different way of *The Golden Bowl,* a technical wager, a matter that is of treatment, a glorifying in the gap between types and text."[2] *When She Was Good* was chided by some of its reviewers for being melodramatic, a kind of literary soap opera, and for exhibiting many of the characteristics associated with that formulaic narrative type: stereotypical characters, pathetic situations, sensational incidents, heightened emotions, constant crisis, etc. And the book is *melodramatic*—like Stephen Crane's *Maggie, A Girl of the Streets* or Frank Norris's *McTeague.* It is not, however, *a melodrama.* For where a melodrama's primary function is, according to John Cawelti, "to assure us of the benevolent moral order of the world," the function of Roth's use of melodramatic devices is to lead us to exactly the opposite conclusion.[3]

The melodramatic devices are used for several reasons. First, a character such as Lucy Nelson perceives life as a soap opera in which she is the beleaguered heroine, and family melodrama is, therefore, an appropriate choice of narrative type for a story of her life presented from her point of view and the point of view of those around her. Second, recognizable narrative types and popular or conventional forms can attract a wide audience to a writer's work, an audience which is currently inaccessible to the experiments in solipsism and surrealism of a Nabokov or a Hawkes. Though popularity is a damning stigma in many critical circles, it is also the only avenue to the mass audience whose consciousnesses Roth's statements about the social function of fiction would seem to determine that he must try to reach. Like novelists since the inception of the form, then, Roth has repeatedly framed his tales in narrative types familiar to a broad audience, only to subvert their expectations *within* the tales themselves—to create a gap, in Kermode's terms, between his texts and his narrative types—in an effort to alter his readers' consciousnesses. Each of his novels clearly rests within the broad outlines of such popular forms: "Goodbye, Columbus," in the outlines of the Horatio Alger success story and the summer romance; *Letting Go* and *The Professor of Desire* in the academic novel and family romance; *When She Was Good* in family melodrama and ladies' magazine romance; *Portnoy's Complaint* in the psychoanalytic confession, sexual memoir, and pornography; *Our Gang* in burlesque humor; *The Breast* in *Mad/Playboy* fantasy and fairy tale; *The Great American Novel* in sports fiction and national epic; *My Life as a Man* in the divorce novel.

This aspect of Roth's fiction is highlighted by the studied banality of the titles he assigns to his stories, and to the excerpts and chapter titles of his novels. Titles like "Defender of the Faith," "Paul Loves Libby," "In Trouble," "A New Man," "Nature Boy," "The Most Unforgettable Character I've Met," "Civilization and Its Discontents," "My True Story," etc. Having used such familiar forms and titles to attract a popular audience usually reserved for Jaqueline Susann or Irving Wallace, Roth then tries, through his *treatment* of his materials, to alter their perceptions and challenge their predispositions. Each of his books focuses on ideas imbedded deep within the American psyche in order to subject those ideas to critical scrutiny. And perhaps none of them is more effective in using this approach than *When She Was Good,* his forgotten novel, which poses profound questions about the American character in its individual and collective, private and public, manifestations.

The same gloomy aura of inevitability which marked Roth's first novel permeates his second, and together they can be viewed as somber companion pieces which explore the lives of the American generation which reached its maturity in the Fifties. *Letting Go,* Roth's contemporary variation on the characters and themes of *The Portrait of a Lady,* investigated the psychological debts and sorrows of the urban, college-educated members of that generation in a Jamesian style and language exactly suited to its subjects. *When She Was Good,* his Midwestern *Madame Bovary,* his contemporary *Main Street,* focuses on the remaining members of that generation: the men and women from small towns and suburbs who never went to college or never finished, those who were seemingly predestined to grow up, marry, raise their children, and die within an afternoon's drive of the places where they were born ... the group Richard Nixon labeled his "silent majority."

Like *Letting Go,* although *When She Was Good* concentrates on the generation of the Fifties its concerns and characters are multigenerational: it recounts the history of five generations of a Midwestern family from the pioneer days of the 1890s through the Cold War era of the Fifties. While the story is grounded in the events of that particular family's life, it is also clearly framed within the context of the wider social milieu of the history of America as a whole during the same period.

Since *When She Was Good* is probably the least familiar of Roth's books to most readers, some summary is in order. Willard Carroll is the son of Norwegian settlers who were as cold and harsh as the Midwestern woods where they struggled to eke out their meager existence. His boyhood in that environment instilled in him the desire for a more civilized, more loving life. "Not to be rich, not to be famous, not to be mighty, not even to be happy, but to be civilized—that was the dream of his life," are the first words of this book about dreams and realities. To Willard, such a life comes to be intimately bound up with the importance of the family and adherence to all the traditional American virtues and values. He settles in Liberty Center, a small town somewhere north of Chicago, marries, gets a secure job with the Post Office, and fathers a daughter, Myra, whom he spoils and overprotects. She grows up to marry a charming n'er-do-well named "Whitey" Nelson, and, when the Depression strikes just as their daughter Lucy is born, Willard takes them into his home "temporarily" until they can get back on their feet. "Temporarily" stretches into sixteen years during which Whitey works irregularly, drinks regularly, and eventually comes to feel that his position as head of his own family has been usurped by his father-in-law, whom his wife and daughter call "Daddy" Will.

Lucy Nelson grows up resenting her father's weakness. Taught that a man should take responsibility for his family, should be "strong" and "true," someone whom his wife and children can depend on to shield them from the vagaries of existence, she hates him for not measuring up to those ideals. Out of shame and anger she withdraws into herself and develops a virulent strain of self-righteousness. When Whitey comes home drunk one night and begins to abuse her mother, she calls the police and has him arrested. Later, after she is married, when she learns that her father almost poked out his mother's eye with a belt buckle during an argument, she returns to the Carroll household, locks Whitey out of the house, and effectively banishes him from Liberty Center. (This is probably the most crucial scene in the entire novel. It appears in all of the many drafts of various versions of the story in the Roth Collection at the Library of Congress. And it would appear to have been the germ of this novel in the same way that the vision of a little girl climbing a tree with soiled underwear was the germ of *The Sound and the Fury.*)

Not surprisingly, she has very few friends. Then she meets Ellen Sowerby, a girl from the rich side of town and, through her, Ellen's cousin, Roy Bassart. Roy is a younger version of her father who has just returned from a hitch in the peacetime army, full of pipe-dreams and easily wounded pride. But he is the first boy who has ever taken an interest in her, the first who ever made her feel feminine—and when she is out with him she is able to escape her home life. Though she quickly realizes that she does not really love him—she *recognizes* that he is like her father—she feels that without him she would have to return to the life of isolation and loneliness which she led before they met. In a classic scene, he eventually seduces her in the back seat of his car and, just as she begins college in nearby Fort Kean, just as her dreams of escaping her family and beginning a new life seem on the verge of realization, she learns that she is "in trouble." Driven by her resentments to refuse the abortion which her father offers to arrange (and which she actually wants), she finally forces Roy to "do his duty," and they are married.

At first she tries to be a submissive and attentive wife, to act out the role she has been taught to assume by her society. But when Roy begins to rationalize his failures and weaknesses and glorify his future prospects—and then suggests that *they* go live with *his* family "temporarily" after their baby is born—she sees herself destined to relive her mother's life and rebels, determined now to change Roy into the man her father never was. As time goes on she feels more and more oppressed by Roy's immaturity and begins to nag and

berate him in public; he runs to his Uncle Julian and leaves her with
their son. Finally, when her last hopes for a more stable future for
herself and her mother seem shattered by Whitey's imminent return
to Liberty Center, she becomes hysterical with rage and paranoia
and drives Roy and their son out of the house. After a brutal confrontation with Roy and his uncle, she flees from her grandparents'
house, half-crazed, and dies of overexposure in the local Lover's
Lane where Roy had first seduced her.

Though summary does not do justice to the novel's awesome,
naturalistic power—reading it one is inevitably reminded of Norris,
Crane, Dreiser, and Sinclair—the story-line *is* just as banal as it
sounds. It is Roth's treatment of his stereotypic materials which
makes *When She Was Good* much more than the obsolete exercise
in nineteenth-century naturalism or the anachronistic "Sumerian
tablet covered with cuneiform scrawl" which it seems to one of his
most recent critics.[4]

Its disruption of simple chronology, its use of changing centers
of consciousness, its repetition of the same incident from several
points of view, its guise of authorial objectivity all testify to its
technical modernity. Revealing all of the novel's major incidents in
the first forty pages, and then spending 250 pages retelling
them—and retelling them in the banal language of the characters
themselves besides—is a particularly modern approach. Through
his linguistic choice, Roth manages to make all of the popular
American clichés about morality, rectitude, family life and marriage, law and order, and male/female relationships tangible factors in the lives of his characters. The limitations of that language
effectively mirror the limitations of possibility and perspective
which are the fundamental antagonists in Lucy's pathetic tale.
Characteristically, Roth's choice of language and narrative viewpoint forces us into the point of view of Liberty Center's inhabitants, compels us to share their restricted perspective.

Within its melodramatic framework Roth's text unconven-
tionally challenges the sympathetic presuppositions of readers ac-
customed to finding in American fiction a series of recognizable
variations on the archetypal male/female relationship, given its
first literary representation in Washington Irving's "Rip Van
Winkle."

Rip is the first in a seemingly endless line of American fictional
heroes who are charming, affable, irrepressible, and irresponsible
boy-men; his Dame—she has no identity or name apart from

his—who hectors him about the chores he doesn't do, the family responsibilities he neglects, the tavern friends he prefers to her, is the first in an equally long line of American wives and mothers, a line which includes Miriam Peck, Goldie Epstein, Lucy Nelson, and even Sophie Portnoy—women who would "civilize" and tame the robust free spirits of the men they married or bore. Dame Van Winkle, like her contemporary descendants, is locked into the role of purveyor of societal conventions and defender of family ideals in the face of the anarchic self who is her husband. In the initial literary confrontation between these two extremes, and in almost all the literary confrontations which succeed it, the male writer presents the conflict from a point of view which is clearly sympathetic to the male combatant. After all, our writers have always seemed to say, all the American boy-man wants is the freedom to "light out for the territory" when he gets the urge—with his trusty gun, his trusty dog, his trusty Indian scout, his trusty Negro slave. In "Rip Van Winkle" this archetypal confrontation ends in an archetypal form of wish-fulfillment: Dame Van Winkle is finally disposed of without Rip's having to accept either guilt or responsibility for her demise, and he wakes up to find himself both emotionally and politically free.

The familiar outlines of this archetypal tale are clearly discernible on the surface of *When She Was Good*. In both "Rip Van Winkle" and *When She Was Good* community attitudes cast the wife as a villain for demanding that her husband accept his responsibilities, and for shrewishly browbeating him in public when he does not, while they see the husband as charming and, though slightly immature, engaging. Alone, we sense, both Rip and Roy would have drifted along happily in the warm glow of male camaraderie; for both, marriage is a disastrous step. Roy is as happy "working on his Hudson" and "shooting the bull" with his Uncle Julian as Rip is roaming the Catskills with his gun and his dog, Wolf, or conversing with the men at the local tavern. Just as Dame Van Winkle reserves her harshest criticism and sharpest tongue-lashings for Nicholas Vedder, the tavern owner who she feels has led her husband astray, Lucy is most adamant in her refusal to be reconciled with Julian because she feels that he is responsible for encouraging the very immaturity she is trying to control and eliminate. Both Rip and Roy groom their sons to follow in their footsteps. In both stories the husbands take off whenever there is a crisis, leaving their wives to fend for themselves and their children as best they can. In both stories the husbands' marital difficulties are resolved by the death of their wives through "natural" causes.

Many of the book's reviewers recognized the outline of this familiar story—the flurry of comment about Lucy as a "ball-breaking bitch," a "castrating American female" who deserved a "bust in the chops," provides a fascinating opportunity for feminist analysis of the biases of male reviewers—but most of them did not recognize that Roth attempted to *reverse* authorial and reader sympathy throughout most of the book. By presenting much of the story through Lucy's eyes, *When She Was Good,* unlike "Rip Van Winkle" and its more typical descendants, attempts to make the reader view the conflict from the woman's perspective. Roth shows *why* Lucy became a paranoiac shrew, *why* she did what she did, *why* a life which begins in a typical desire to do and be good becomes a masochistic extravaganza instead. In the process, he provides devastating insights into the toll in pain and pathology which the archetypal male/female roles can exact from all concerned.

The core of Lucy's behavior is that while she has totally accepted the idealized versions of American masculinity and femininity, in her own life she must contend with the reality of men and women who are characters drawn from "Rip Van Winkle," not "Father Knows Best." The disparity between those ideals and that reality, between what she has been led to expect and what she gets, drives her to manic self-righteousness and, finally, to death.

Asked about the symbolic elements in *The Old Man and the Sea,* Ernest Hemingway said that "I made a real old man, and a real boy, and a real sea and a real fish and real sharks. But if I made them good and true enough they would mean many things."[5] Like Hemingway's novel, Roth's tale is a fable about a particular character caught in a particular set of circumstances which reverberates with more universal implications. Though he seems to have been concerned with altering the traditional view of American male/female relationships in *When She Was Good,* Roth most certainly did *not* intend that the reader sympathize with Lucy throughout. Instead he sought a dual reaction: that the reader see things from Lucy's point of view, and therefore see traditional roles from a new perspective; and that the reader also ultimately be forced to disassociate himself from her most hysterical excesses and recognize them as just that—excesses.

Alix Kates Shulman, author of *Memoirs of an Ex-Prom Queen,* sensed this duality when she observed that *When She Was Good* was one of the few novels about the Fifties written by a male which "though widely hailed as the definitive portrait of the Great American Bitch, seems to recognize, even to understand, the Middle-American girl's plight—and yet still manages to blame her for the consequences."[6]

Though this duality may be assigned to an inability of the male author totally to identify with his female heroine, that perspective ignores the fabulistic element which underlies the novel. Roth's story is not just a case study of one aberrant member of American society; it is also a fable designed to show a fundamental weakness in the character of the larger society of which Lucy is a part.

Roth suggested both of his intentions in the *Literary Guild Magazine* (July 1967) at the time of the novel's publication in a comment reminiscent of Hemingway's in its emphasis on both the particularity and universality of his tale. "I have located the novel 'in the middle of America,' " he wrote. "Of course, Lucy's hysterical moralizing, her pitiless rectitude, her obsessive concern for what is virtue and what is vice—none of this horrific small-mindedness is by any means indigenous to our country. I would not expect the reader to see Lucy as 'typical' or 'representative' or 'symbolic.' She is bizarre, she is singular, she is 'a case'—and yet I would hope that in her rhetoric and behavior—in the particular style her anguish takes—there will be much that American readers will find altogether ordinary and recognizable. For it has always seemed to me that though we are, to be sure, not a nation of Lucy Nelson's, there is a strong American inclination to respond to life *like* Lucy Nelson—an inclination to reduce the complexities and mysteries of living to the most simple-minded and childish issues of right and wrong. How deeply this perverse moralistic bent has become imbedded in the national character and affected our national life is, I realize, a matter of debate; that it is even 'perverse' is not a judgment with which everyone would readily agree. What destroys Lucy (some readers may hold) has nothing whatsoever to do with the rest of us. I am of a different opinion."

Lucy's character is singular because it is carefully defined as a result of her particular background and accumulated experiences; "and yet" that background and experience took place "in the middle of America." Roth's fable rests in the qualities in Lucy's behavior, character and rhetoric which he saw as imbedded "in our national character"; in the implicit parallels between her attitudes and the national attitudes which they—in their own particular way—reflect.

In spite of his disclaimer, Roth's characters, settings and incidents are firmly grounded in typical American reality. The war in the back seats of Liberty Center's Lovers' Lane, the athletic hero-worship, the gossip, class distinctions, and dreams he describes are a very real part of most small-town life. The kindly old postman, the all-suffering piano teacher, the flinty old grandmother, the aimless GI, the girl "in trouble," the father who drinks too much (though not as much as the town drunk), are the people who populate those towns. Their typicality is best understood in relation to George Lukacs's definition of the "type"—a notion which helps to explain how Roth's novel can be both realistic and a fable at the same time. "Realism," Lukacs wrote, "is the recognition of the fact that a work of literature can rest neither on the lifeless average, as the naturalists suppose, nor on an individual principle which dissolves itself into nothingness. The central category and criterion of realist literature is the type, a peculiar synthesis which binds together the general and the particular both in characters and situations. What makes a type a type is not its average quality, not its mere individual being, however profoundly conceived; what makes it a type is that in it all the humanly and socially essential determinants are present in their highest level of development, in the ultimate unfolding of the possibilities latent in them, in the extreme presentation of their extremes, rendering concrete the peaks and limits of men and epochs."[7]

The complexity of *When She Was Good* is suggested by the fact that while Roth's characters are typical in this sense (as are the characters in most of his fiction) and, therefore, his tale is realistic according to Lukacs's sense of the term, Roth frames his story in formal devices designed to create an aura of myth and legend about it—as Hemingway had done in *The Old Man and the Sea* and Carson McCullers did in her *Ballad of the Sad Café*. He sets his tale in the recent past, for example, recognizing that Americans evidence a "dedication to the past so brief that it was legend before it hardened into fact." He makes the story's geographical location intentionally vague: while critics placed it in Michigan, Minnesota, Illinois, and Wisconsin, all we really know is that Liberty Center is somewhere north of Chicago. The name of his town, Liberty Center, metaphorically suggests its symbolic nature and is an ironic commentary on the pathetically limited perspectives and possibilities of its inhabitants as well. The narrative begins in an omniscient, objective, third-person voice, gradually shades into the voice of Willard Carroll, then into the voices of Roy and Lucy, before concluding in the same objective voice in which it began. The effect of framing the story in a prologue and epitaph narrated in this omniscient voice is two-fold. It distances the action and assigns it a legendary, folkloric quality; and, like the choruses in Greek tragedy, it serves to set the scene and comment on the final outcome, producing the effect of ironic understatement in the book's closing pages. Within this framework, the characters' language is tightly controlled so that it maintains a typical tone and vocabulary throughout.

"What destroys Lucy (some readers may hold) has nothing whatsoever to do with the rest of us. I am of a different opinion," Roth wrote. Lucy's pathetic tale, published in 1967 as Eugene McCarthy began his presidential campaign, in the same year that Norman Mailer's fable *Why Are We in Vietnam?* appeared, reflects Roth's opinion by mirroring that other, national tale of pathetic involvement which followed a similar pattern with equally disastrous results. The emphasis Roth placed on the national quality of Lucy's story in his essay is underlined by some of the titles he considered for the book—*The American Way, An American Girl, Saint Lucy of the Midle West* and *An American Saint*—and by his titling one of the published excerpts from the book "O Beautiful for Spacious Skies."[9] In 1974 interview he said that "there was a time when *I* at least came to associate the 'moral' rhetoric the heroine of *When She Was Good* employed to disguise from herself her vengeful destructiveness, with the kind of language our government used when they spoke of 'saving' the Vietnamese by systematic annihilation" (RM, p. 11).

When She Was Good does not only reflect the *rhetoric* of the United States Government during the Vietnam War years and the period immediately before and after them. It reflects our government's *behavior* during those years as well.

Lucy's behavior is, in part, prompted by her mother's habitual weakness in the face of the "enemy," her desire to "accommodate"—just as our involvement in Southeast Asia evolved out of a Cold War mentality spawned in part by McCarthyism and its charges that our leaders had been too "soft on Communism." Myra Nelson failed to have a happy marriage, failed to make her husband meet his responsibilities as Lucy sees them, but

Lucy feels that that was because her mother was too weak; like America after World War II, Lucy has supreme confidence in her own power and moral rectitude. She will succeed where others have failed. She is defending the good, she feels, and while others may criticize her actions now, in time they will realize that what she has done she has done *for their own good*. Lucy's involvement with Roy, like our national involvement in the swamp of Vietnam, is a gradual one which she keeps resolving to end until it is too late for her to withdraw without losing her honor and self-respect. She even circles "withdrawal dates" on her calendar, but keeps postponing them because of the forces of obligation, circumstance, and vanity. When she begins to realize that she is caught—when she learns that she is "in trouble"—she attempts, at first, to cover up the actual degree of her involvement. As the opposition to her behavior grows, she withdraws further into herself and refuses even to speak to those around her with whom she disagrees.

In spite of her sense of moral superiority, she cannot help but wish at times that things had been different, that those around her had been stronger and more decisive in their opposition to her rhetoric. Her thoughts could as easily be those of government leaders in the Sixties who found themselves trapped in an unpopular war because their strength after World War II—both moral and physical—had been so absolute, and those who opposed their policies had been so silent and so impotent for so long, that they felt no real compulsion to limit their use of that power until it was too late. "If only they'd said *no*," she thinks. "NO, LUCY YOU CANNOT. NO, LUCY, WE FORBID IT. But it seemed that none of them had the conviction any more, or the endurance, to go against a choice of hers.... She could do whatever in the world she wanted..." (p. 150).

Caught in a relationship she had tried to terminate but could not escape because of her own self-righteousness, she resorts to attempting to impose her will by escalating her use of rhetoric and force, both within and outside of her home. With each subsequent minor success, or apparent success, she gains greater confidence about the rectitude of her attitudes—more than once she thinks she sees the "light at the end of the tunnel"—greater confidence in her ability to master the situation. With each success she grows more deaf to the discontent and dissension she is causing within her own home, more insensitive to her alienation of her son, Eddie's, affections. (Eddie would have been college-age during the late Sixties.)

Just "how deeply" this "perverse moralistic bent" which *When She Was Good* documents in the private sphere became "imbedded in our national character and affected our national life" in the post-World War II period—just how it informed the paradox of our monstrous good intentions in Vietnam—has been thoroughly documented by David Halberstam in *The Best and the Brightest* (1972).

Lucy feels that she will succeed in the battle to make her boy-man accept his responsibilities, in spite of the experience of the women around her; in an interview Halberstam observed that "when we went into Vietnam, we thought the world was ours, that we were supermanagers in a supercentury, that America could do no evil." Though Lucy sees that Roy is like her father, she feels that she will be able to accomplish what her mother could not; in the post-World War II period, "we were the can-do society, and when some experts tried to warn us that the French had failed at the same task in Vietnam, there was this American arrogance that said if the French failed, it was because they were a decadent European nation that had lost too many wars." When Lucy wins her first skirmish to keep Roy and force him to meet his obligations, by standing up to his Uncle Julian's lawyer in a telephone conversation, she feels that she has achieved an important victory which will make it easier for her to handle any future confrontations; Halberstam pointed out that "Kennedy's advisers all used the Cuban Missile Crisis as a test run for Vietnam. They thought it set the pattern: Use just so much force, but not too much; keep the phone line open... and squeeze." As the final confrontation between Lucy and Roy's family approaches, she thinks that she will be able to cow Julian and force him into submission because she knows about his adulterous affairs; again, according to Halberstam, the government people who bug "believe that if you know a little gossip about somebody, you've got some power over them ... it makes them feel a little stronger and more self-righteous." Both *When She Was Good* and *The Best and the Brightest* chronicle a devastating loss of American innocence.[10]

Through the story of a single American girl, then, Roth makes a comment on the social circumstances which prevailed at the time the book was written. *When She Was Good* is anything but an anachronistic book; its spirit is as profoundly tied to the spirit of the Sixties as is *Portnoy's Complaint*'s. Roth's dual focus in on the nature of the male/female relationships which began to be challenged during that period, and on the American self-righteousness which destroyed Lucy and alienated a sizable minority of the American people at the same time. By building up our sympathy for Lucy and her particular predicament and then forcing us to disassociate ourselves from her excesses—*whatever our sympathies with her desire to do the right thing may have been up to that point*—he attempted to alter his readers' perceptions of our national excesses as well. "When she was good, she was very, very good, but when she was bad she was horrid," goes the nursery rhyme which gives the book its title. Roth apparently hoped that we would perceive that the "She" in his title refers to both Lucy and the America of which she is a part.

Halberstam's judgment of Richard Nixon in 1973 applies to Lucy Nelson and her Amerca as well: "I think that he believes that he's a moral force. All men convince themselves of their own mythology." That fact is the source of the danger and the perversity, for the greatest atrocities in the personal and collective history of mankind always seem to be perpetrated in morality's name. Often when we are most "good" we are most horrid. Roth's perception of that paradox is at the heart of this fiction, and it is the reason why *When She Was Good,* more than ten years after its initial publication, seems "better, finer and more provocative than most novels about which one is easily enthusiastic."[11] The reason why, in spite of the critical misunderstanding which greeted it in 1967 and the neglect which has followed it since, it has, to date, gone through seventeen paperback printings and continues to be read.

CHAPTER 6

Paleface, Redskin, Redface

L OUIS D. Rubin's description of the essence of "The Great American Joke" provides a useful frame of reference for investigating the radical shift in Philip Roth's fictive techniques after *When She Was Good.* "Out of the incongruity," Rubin writes, "between mundane circumstance and heroic ideal, material fact and spiritual hunger, democratic, middle-class society and the desire for cultural definition, theory of equality and fact of social and economic inequality ... between what men would be and must be, as acted out in the American experience, has come much pathos, no small amount of tragedy, and also a great deal of humor...."[1]

In *Goodbye, Columbus* Roth explored the incongruity between spiritual ideals and material realities in contemporary American society through realistic social satire. In *Letting Go,* his contemporary tragedy, he combined Dreiserian determinism with Jamesian psychological realism in an effort to portray the incongruity between the ideal view of man as a free, morally responsible choice-maker and the everyday reality of settling for something much less than unfettered freedom of choice. In *When She Was Good* he created a powerful fable of the incongruity between professed ideals and actual deeds, good intentions and evil consequences, in our private and public lives, through the pathetic tale of a typical small-town girl of the Fifties.

All of these books were given the serious critical attention they deserved. It was generally conceded that, even if Roth did not always succeed in his attempts at capturing the essence of contemporary American society, he was a talented writer who seemed dedicated to taking worthwhile risks in thoroughly respectable and *serious* channels. In the three books he wrote next, however, he approached his recurrent themes from another direction—through

comedy and humor reminiscent of the raucous and ribald native
American humor of the nineteenth century—and the critical attitude toward his work almost immediately became more hostile.

To readers of Roth's first three books, "Whacking Off"—the
episode from *Portnoy's Complaint* published in *Partisan Review*
shortly after *When She Was Good* appeared which innaugurated
his most purely comic period to date—came as quite a shock. The
title *alone* was enough to alienate many of the critics who had
praised his earlier books. The story's basic themes were familiar, of
course, and so were its characters. But the language! the subject
matter! the treatment! the (lack of) form!

Discussing the story and its author quickly became a preoccupation in literary circles: Could the same Phillip Roth who had
declared himself a disciple of James and Flaubert, had written contemporary American variations on the characters and themes of
The Portrait of a Lady and *Madame Bovary,* had defended the
values of "moral" art—could he have actually turned his talents to
writing what seemed destined to become what Anatole Broyard was
to describe as the *"Moby Dick* of masturbation"? Or rather: Since
Roth had apparently done just that, *why?* The slogans scrawled on
every wall, the obscenities chanted in the streets weren't enough?
Had the "trashing of culture" actually begun to infect the young
writers the Establishment had taken to its bosom?

Roth's comments in the self-interview "Reading Myself" can
help to furnish some of the answers to these questions. In that discussion of *The Great American Novel* he delineates the opposite
poles of a dichotomy between the contradictory impulses of the
"paleface" and the "redskin." In a 1939 essay Philip Rahv posited
an opposition in American literature between the "thin, solemn,
semiclerical culture of Boston and Concord" (paleface), and the
"low-life world of the frontier and the big cities" (redskin). According to Rahv, a paleface like Henry James or T. S. Eliot
"continually hankers after religious norms, tending toward a refined estrangement from reality ... at his highest level the paleface
moves in an exquisite moral atmosphere, at his lowest he is genteel,
snobbish, and pedantic" (RM, p. 82). The redskin like Whitman or
Twain, on the other hand, is characterized by "reactions" which
are "primarily emotional, spontaneous, and lacking in personal
culture.... In giving expression to the vitality and to the aspirations of the people, the redskin is at his best; but at his worst he is a
vulgar anti-intellectual, combining agression with conformity, re-

verting to the crudest forms of frontier psychology'' (RM, pp. 82–83).

As Roth sees it, in postwar America "a lot of redskins—if not to the wigwam then to the candy store and borscht belt born—went off to the universities and infiltrated the Departments of English, till then almost exclusively the domain of the palefaces." The result, he says, was that a group of writers like himself evolved—he calls them "redfaces"—who found themselves *"fundamentally ill at ease in, and at odds with, both worlds"* (p. 83). To Roth, "being a redface accounts as much as anything for the self-conscious and deliberate zig-zag that my own career has taken" (pp. 83–84). For "one of my continuing problems as a writer has been to find the means to be true to these seemingly inimical realms of experience that I am strongly attached to by temperament and training—the aggressive, the crude, and the obscene, at one extreme, and something a good deal more subtle and, in every sense, refined, at the other" (p. 82).

The redface like himself, he concludes, "sympathizes equally with both parties in their disdain for the other, and, as it were, re-enacts the argument within the body of his own work. He can never in good conscience opt for either of the disputants; indeed, bad conscience is the medium in which his literary sensibility moves" (p. 84).

Roth's early writing, we have seen, was influenced by the highly serious, "paleface" view of art propounded by Henry James and his academic adherents. But even as he wrote *Goodbye, Columbus, Letting Go,* and *When She Was Good* with this view of the sacramental nature of the fictionist's enterprise in mind, Roth felt that other impulse—the amoral, comic impulse of the redskin—which he was at first reluctant to acknowledge, even to himself. This impulse—perceptible in "Epstein," the conclusion of "The Conversion of the Jews," the Uncle Asher episodes in *Letting Go,* and the Uncle Julian episodes in *When She Was Good*—was not personified by James, Tolstoy, Flaubert, or Mann, but by the popular radio and burlesque comedians like Henny Youngman, and by two of the characters from his Newark boyhood whom Roth calls Jake the Snake H. and Arnold G.

Henny Youngman impressed the young Roth because "he argued by his schlemieldom that it was in the world of the domestic squabble and unending social compromise, rather than on the concert stage, that the Jews of his audience might expect to spend their lives" (RM, p. 81). (Though the tone is quite different, the theme is *Letting Go*'s.) He recalls Jake the Snake as a "middle-aged master of invective and insult, and repository of lascivious neighborhood gossip ... who owned the corner candy store in those years when I preferred the pinball machine to the company of my parents." Arnold G. was Roth's older brother Sandy's "navy buddy ... an unconstrained Jewish living room clown whose indecent stories of failure and confusion in sex did a little to demythologize the world of the sensual for me in my adolescence. As Jake the Snake demythologized the world of the respectable. As Henny Youngman ... demythologized our yearning for cultural superiority ..." (p. 81). In his interview with Alan Lelchuk on *Our Gang,* Roth mentioned the comedy routines of Olson and Johnson, Laurel and Hardy, Abbott and Costello, the Three Stooges, and Charlie Chaplin as "models" for the "broadly comic" style he was seeking in that book (RM, p. 46).

While references to Jake the Snake and Henny Youngman as "influences" on his writing may at first seem facetious, they should not be passed off lightly. They are included in one of Roth's most important self-analyses; and they underline an essential point which he has been making repeatedly since *Portnoy's Complaint* appeared in 1969: the sources of his comic techniques are oral and popular *as well as* literary. Ignoring that fact cannot help but mislead the critic and his readers. To the student of native American humor, Jake the Snake and Arnold G. are anything but unfamiliar characters: they seem to be Southwest storytellers miraculously transported from their well-worn perches atop nineteenth-century cracker barrels to the candy store and living room of Roth's Newark in the 1940s. It was in the writing of the nineteenth-century humorists—especially those of the Old Southwest, Mark Twain's predecessors and contemporaries—that oral and literary strains most fully combined into a popular literary form. And it is with that popular humor that Roth's comic fiction has the clearest affinities.

Choosing native American humor as a perspective on Roth's comic fiction is hardly arbitrary: his knowledge of the writing of the nineteenth-century humorists can be documented. As a graduate student at the University of Chicago, he studied native American humor as well as Henry James. While there he took several courses with two of the pioneers in the study of that writing, Napier Wilt and Walter Blair, and he specifically recalls reading Blair's ground-breaking work, *Native American Humor* (1937), at that time.[2] The permanence of the impression this exposure to the earlier humorists had on his own comic imagination is suggested by his dedicating *Our Gang* to Wilt (not *When She Was Good* or *The Breast,* but his political satire, *Our Gang*), and by his inscribing Blair's copy of *The Great American Novel,* "To Walter Blair, who introduced me to the tall story."[3] When Lelchuk asked him to cite American *literary* precedents for the type of bitter political satire in *Our Gang,* Roth immediately mentioned the work of several of the nineteenth-century humorists: James Russell Lowell's *Biglow Papers* and David Ross Locke's "Petroleum V. Nasby" letters (RM, p. 44).

Of course knowledge of native American humor is not affinity; and Roth's knowledge would be a little assistance in understanding his own writing if he had not been predisposed to respond to that humor as somehow consonant with his own talents and fictional objectives. His comments in "Reading Myself" and the *Our Gang* interview indicate that just such a temperamental kinship with these earlier redskins did exist. Though the impulse to portray the incongruities and myths which Rubin describes as at the heart of the "Great American Joke" through comedy was apparently dormant in Roth from the start, however, his early reverence for art as a highly serious moral vocation and his aspirations for cultural acceptance precluded his surrendering to that impulse at the beginning of his career. Only *after* he had attempted to treat those incongruities through acceptably serious means and found himself (and many of his critics) dissatisfied with the results, could he allow the redskin in him to have his say. By 1967 a complex of personal, literary, and social pressures encouraged the necessary self-confidence and self-liberation. *Portnoy's Complaint, Our Gang,* and *The Great American Novel* were the result.

When he finally did turn to humor, Roth naturally used the methods that he felt would be most effective in highlighting the contrasts he was trying to explore—and his knowledge of the techniques of the nineteenth-century humorists came to the fore. Within this broad context his three comic novels may be viewed as a sequence marked by its movement from satiric to more purely comic content.

CHAPTER 7

In the American Grain
(Portnoy's Complaint)

M ENTION Philip Roth's name in conversation and nine times out of ten the response will be *"Isn't he the one who wrote that dirty book about ....?"* For of all his novels *Portnoy's Complaint* is by far the best known—*Goodbye, Columbus* rivals it, but as a movie, not as a book—the one most firmly rooted in the popular consciousness. Almost half a million people bought the book in hardcover, millions more have read it in paperback. And those who have not bought or read the book seem at least to have heard of it by word of mouth, or through feature articles which appeared in mass-circulation magazines such as *New York, Time, Life,* and *Newsweek* when it first appeared in 1969. Eventually, the Portnoys may very well join Hawkeye, Huck Finn, and Holden Caulfield as permanent characters of American popular lore; discussion of the book's popular impact would seem to be mandatory in any popular history of the Sixties on the order of Frederick Lewis Allen's *Only Yesterday*; and when the literary history of the period is finally written it will certainly agree with Albert Guerard, Morris Dickstein, and many of the book's reviewers in their judgment that—for good or ill—it is one of the decade's cultural milestones as well.[1]

Although we may be willing to grant that *Portnoy's Complaint* is funny, true, even touching at times, the uneasy feeling persists, however, that any novel which revels in Jewish-Gentile stereotypes, overflows with obscenity, and treats masturbation, fellatio, cunnilingus, a *ménage á trois,* and assorted sexual deviations (with liver and other objects animate and inanimate) must be, *a priori,* pornographic and unworthy of extended critical examination. This feeling persists in spite of the fact that we know prurient *intention,* not

sexual *matter,* defines a work as pornographic. Though we may recall Henry James's assertion that the reader should grant the writer
his *donnée* and evaluate a literary work by the success or failure of
the author's *treatment* of his chosen materials, when that *donnée* is
explicitly sexual and patently obscene we tend to balk. With
Emerson (paleface extraordinaire), we may recognize that, in
theory at least, "thought makes everything fit for use," that "the
vocabulary of an omniscient man [i.e., a poet, an artist] would
embrace words and images excluded from polite conversation.
What would be base, or even obscene, to the obscene, becomes il-
lustrious, spoken in a new connection of thought.... The meaner
the type, the more pungent it is, and the lasting in the memories of
men."[2] But like Emerson suddenly confronted with Walt
Whitman's *Leaves of Grass,* when we find our theoretical liberality
challenged by a novel like *Portnoy's Complaint,* which not only
uses such words but incessantly shouts them at us in capital letters,
our moral reservations frequently overshadow our critical
receptivity—at least in public.

Yet our task as readers and critics is fundamentally the same as it
is when we approach any other work of the imagination: we must
try to judge whether the words and images employed by the author
are those best-suited to the subject—whether, in the case of
Portnoy's Complaint, words and images commonly designated obscene by polite society have been made "fit for use" by the quality
and integrity of the author's thought, by the power of the overall
conception of the work in which they play such a prominent part.

The history of the evolution of that conception is, like that of
most works of art which arouse and hold critical interest, essentially a record of an artist's struggle to blend content and form in
the service of a particular vision. A record, in this instance, of
Roth's quest for a voice and a treatment which would allow him the
imaginative freedom to combine realistic detail and comic
fantasy—the impulses of the paleface and the redskin—in an effort
to capture the tenor of contemporary American life in a way that
his first two, strictly controlled, novels could not. "After such
knowledge as the Grimes case offers to the creative imagination,"
one of Roth's correspondents had written after reading "Writing
American Fiction," "it becomes clear that the writer who dares to
handle this much American experience will have to have not only
Ralph Ellison's wariness and distrust, but his capacity for high
comedy—for the mode of comic insight (one finds it occasionally in

Faulkner and Fitzgerald and Nathanial West as well) which allows
for the appalling paradoxes of American life but does not forgive
them or those who create them...."[3]

Roth apparently agreed, and as early as 1961 the basic outline of
the central characters, themes, and situations of *Portnoy's
Complaint* were already on his mind. In "The New Jewish Stereotypes," an essay published in that year, he summarized those materials as they had been repeatedly presented to him in the stories of
his students at Iowa. His summary is lengthy but worthy of extended quotation. "There were several Jewish graduate students in
the class I taught at the Writing Workshop of the State University
of Iowa," he wrote,

and during one semester three of them wrote stories about their childhood,
or at least about a Jewish childhood.... Curiously enough, all of the
stories had similar situations and similar characters. The hero in each of
them was a young Jewish boy, somewhere between ten and fifteen, who
gets excellent grades in school and is always combed and courteous. The
stories are told in the first person and have to do with the friendship that
grows up between the hero and a Gentile neighbor or schoolmate. The
Gentile is from the lower class and he leads the Jewish boy, who is of the
middle class, into the mysteries of the flesh. The Gentile boy has already
had some kind of sexual experience himself. Not that he is much older
than his Jewish companion—he has the chance for adventure because his
parents pay hardly any attention to him at all.... This leaves their off-
spring with plenty of time to hunt girls. The Jewish boy, on the other
hand, is watched—he is watched at bedtime, at study-time, and especially
at mealtime. Who he is watched by is his mother; the father we rarely
see....what the hero *envies* the Gentile boy is his parental
indifference—because ultimately he envies the Gentile his sexual adventure. Religion is not understood as a key to the mysteries of God, but to
the mysteries of sex....

I must hasten to point out that in these stories the girls to whom their
Gentile comrades lead the heroes are never Jewish girls. The Jewish girls in
the stories are mothers and sisters. The sexual dream—for whatever
primal reason one cares to entertain—is for the Other. The dream of the
shiksa.... Though there may be biographical fact at the bottom of these
stories ... the satisfactions that are derived through the manipulation and
interpretation of the real events are the satisfactions of one's dreams ...
what the heroes of their stories learn at the end—as their Gentile comrades
disappear into other neighborhoods and into maturity—is the burden of
their reality. (SD, pp. 15–16)

In "Writing American Fiction" Roth asked why *all* of our fictional heroes didn't "wind up in institutions like Holden Caulfield, or suicides like Seymour Glass" (p. 226). And leaving the investigation of contemporary social life to the *amor-vincit-omnia* boys, he said in the same essay, "Would indeed be unfortunate, for it would be somewhat like leaving sex to the pornographers, where again there is more to what is happening than first meets the eye" (p. 231). *Portnoy's Complaint* finally grew out of four projects that Roth worked on between 1962 and 1967. Through these four projects the bare bones of the folkloric materials his students had presented to him, the psychiatric setting, and the sexual subject matter gradually coalesced to form the vision and voice of his novel. He traces this process in a 1974 essay appropriately entitled "In Response to Those Correspondents, Students and Interviewers Who Have Asked Me: 'How Did You Come to Write That Book, Anyway?' "

Each of the abandoned projects, as he now sees it, was "a building block for what was to come," but each "was abandoned in turn because it emphasized to the exclusion of all else what eventually would become a strong element in *Portnoy's Complaint,* but in itself was less than the whole story." The first of these projects, begun a few months after the publication of *Letting Go* at the same time that he was working on *When She Was Good,* was a "dreamy, humorous manuscript of about two hundred pages titled *The Jew-boy,* which treated growing up in Newark as a species of folklore." He ultimately found it "unsatisfying" because it "tended to cover over with a patina of 'charming' inventiveness whatever was genuinely troublesome to me and ... intimated much more than I knew how to examine or confront in a fiction" at that time (RM, p. 33). "Yet there were things that I liked and, when I abandoned the book, hated to lose: the graphic starkness with which the characters were presented and which accorded with my sense of what childhood had felt like; the jokey comedy and dialogues that had the air of vaudeville turns; and a few scenes I was fond of, like the grand finale where the Dickensian orphan-hero (first found in a shoebox by an aged *mohel* and circumcised, hair-raisingly, on the spot) runs away from his loving stepparents at age twelve and on ice skates sets off across a Newark lake after a little blond shiksa whose name, he thinks, is Thereal McCoy" (RM, p. 34).

The second project was a play called *The Nice Jewish Boy,* written between 1962 and 1964 with the help of a Ford Foundation grant in playwrighting and read as a workshop exercise at the

American Place Theatre in 1964 with Dustin Hoffman in the title role. Like *Letting Go* and *When She Was Good, The Nice Jewish Boy* used realistic conventions which, to a certain extent, inhibited Roth's ability to explore the more fantastic elements of his character's "secret life." Though the play also had dialogue and comic touches he liked, he finally felt that "the whole enterprise lacked precisely the kind of inventive flair and emotional exuberance that had given *The Jewboy* whatever quality it had ... So: the struggle that was to be at the source of Alexander Portnoy's difficulties, and motivate his complaint, was in those early years of work so out of focus that all I could do was recapitulate his problem technically, telling first the dreamy and fantastic side of the story, then the story in more conventional terms and by relatively measured means" (p. 35).

Roth goes on to describe this dichotomy as "symptomatic" of Portnoy's dilemma. But, as "Reading Myself" makes clear, it is also symptomatic of the contending influences, allegiances, and aspirations that were at the heart of Roth's own *artistic* dilemma during this transitional period. How to join the fantastic and the real, the amoral and the moral, the language and humor of Jake the Snake and the moral thrust of James's art—these were the unresolved questions which Roth had to answer technically before *Portnoy's Complaint* could finally become a coherent artistic whole.

Writing *When She Was Good*—"with its unfiery prose, its puritanical, haunted heroine, its unrelenting concern with banality"—oppressed Roth's spirit, frustrated his imagination, and, according to Albert Goldman, even led him to talk of giving up his writing career entirely.[4] When he finally managed to complete it midway through 1967, he was "aching to write something extravagant and funny," to "get in touch with another side of" his talent (RM, p. 21). And the sense of freedom and relief he felt expressed itself in a third project, an uncensored monologue, "very foul indeed, beside which the fetid indiscretions of *Portnoy's Complaint* would appear to be the work of Louisa May Alcott" (RM, p. 36). Conceived as a lecture accompanied by a slideshow, it "consisted of full-color enlargements of the private parts, fore and aft, of the famous," accompanied by a running commentary. "It was blasphemous, mean, bizarre, scatological, tasteless, spirited, and largely out of timidity, I think, remained unfinished ... except that buried somewhere in the sixty or seventy pages were several thousand words on the subject of adolescent masturbation, a personal interlude by the lecturer, that seemed to me on rereading to be funny and true, and worth saving . . .'' (p. 36).

"Not that at that time,'' Roth continues, "I could have set out directly and consciously to write about masturbating and come up with anything so pointedly intimate as this. Rather it had required all the wildness and roughousing—the *merriment,* which is how I experienced it—for me even to *get* to the subject. Knowing what I was writing about . . . was simply unpublishable—a writer's hijinks that might just as well not see the light of day—is precisely what allowed me to relax my guard and go on at some length about the solitary activity that is so difficult to talk about and yet so near at hand. For me writing about the act had, at the outset at least, to be as secret as the act itself'' (RM, pp. 36–37).

At the same time that the redskin in Roth was so merrily at work trying to outdo Mark Twain's *1601* and his lecture on onanism—in the style of the literary comedians and comic lecturers of the nineteenth-century's lyceums and chautauquas—the paleface began a fourth project.

Simply titled *Portrait of the Artist,* this manuscript of several hundred pages was a strongly autobiographical piece based on the experiences of his own Newark boyhood which was eventually transformed into parts of both *Portnoy's Complaint* and *My Life as a Man.* "By sticking closely to the facts,'' Roth writes, "and narrowing the gap between the actual and the invented, I thought I could somehow come up with a story that would go to the heart of the particular Jewish ethos I'd come out of. But the more I stuck to the actual and the strictly autobiographical, the less resonant and revealing the narrative became'' (p. 37).

However, in *Portrait of the Artist* he invented as upstairs neighbors to the central character a family named Portnoy—a composite portrait, Roth tells us, loosely based on the families in his neighborhood—who had a son named Jack, Jr. Gradually the Portnoys began to take over his story, and as they did Roth realized that the family they were coming to resemble most was not any of the particular ones he had known as a boy, but the folkloric one his students had described in their fiction at Iowa. As he "played'' with this material, he chose not to treat the folklore *as* folklore—as he had done in *The Jewboy* by "emphasizing the fantastical, the charming, the quaint, the magical and the 'poetic' ''—but instead, "under the sway of the autobiographical impulse that had launched

Portrait of the Artist, I began to ground the mythological in the recognizable, the verifiable, the historical. Though they might *derive* from Mt. Olympus (by way of Mt. Sinai) these Portnoys were going to live in a Newark and at a time and in a way I could vouch for from observation and experience" (pp. 39–40).

Roth finally abandoned *Portrait of the Artist,* as he had earlier abandoned *The Jewboy, The Nice Jewish Boy,* and the slideshow—but dialogue, scenes, and characters from all four of these projects became a part of *Portnoy's Complaint.* And the approach to his materials which he had decided upon while writing *Portrait of the Artist*—grounding the mythological and fantastic in the recognizable, verifiable, and historical—was one that he would use in *Our Gang, The Great American Novel, The Breast,* and *My Life as a Man,* as well as in *Portnoy's Complaint.*

He recast parts of *Portrait of the Artist* into a story he published at about this time, "A Jewish Patient Begins His Analysis" (the indefinite article suggests the material's folkloric roots), which eventually became the first part of *Portnoy's Complaint.* A relatively restrained and realistic first-person narrative, the story was presented as the childhood reminiscence of one Alexander Portnoy delivered as a prepsychoanalytic monologue. There was nothing spectacular or radical about either the content or the style: Roth had used the psychoanalytic situation before—notably in *Letting Go,* where Libby Herz visited a Dr. *Lumin* in the hope that he would shed some light on her problems, in some of the early drafts of *When She Was Good,* and in the 1963 story "Psychoanalytic Special"—and, as Theodore Solotaroff has pointed out, the story's revelations about the tensions in Jewish family life were "hardly news" either. "Nor did a psychoanalytic setting seem necessary to elicit the facts of Jack Portnoy's constipation or Sophie's use of a breadknife to make little Alex eat."[5]

But the story was a crucial breakthrough, nevertheless, a beginning because "strictly speaking, the writing of *Portnoy's Complaint* began with discovering Portnoy's voice—or more accurately his mouth—and discovering along with it, the listening ear: the silent Dr. Spielvogel. The psychoanalytic monologue ... was to furnish the means by which I thought I might convincingly draw together the fantastic elements of *The Jewboy,* and the realistic documentation of *Portrait of the Artist* and *The Nice Jewish Boy.* And a means too of legitimizing the obscene preoccupations of the untitled sideshow on the subject of the sexual parts" (RM,

p. 41). Shortly after "A Jewish Patient Begins His Analysis" was published in *Esquire* (April 1967), "Whacking Off" and "The Jewish Blues" appeared. And from the very first sentence of "Whacking Off"—"Then came adolescence—half my waking life spent locked behind the bathroom door, firing my wad down the toilet bowl, or into the soiled clothes in the laundry hamper, or *splat,* up against the medicine-chest mirror ..."—the need for the psychoanalytic setting became clear.

In each of his earlier fictions Roth had attempted to find the most effective means to convey the feel of our cockeyed world, the quality of the social being's private life, the forces at work in those public and private worlds as a particular, representative individual perceived them. In *Portnoy's Complaint* he found a new, perhaps ideal, way of telling that tale. His desire to find the "aesthetically appropriate vessel" to express that feel fully and originally—and to express the interrelationship of fantasy and reality which he saw as central to it—was a central factor in his decisions to scrap each of the projects which paved the way for *Portnoy's Complaint. The Jewboy* and the slideshow were too fantastic; *The Nice Jewish Boy* and *Portrait of the Artist* were too realistic. The fantastic nature of the former two undermined their credibility as felt life; the realistic conventions of the latter two militated against their adequately capturing that feel and its confusion of the realms of fantasy and reality. Through the device of the psychoanalytic monologue Roth managed to combine the best features of both approaches.

The advantages of this stylistic choice are numerous. The psychoanalytic setting provides a realistic justification for Portnoy's vehement soul-baring and finger-pointing, for his use of words and images which would be unacceptable in a more public context, and also for his emphasis on sexual memories. It also provides him with an audience, essential since Portnoy is both analysand and performer, character and author in his own serio-comic tale. The dramatic monologue which this setting provokes has the effect of locking us into Portnoy's vision of the world; and his viewpoint is unqualified by any other (until the punch line), reveals as no other could *his* interpretation of the burden of his reality. Through the monologue we learn what reality feels like to him and, in the process, we are forced (as he is) constantly to question where the line between objective reality and his pathological fantasies lies. We are, in other words, forced to consider the interpenetration of reality and fantasy in *a* life, and are, by extension, made conscious of the same interpenetration in *our* lives. The monologue form also permits digressions, exaggerations, repetitions, descriptions, and oversimplifications which, while vital to our understanding of Portnoy's character and psychology, would be less acceptable in another narrative context.

Critical discussion of *Portnoy's Complaint* has focused almost exclusively on its ethnic dimensions, but it is also important to recognize that Roth's novel is very much in the American grain in spite of its Jewish specifics. Its essential conflicts, its themes, its characters, its language and comic technique all link it to classic works of the American imagination, works to which it is finally related like a foul-mouthed nephew with a Yiddish accent. Perhaps nowhere is the novel's distinctly American character more marked than in its style—the concrete result of those four abandoned projects—and in its use of that style to achieve freedom of consciousness and expression for both its author and its hero.

"The classic American writers," Richard Poirier argued in *A World Elsewhere: The Place of Style in American Literature,* "try through their style to temporarily free the hero (and the reader) from systems, to free them from the pressures of time, biology, economics, and from the social forces which are ultimately the undoing of American heroes and quite often their creators. What distinguishes American heroes of this kind ... is that there is nothing within the real world, or in the systems which dominate it, that can possibly satisfy their aspirations ... they tend to substitute themselves for the world."[6]

The heroes of *Goodbye, Columbus, Letting Go,* and *When She Was Good,* as we have already seen, were plagued by just such unsatisfiable aspirations to freedom, just such inclinations toward solipsism—and so is Portnoy: "Nothing but self. Locked up in me!" he moans. But in *Portnoy's Complaint* the style and form of the narrative itself work to achieve such freedoms as well, in a way that they do not in the earlier books. Although Poirier does not discuss Roth's work, his comments can illuminate the connection between Roth's use of style in *Portnoy's Complaint* and the novel's profoundly American character. There is a parallel, Poirier observed, between "the writer, struggling to express himself in language," as Roth had in his abandoned projects, "and the defiant hero, contending with the recalcitrant materials of reality,"[7] as Portnoy does in his life and monologue. In *Portnoy's Complaint* and the major works which succeed it, that parallel—implicit from the beginning in Roth's preference for first-person narrators who shape their own retrospective stories—becomes increasingly more explicit as the identities of "artist" and hero merge. That process culminates in *My Life as a Man.*

The artistic defiance which Poirier saw as the source of the styles of the classic American writers manifests itself in characteristics which also mark *Portnoy's Complaint.* Our writers, Poirier says, try in the face of overpowering social realties to create environments in their fiction that "might allow some longer existence to the hero's momentary expansion of consciousness";[8] in the face of similarly overpowering realities, Roth uses the psychoanalytic session to provide the occasion for a similar expansion. To Poirier, American fictions are characterized by "extravagances of language" which are "an exultation in the exercise of consciousness momentarily set free";[9] Roth told George Plimpton that Portnoy is "obscene because he wants to be saved" (RM, p. 19), and Portnoy's use of obscenity is an attempt to break free from the hold of the conditioning which he is struggling to overcome. The monologue rather than the dialogue, according to Poirier, has been the most congenial form for our classic writers, as it has been for Roth. American writers are dedicated to the effort to liberate consciousness—an effort with which Roth allied himself early in his career—and their concerns have produced a long line of heroes who are, Poirier observed, cast as liberators in their fictional worlds; as Assistant Commissioner for the City of New York Commission on Human Opportunity, Portnoy, like Hawkeye and Huck, is assigned such a liberator's role. Portnoy, like Holden Caulfield or Isabel Archer, is a "stock character" who enacts what Poirier calls "the American hero's effort ... to express the natural self rather than merely to represent, in speech and manner, some preordained social type."[10] The environment American writers have characteristically struggled to create through their language is, again according to Poirier, one in which "the inner consciousness of the hero can freely express itself, an environment in which he can sound publicly what he privately is"—or thinks he is;[11] and that is exactly the kind of verbal space which Roth struggled to create in *The Jewboy, The Nice Jewish Boy,* and *Portrait of the Artist*—a linguistic environment he finally achieved in *Portnoy's Complaint.*

This perennial effort to free the hero and his consciousness from social strictures of heredity and environment is, of course, inevitably an unsuccessful one. Since the "world elsewhere," the "city of words" which our authors seek to create, is one which must be wholly built of language, the complete freedom which the author and his defiant hero seek constantly eludes them both. To communicate verbally is to use conventions and, to a certain extent, to be bound by them. In recognition of that ultimate failure of freedom, Poirier pointed out, "American writers are at some point always forced to return their characters to prison. They return them to 'reality' from environments where they have been allowed most 'nakedly' to exist, environments created by various kinds of stylistic ingenuity";[12] and so in *Portnoy's Complaint* Dr. Spielvogel must have the last word—a punch line promising that reality will now have its day. Poirier argues, however, that our writers' failures to achieve the freedom they seek are never complete if they can create that expansion of consciousness even fleetingly. And in that effort, writers as different as Melville, James, and Roth are "quite willing, for themselves and for their heroes, to accept the appearance of failure in the interests of this free exercise of consciousness"[13]—an assertion which helps to explain the artistic pressures which produced *Our Gang, The Great American Novel,* and *The Breast* as well as *Portnoy's Complaint.*

Roth's exercise of style as a means to freedom of consciousness and expression, then, is in the American grain; and so is the subject which that style is meant to expose and explore—Portnoy's *complaint.* For like his American forebears, Alexander Portnoy wants most of all to be free—of his past and its burdens, of the weight of a culturally formed conscience and consciousness. Like Ahab, Huck, and Holden, like the heroes and heroines of *Goodbye, Columbus, Letting Go,* and *When She Was Good,* he seeks impossibly total satisfactions, impossibly complete freedoms from his environment, and lashes out at the world where he cannot find them. And reaction to his particular experience of the traditional American conflicts—of self vs. society, freedom vs. responsibility, pleasure vs. duty, self-definition vs. societal definition—is to pursue equally traditional American dreams of escape.

Part of him, for example, longs for the comforts of the "old agrarian dream" of escaping back to nature and the "good and simple life" he sees in Iowa and Vermont (PC, p. 186); but instead of capturing that idyllic world beyond social pressures—as Huck did (for a while) on his raft, and John Hawkes's Skipper does on his floating Caribbean isle—Portnoy feels compelled to reject it, manages only to soil the virgin land with his misspent semen. He longs nostalgically for the simplicity and male camaraderie of the softball diamond ("Oh, to be a center fielder, a center fielder—nothing more") and the Turkish bath (a habitat where he could be natural, "A place without *goyim* and women"); but he is inexorably drawn to the forbidden *shiksa*. Where Hawkeye, Rip, and Huck—heroes of another century—could "light out for the territory" and thereby temporarily elude civilization's grasp, for contemporary heroes like Holden and Alex there is no longer any unspoiled frontier to light out *for*—except, perhaps, the internal frontier of madness. So Holden wanders frustrated through a grimy and debased urban wilderness and longs to be a catcher in a field of rye where innocence, not hypocrisy, will rule. And Alex reverses the nineteenth-century vectors, flees *to* Europe (as Paul Herz had thought of doing and Gabe Wallach had done) in his desperate search for an escape route. But the Old World decadence of Rome and Greece only produces further degradation and guilt; and exile *to* Israel—the modern American Jew's romantic vision of the last frontier—renders him guilty *and* impotent. Like Holden, Alex cannot escape his civilization's discontents through physical flight because he has already *internalized* them. He is a victim of what Tony Tanner has characterized as the American hero's worst nightmare—conditioning. And he can find no escape from it except obscenity and the psychiatrist's couch—and even *there* he is not really free.

As sociologist Alan Segal observed in the *British Journal of Sociology* in 1971, the central irony of Portnoy's plight is that the very nature of his rebellion against his parents and his past—the primary element in his character, the source of his most extreme behavior—is clear evidence of the extent to which his character and actions are determined by exactly the values he is trying to escape. His mode of rebellion against social conditioning, in other words, is totally conditioned. Segal explains it this way: "Portnoy's dilemma is that he faces two alternatives almost equally unsatisfying and untenable: one, that he comply with his parents' wishes, thus getting them off his back but incurring his own permanent displeasure; two, that he pursue short-lived and specific satisfactions which involve the constant complaints of his parents and which, he fears, will lead to his public unmasking as some kind of sexual pervert. He has determinedly turned his back on the former possibility, is compelled to pursue the latter, yet yearns for a third alternative which is not forthcoming."

More importantly, Segal perceives that "Portnoy is trapped because he can only express his desires for independence from the Jewish world against [the WASP world] and in terms of the Jewish scheme of things. . . . Portnoy's complaint is this: in order to overcome his condition he must shed the Jewish identity with which he has been imbued. But this would involve the undermining of the channel of his independence—sex with the *goyim* on a compulsive scale—which is ironically both his present emancipation from the Jewish world and his imprisonment in its scheme of things."[14] Like Gabe Wallach and Paul Herz, he is more his parents' son than even he realizes. Considering his antipathies, the ultimate irony of his monologue is how often he sounds and acts exactly like the mother he attacks with such verbal gusto.

Portnoy mocks his mother for complaining that she was always "too good," yet he honestly believes that "I am too good too, Mother, I too am moral to the bursting point—just like you!" (p. 124). The books in his parents' home, he says, were chiefly books "written by Sophie Portnoy, each an addition to the famous series of hers entitled, *You Know Me, I'll Try Anything Once*" (p. 93). He is also the hero of his own melodramatic series, *Portnoy's Complaint* or *"My Modern Museum of Gripes and Grievances."* Sophie's tales all show a flair for self-dramatization, and in her epic she casts herself as "a woman on the very frontiers of experience, some doomed dazzling combination of Marie Curie, Anna Karenina, and Amelia Earhart" (p. 93). He sees *himself* as Oedipus, Cordelia, Raskolnikov, and Daedalus—and as Alexander the Great, Alex in Wonderland, Joseph K., John Lindsay's Profumo, and Duke Snider (as well as Al Port, Al Parsons, Alexander Porte-Noir, Alton Peterson, Anthony Peruta, "Big Boy," "The Knight on the White Steed," and the son in a Jewish joke). In his story as in hers, "nothing is ever said once—nothing!" (p. 99).

She overdramatizes, speaks in capital letters, exaggerates *ad absurdum:* "Alex . . . *tateleh,* it [the effect of eating French fries] begins with diarrhea, but do you know how it ends? With a sensitive stomach like yours, do you know how it finally ends? *Wearing a plastic bag to* do your business in!" (p. 32). But he has refined the family tradition of verbal overkill to an art.

Sophie and Jack blame all their troubles on the *goyim*; Portnoy blames all his trouble on *them*. He ridicules his mother for feeling superior to her neighbors because she gives the black housekeeper a whole can of tuna for lunch—"and I'm not talking *dreck,* either. I'm talking Chicken of the Sea, Alex ... even if it is 2 for 49"—and then runs scalding water "over the dish from which the cleaning lady has just eaten lunch, alone like a leper" (p. 13). But he is guilty of far greater hypocrisies. Though he prides himself on his position as Assistant Commissioner for Human Opportunity—a post which charges him to "encourage equality of treatment, to prevent discrimination, to foster mutual understanding and respect"—he denies all of these ideals in every one of his personal relationships. He treats the women in his life like objects, goes so far as to deprive them of their names and refer to them as The Pilgrim, The Pumpkin, The Monkey, and the Jewish Pumpkin. He rages at his parents, *"I will not treat any human being* (outside my family) *as inferior!"* Though he describes his affair with The Pilgrim as "something nice a son once did for his dad," from the evidence in his monologue there is little to suggest that the adult Alex *ever* did *anything* nice for his dad—or for anyone else close to him. His mother would have a "conniption" if he were to marry a *shiksa*; and in spite of his protestations that his religion means nothing to him, when The Pumpkin, whom he is planning to marry at the time, says that she sees no reason to convert to Judaism, the vestiges of religious pride cause him to reject her just as his mother would.

In spite of his bitter resentment of his mother's disciplinary measures against him when he was a child, their views of just reward and punishment hardly turn out to be very far apart. Her sense of values is so deeply ingrained in him that the behavior of his two sexually knowledgeable adolescent friends, Mandel and Smolka, was adequately explained for him—as it would have been for his mother and Roth's students at Iowa—by the fact that one was *"a boy without a father"* and the other had *"a mother who works."* When he learns that Mandel is now a salesman and Smolka is now a professor at Princeton—Princeton!—Alex is flabbergasted. "Why they're supposed to be in jail—or the gutter. They didn't do their homework, damn it!" (p. 176).

Though the irony which these parallels point up is not totally apparent to Portnoy, he does sense the futility of his attempts at rebellion. His obscenity is both a product and a symptom of his awareness of his condition. Raised in Sophie and Jack Portnoy's home, he *is* fully aware of the overwhelming power of *words.* He knows, for instance, that in the right context the word "cider" can cause tears, and that the word "CANCER" can cause hearts to stop and prayers to rise from the throats of adolescent atheists. He knows that the words "Jew" and *"goyim"* can define and circumscribe a world, that "love" can smother and "fear" can debilitate and warp. He knows that some words ("conniption," "aggravation," "spatula") seem to be Jewish words, and that using the *wrong* words can ruin his chances with the *shiksas* at Irvington Park (or Mary Jane Reed's chances with him).

So Alex is anything but a "hip" young Sixties man who uses obscenity almost unconsciously as an indication of his liberation from the older mores and taboos. *To Portnoy obscenity is an achievement*—and a weapon. He uses it *because,* like his parents and the society whose sexual conventions he is struggling so hard to violate, *he* thinks it is "dirty" too. He knows that the words he uses offend; they are meant to. He is obscene because he believes that through language he can break down the battlements of his own moral defenses—defenses which have been imposed on him by his society. But since he *has* internalized his Jewish and American societies' values, by talking and acting "dirty" all he really manages to do is increase the guilt which binds and tortures him. The guiltier he feels, the more frustrated he becomes; the more frustrated he becomes, the more vehement is his obscenity and his sexual promiscuity. Until finally he is literally speechless, caught in the whirlpool of this vicious circle, only able to express himself through an anguished howl of pain at his conditon.

"*Why* must you use that word all the time?" Portnoy's Jewish Pumpkin asks two pages before that closing howl (p. 270); and "Why he must," Roth told Plimpton, "is what the book is all about" (RM, p. 19). It is finally fair to say of the "bad" language in *Portnoy's Complaint* what James M. Cox has said of the "bad" language in *Huckleberry Finn:* it is a perfect expression of the conflict in the book.[15] That language places *Portnoy's Complaint* in the tradition of native American humor, and that central conflict indicates his relationship to the characters of Roth's earlier and later fiction.

The interpenetration of reality and fantasy has been one of native American humor's most persistent subjects; obscenity has always been one of the staples of its techniques. Although the discussion of *The Great American Novel* which appears below has been designed to detail the techniques of the nineteenth-century humorists which Roth has drawn on in *all* his comic fictions, since the obscenity of *Portnoy's Complaint* is so pronounced and so often lamented its literary precedents warrant brief comment here as well. Aristophanes, Chaucer, Rabelais, Swift, James Joyce, and D. H. Lawrence aside, Roth's language is clearly part of an American tradition represented by George Washington Harris's *Sut Lovingood's Yarns*—published in 1867, exactly one hundred years before "Whacking Off"—and the other major works of the humor of the Old Southwest. As Walter Blair has pointed out, these humorists were all "consciously or unconsciously, local colorists, eager to impart the flavor of their particular locality,"[16] just as Roth's novel imparts the flavor of his boyhood Newark. If Portnoy is a foul-mouthed nephew with a Yiddish accent, Sut is one of his uncles, and Simon Suggs, Mike Fink, Davy Crockett, Jim Doggett, and Pap Finn are all members of the same raucous, rough-and-tumble family.

Native American humor has *always* been in bad taste. Like the oral tales which are such a decisive factor in that humor's form and content—whether the tales are exchanged in Jake the Snake's Newark candy store or Pat Nash's Tennessee grocery—*Portnoy's Complaint* is marked by its homespun diction, its word coinage, its informal but rhythmical sentences, by onomatopoeia and assorted similes, metaphors, hyperboles, synecdoches, and other ludicrous imagery. As Blair has noted, these oral tales "typically mingle the circumstantial and the precise with the outrageous and the imprecise. Though meticulous about dates, dimensions, and techniques, the storyteller unashamedly introduces men and animals that are impossible monsters."[17] Blair's comments are echoed in Roth's description of the approach to his materials which he discovered while writing *Portrait of the Artist*. And this combination of realism and fantasy explains why Sophie Portnoy is no more a wholly realistic description of a Jewish mother than the Big Bear of Arkansas was of a real bear. Roth makes Portnoy the quintessential son of a quintessential Jewish family, gives that mythological son mythological parents, and then squarely locates them behind the venetian blinds and bathroom doors of a recognizably historical Jewish community.

As mythological personages, exaggerations of common characters, the Portnoys are a composite of many of Roth's other, more realistic, characters. Jack Portnoy, who pounds the Harlem pavement trying to sell insurance, is much like Leo Patimkin, Paul Herz's father, and the fathers of Nathan Zuckerman and Peter

Tarnopol; his more successful brother, Hymie, is like Leo's older brothers Ben. Mordecai Wallach is ruled by a wife who is "Very Nice to People"; Jack is dominated by a wife who is "too good." Like Mordecai, Jack suffers from chronic constipation, but both men's problems—like both their sons' verbal diarrhea—are a product of their "sympathies," not their sympathetic nervous systems.

Sophie Portnoy and Mary Jane Reed are also familiar. Like *Letting Go* and *My Life as a Man, Portnoy's Complaint* focuses on the women who are central to the hero's dilemma. Like Neil's Aunt Gladys and Roy Bassart's mother, Alice, Sophie is a contemporary Mrs. Partington or Aunt Polly, dedicated to overprotecting and controlling her boy in the name of religion and civilization. Mary Jane, like Libby and Lucy, Martha Reganhart, Lydia Jorgenson Ketterer, Maureen Johnson Tarnopol, and Helen Baird, is an all-American *shiksa* who is both predator and prey of the Jewish lover she is drawn to. Like *When She Was Good's, Portnoy's Complaint's* subject is "a grown child's fury against long-standing authorities believed" by its hero to have misused their power (RM, p. 9).

Like all of Roth's hero's, Portnoy is torn between the redemptive impulses of the moralist and the less-worthy impulses of the self-indulgent libidinous slob. Paul and Gabe's conflicting imperatives are his, and so are Kepesh, Zuckerman and Tarnopol's tendencies to self-dramatization. Like them Portnoy feels called upon to redeem the neurotic woman he is involved with; like them, he both shuns and covets that role. He is, like all of Roth's heroes, "locked up in self," struggling to come to terms with the burden of his past, to submerge the pleasure principle to the reality principle and emerge from the process whole.

Albert Goldman summed up the book's significance when he said that Roth has "explored the Jewish family myth more profoundly than any of his predecessors, shining his light into all its corners and realizing its ultimate potentiality as an archetype of contemporary life." For, in spite of its Jewish specifics, "*Portnoy's Complaint* boldly transcends ethnic categories. Focusing its image of man through the purest and craziest of stereotypes, the book achieves a vision that is, paradoxically, sane, whole and profound."[18] And profoundly American.

CHAPTER 8

The Official Version of Reality
(Our Gang)

I N *Our Gang* and *The Great American Novel* Roth shifted his focus from the social being's private life to the public life of the American society which had had so much to do with his earlier heroes' personal woes. As "Jewish fiction" both of these books are inexplicable (and indefensible), but as further explorations of the relationship between reality and fantasy in our "cockeyed" contemporary world, and as further efforts of their author to find freedom of expression, they are logical outgrowths of Roth's earlier concerns. Like *When She Was Good* and *Portnoy's Complaint,* both of these books treat folkloric materials—here the popular lore is of Tricky Dick and the national pastime, baseball—and Roth's treatment of those materials in each of them is an extension of the comic techniques he first used in his previous novel. Each is firmly rooted in the consciousness and ego of an obsessed self—as his previous and subsequent narratives are—but the emphasis in *Our Gang* and *The Great American Novel* is on scrutiny of public, rather than private, illusions and myths, the illusions and myths with which we are all forced to live regardless of our private obsessions.

"To begin writing fiction as an attack," Roth said in 1963, "is a deadly kind of beginning" (SD, p. 70). Yet throughout his career he has temporarily disregarded his own reservations and been drawn into writing satiric attacks by public events and political utterances which have aroused his sense of moral outrage. At Bucknell he wrote a long "free-verse poem about McCarthyism" for the *Et Cetera* (RM, p. 11). At Chicago he dissected President Eisenhower's pietistic rhetoric in an essay entitled "Positive Thinking on Pennsylvania Avenue," and satirized literary politics in one titled "Mrs. Lindbergh, Mr. Ciardi, and the Teeth and Claws of the Civilized World." After a visit to Cambodia in 1970 he made a Swiftian "Modest Proposal" that the United States bring a speedy end to the war in Southeast Asia by dropping goods instead of bombs on the populace. In each of these cases his purpose seems to have been much the same as the one he avowed in his discussion of the impulses which produced *Our Gang:* to turn his own "indignation and disgust from raw, useless emotion into comic art."[1]

"I am proud to say," he told an interviewer, "that Richard Nixon was known as a crook in our kitchen twenty-odd years before this dawned on the rest of America as being within the realm of possibility" (RM, p. 11). In "Writing American Fiction," published in 1961, he cited Nixon as *prima facie* evidence of the validity of his observations about the fantastic nature of American social reality; and in that essay, as in *Our Gang,* his primary target was Nixon's *rhetoric.* "Several months back," he wrote then, "most of the country heard one of the candidates for the presidency of the United States, the office of Jefferson, Lincoln, and FDR, say something like, 'Now if you feel that Senator Kennedy is right, then I sincerely believe that you should vote for Senator Kennedy, and if you feel that I am right, I humbly submit that you vote for me. Now I feel, and this is certainly a personal opinion, I am right....' and so on.... It still seems to me a little easy to pick on Mr. Nixon as someone to ridicule, and it is not for that reason that I have bothered to paraphrase his words here. If one was at first amused by him, one was ultimately astonished. As a literary creation, as some novelist's image of a certain kind of human being, he might have seemed believable, but I myself found that on the TV screen, as a real public image, my mind balked at taking him in. Whatever else the television debates produced in me, I should like to point out, as a literary curiosity, they also produced a kind of professional envy.... I found myself beginning to wish that I had invented it. That may not, of course, be a literary fact at all, but a simple psychological one—for finally I began to wish that *someone* had invented it, that it was not real and with us" (RM, p. 120). But Richard Nixon, however much Roth and others might have wished it were not so, was indeed both real and with us in 1960. Even more incredibly, a decade later he was not only still real and still with us, but he had undergone another incarnation as the "New Nixon"—and he was our *President.*

His abuse of language was no longer harmlessly amusing, no longer just a joke, as it had been in 1960 when he was powerless; and Nixon himself was no longer so easy to ridicule. By 1971 he was protected by the dignity and reverence Americans have traditionally granted their Chief Executive—had incorporated the imperial "we" into his speech and constantly reminded us of his position by referring to himself as "The President"—and his statements, no matter how absurd, had become the "Official Version of Reality."

Throughout his career in public life, most notably in his "Last Press Conference" in 1962 and during the Watergate period, Mr. Nixon and his supporters have complained that he has been treated harshly by the press, the media, the intellectuals, and the other opinion-makers whom they branded the "effete snobs," the "nabobs of negativism," of the "Eastern Liberal Establishment." And to a certain extent their complaints have been justified. For in Richard Nixon many of the members of those groups—by inclination and vocation writers, like Roth, who are concerned with the meaning and usage of words—have always seen the apotheosis of the opportunistic politician who twists and corrupts the language for his own purposes. Thus Roth was far from alone in his long-standing anti-Nixonian ire. Emile de Antonio's film *Millhouse* and Gore Vidal's play *An Evening with Richard Nixon*—both of which appeared within a year of *Our Gang*—sought to use Nixon's own words to expose him as a duplicitous demagogue. (Like *Our Gang*'s last chapter, Vidal's play takes place in Hell.) In *D Hexorcism of Noxon D Awful* (1969) Ishmael Reed attempted to "make a crude, primitive fetish... that would put a 'writing' " on the man he saw as an enemy of the people.[2] Cartoonists Philip Guston *(Poor Richard),* Jules Feiffer, Herblock, and David Levine caricatured him mercilessly. In his *Nixon Agonistes: The Crisis of the Self-Made Man* (1971), Garry Wills presented an exhaustive analysis of the man and his career which portrayed him as a latter-day Uriah Heep. And just a month after *Our Gang* was published, Jeff Greenfield, writing in the *Village Voice,* analyzed and dissected Nixon's rhetoric in the journalistic essay as devastating as H. L. Mencken's essay on President Harding's "Gamalielese."[3]

What distinguishes Roth's effort from these others is not so much its accurate mimicry of Nixon's numerous verbal tics—such mimicry is only to be expected from a writer whose ear for American speech has been characterized as the "finest since Sinclair Lewis." Its originality lies instead in its application of the comic techniques of Swift and, perhaps more importantly, the nineteenth-century native American humorists, in an effort to expose and deflate its subject—to counterbalance the dignity and reverence which shielded him by ridicule and disdain.

Our Gang began, like the *Et Cetera* and *Chicago Review* satires, as a specific response to what Roth considered one of his subject's particularly offensive public statements. He was angered by the moral insensitivity he saw in the contradiction between President Nixon's espousal of the rights of the "unborn" at the same time that he was also expressing support for the officer accused of ordering the massacre of all the inhabitants—born and unborn alike—of the Vietnamese village of My Lai. Roth's outrage at this moral myopia was expressed in a Swiftian disputation written in the heat of anger. Titled "Imaginary Conversation with Our Leader," it appeared in the *New York Review of Books* in May 1971, a month after Nixon made his antiabortion statement at San Clemente. This piece, which became the book's first chapter, was clearly occasional and specifically focused on exposing the opportunism and casuistry which he saw in Nixon's public statements. A month later the "Imaginary Press Conference with Our Leader," which became *Our Gang's* second chapter, was published, and the target of Roth's satire expanded to include the decay of public language in the news media, religion, and sports as well as in politics. His attack on *Nixon's* rhetoric, in other words, burgeoned into a full-length "impersonation, a parody, of Nixon's style of discourse and thought," *and* of the "high seriousness with which 'responsible' critics" continue to take his public statements (RM, p. 52).

Apparently what led Roth to continue his satire was his recognition of the opportunity his subject provided for him to awaken his readers' consciousnesses to both the decay of public speech and the fantastic quality of contemporary reality—two of his most persistent concerns. He suggested as much in the interview titled "Writing and the Powers-That-Be," when he said that what engrossed him about his subject in *Our Gang* was "*expressiveness* rather than bringing about political or social change" (RM, pp. 12–13); and when he told Alan Lelchuk that the book was intentionally shocking, "in execrable taste," so that it might "dislocate the reader," and "get him to view a familiar subject in a way he may be unwilling to, or unaccustomed to" (RM, pp. 48–49).

His inspiration came from the passage in George Orwell's essay "Politics and the English Language," which he used as one of *Our*

Gang's epigraphs: "... one ought to recognize that the present political chaos is connected with the decay of language and that one can probably bring about some improvement by starting at the verbal end.... Political language—and with variations this is true of all political parties, from Conservatives to Anarchists—is designed to make lies sound truthful and murder respectable, and to give the appearance of solidity to pure wind." The political chaos, like the fantastic reality, is connected with the abuse of language; and Roth's approach to the connection Orwell points out is to show a politician who *literally* tries to make murder respectable, and in the process constructs a version of reality that is "pure wind."

So: *Nixon's* antiabortion statement becomes an issue in President Trick E. *Dixon's* reelection campaign; reality shades into fantasy. In order to make the issue work to his advantage—and to forestall the Democratic gains expected as a result of the recent enfranchisement of the eighteen- to twenty-one-year-olds—Dixon proposes to extend the vote to the unborn and declares himself the candiate of "Prenatal Power." When his motives are challenged and his opponents transform his "pro-life" position into a "pro-*fornication*" one, Tricky develops a strategy designed *literally* to silence them and make his lies not only respectable but the "Official Version of Reality." As a part of his strategy to eliminate the Boy Scouts protesting in the streets of Washington, he invades Denmark and captures Elsinore, Hamlet's castle. But before he can reap the benefits which will most certainly accrue from such a bold stroke taken in the interests of "national security," he is assassinated: stuffed in a twist-tie plastic bag and left to suffocate from his own hot air. However, Dixon—a political animal even in death—is soon running for office in Hell, using the same tactics (and many of the same words) which were the hallmarks of his actual counterpart's earthly campaigns in his battle for the post of Satan.

Where Nixon's *Six Crises* was, according to Garry Wills, "a saga of moral education," the six crises which make up *Our Gang* are a saga of an amoral ambition which persists even beyond the grave. Five of the book's six chapters are dominated by the ego and solecistic language—public and private—of President Trick E. Dixon. In each of the chapters which record his public utterances (1, 2, 4, and 6), Tricky callously uses the dignity of his office to manufacture and perpetuate a *fictional* reality—a construct which is a fantasy in spite of its becoming the authorized version of events—for his audiences. In Chapter 5, though Tricky is dead, the rhetoric of the government and the media go on performing the same function, and thereby show themselves to be accomplices in the abuse of language which Tricky personifies. The only chapter which does not take place in the public eye, Chapter 3, is designed to expose Dixon's character even more fully—designed to suggest that even our worst fears about him have been valid—and to show the petty, insecure private man behind the dignified, presidential public facade. In part, it seems provided just in case some readers may have missed the point of the public chapters—which is highly unlikely since subtlety is as inimical to *Our Gang* as truth is to Dixon.

In that lack of subtlety, and in its use of deflationary parady, burlesque, *reductio ad absurdum,* blatantly *ad hominem* attack, buffoonery, and abusive language, *Our Gang* fits neatly into the ranks of American political satire. The Andy Jackson of Seba Smith's *Jack Downing Sketches,* the Calhoun, Webster, and Polk of James Russel Lowell's *Biglow Papers,* the "Androo" Johnson of David Ross Locke's "Petroleum V. Nasby" letters, the Abe "Linkhorn" of George Washington Harris's *Sut Luvingood's Yarns,* the King Leopold and Czar Nicholas of Mark Twain's late soliloquies, and the wide variety of targets of Charles Farrar Browne's "Artemus Ward" lectures are all nineteenth-century American precedents for the portrait of Dixon in Roth's book. All of these works are marked by their lack of restraint, their impudence, and their consciously indecorous bad taste. The only constraint their authors display is a common sense of their obligation to use their artistic powers to take their subjects to task for their corruption, incompetence, and duplicity. Their humor is, at base, a serious matter.

Roth explained his notion of satire to Lelchuk in a way which clarifies his link to the earlier humorists. "True," he said, "when we all learned about satire in school, we were told that it was a humorous attack upon men or institutions for the purpose of instigating change or reform, or words to that effect about its ameliorative function. Now, that's a very uplifting attitude to take toward malice, but I don't think it holds water. Writing satire is literary, not a political, act, however volcanic the reformist or even revolutionary passion in the author. Satire is moral rage transformed into comic art..." (RM, p. 53). The likelihood, in other words, that Presidents Jackson, Polk, Lincoln, Andrew Johnson, or Nixon would come to see the error of their ways and change as a result of the satires directed at them by their enemies is rather slim. That is what Roth means when he speaks of satire as being not so much a "political" act as a *literary* act. Satire *can* change its *readers'* perceptions, and that ameliorative function is the one Roth has sought to satisfy in all his writing. Thus, at its best, such satire is a "personal grouse against life" transformed into art; at its worst, it is just a personal grouse.

Within this common intentional framework, the characteristically American satires mentioned above are also alike in their central concerns and comic approaches. Each of them is concerned with the incongruity between democratic ideals and the antidemocratic strain its author sees in the officials he is attacking; each treats that incongruity in terms of conflicts between reality and fantasy which the comic form is suited to explore; each focuses on the devaluation of language practiced by the public officials who are the subjects of its scorn.

Roth's Dixon, and the rest of the political, media, and institutional custodians of our language and official reality are all cast as either comic-strip villains or baggy-panted clowns. Dixon and his entire administration are reduced, as the book's title suggests, to the ludicrously funny children in a popular series of short movie comedies, which one reviewer aptly described as "Diabolical Keystone." Spanky, Buckwheat, Alfalfa, and their friends are replaced by Tricky, his saccharine wife, Pitter, Dixon's cohorts (Attorney General Malicious, former-President Poppapower, Secretary of Defense Melvin Lard, former-Senator Joseph McCatastrophy, the Rev. Billy Cupcake), his enemies (John and Robert Charisma, Gov. George Wallow of Alabama, Senator Hubert Hollow, former-President Lyin' B. Johnson, New York Mayor John Lancelot), and the members of the electronic and print media (Mr. Daring, Mr. Shrewd, Mr. Respectful, Mr. Asslick, and the dean of Washington political commentators, Erect Severehead). Names in the book are assigned according to what would appear to be a rather simple principle: public figures of whatever party who take part in formulating and perpetuating the official version of reality are given satiric or deflationary names of one kind or another; all other characters retain their own names. Thus Nixon becomes Dixon, Kennedy becomes Charisma, Humphrey becomes Hollow—but Joan Baez, Jane Fonda, Curt Flood, et al., keep their own names.

But in this version of the *Our Gang* comedies, pint-sized prank-sters full of mischief and cute schemes, in and out of "scrapes"—harmless, clever, engaging, and appealing scamps—become full-sized con-men, with heartless and harmful schemes which threaten us all. Nothing is too crude or too low, the theory behind such satire goes, as long as it serves the purpose of reducing the exalted leaders to the point where their flaws can be suggested or exposed. Thus the comedy is Keystone because of its slapstick and vaudevillelike *schtick*. But underlying the humor, just beneath the surface and never completely out of mind, is the uncomfortable recognition that though Tricky Dick and his friends are outrageous parodies, fictional constructs as unreal as Sophie Portnoy or the Patriot League, they are also just real enough to make us stop between laughs and shudder.

When *Our Gang* was published in 1971, one of its reviewers observed that it was so topical that in twenty years it would be unreadable without footnotes which would crawl halfway up every page. Several others argued, Murray Kempton among them, that in spite of Roth's comic talent his imagination was unable to parody an original who was endlessly capable of parodying himself. From the vantage point of today, the first statement seems premature; the second terribly accurate. For the revelations of White House chicanery and wrongdoing which have surfaced since *Our Gang* was written have confirmed the wisdom of Roth's choice of a subject through which to convey the interpenetration of reality and fantasy. In the wildest flights of his vindictive imaginative fantasy, Roth came disconcertingly close to the *realities* of one of the most corrupt administrations in the two-hundred-year life of our Republic. Reading *Our Gang* now, with 1974's most important work of fiction, *The White House Transcripts,* and the media coverage of Richard Nixon's resignation in mind, makes Roth's fiction all the more fascinating.

In 1971 we laughed at the Tricky Dixon who incessantly referred to his book *Six Hundred Crises* in difficult situations, but we couldn't help feeling that such constant repetition was a rather cheap joke. But the *White House Transcripts* and the testimony before the Watergate Committee show that Richard Nixon referred to his *Six Crises* in exactly the same obsessively self-aggrandizing way. In *Our Gang,* Tricky and his closest advisers spend hours in their underground bunker—in a parodic dark night of the soul—debating the merits and deficiencies of possible "game plans," and scapegoats for their covert scheme to massacre Boy Scouts; and Tricky in private is a portrait of inconclusive, insecure, irrational leadership. We now know that Haldeman, Erlichman, and Nixon spent endless hours in the Oval Office discussing their "scenarios" for handling the "problem area," for protecting themselves and "screwing" their enemies, for finding an acceptable scapegoat—"The Big Enchilada." And the Nixon we see in the *Transcripts* is as indecisive and muddleheaded as the Dixon of Roth's bunker. (After reading *Our Gang,* it is almost impossible to read the conversations in the *Transcripts* without picturing Nixon and his fellow conspirators in Whittier College football uniforms.)

Dixon invades Denmark in an effort to shift attention from his domestic problems, invoking "national security" as his cover; according to some news reports at the time, Nixon, in the last weeks of his presidency, may have alerted the U.S. Sixth Fleet in the Mediterranean—and thus raised the possibility of imminent confrontation with the Soviet Union in the Mideast—out of similar motives. He most certainly timed foreign-policy initiatives with his domestic problems in mind. The examples of the parallels between Roth's Dixon and Nixon are almost endless—and they do not stop in 1971. As Watergate began to unravel, Roth wrote another parody, "The President Addresses the Nation," which appeared in June 1973. In it the president explains on national television why he cannot accept Congress's decision to impeach him and has, therefore, declared martial law. Shortly before Mr. Nixon resigned, he considered rejecting a decision on the tapes made by another branch of the government, the Supreme Court. And shortly after he resigned—using phrases remarkably similar to those in parts of Roth's parody written a year before—Pentagon sources reported that Defense Secretary James Schlesinger had taken precautions during the final days of the Nixon presidency to make sure that such a military takeover would be impossible.

As Watergate began to make headlines across the nation, Roth could not help but say "I told you so." In his preface to the Bantam "Watergate Edition" of *Our Gang*—which appeared in May 1973 as the Senate Watergate Hearings were concluding—he wrote that "My publisher asked me if there is any statement I would like to make about my 1971 Nixon book, *Our Gang,* as a result of what I read in the press and see on television about the Watergate scandal. Yes, there is. I wish publicly to apologize to President Nixon. Only now do I realize that I had no right whatso-

ever to depict him back then, if only in fiction, as a moral hypocrite, a lawless opportunist, a shameless liar, and a thorough-going
totalitarian at heart. What evidence did I have to support such a
fantasy? My fellow Americans, what evidence did any of us
have? . . . We—alas, I—had nothing even faintly resembling the in-
criminating evidence that is now to be found every morning in the
daily newspaper and every night on the evening news" (p. ix).

A year later when he wrote the preface to the "Pre-Impeachment
Edition" (May 1974), *The White House Transcripts* had been published and the evidence showed that, if anything, he had not gone
far *enough:* "as a result of the release and publication of *The White
House Transcripts,* Bantam Books is no longer 'asking' me for
introductions—they are demanding an explanation. To be sure they
have no quarrel with me about the depiction of 'Tricky.' . . . What
disturbs them about *Our Gang* is that in it I failed to give any indication whatsoever of the profanities that apparently punctuate
President Nixon's conversation. . . . I had no more reason than any
other American to believe that the close associate of President
Eisenhower, the Quaker who attends Sunday worship services in
the White House conducted by Billy Graham, Tricia's father, Pat's
husband, David Eisenhower's father-in-law, could possibly use language as indecent—well, to be utterly candid about it, as indecent
as the language in some of my own fiction" (p. ix).

Roth's fantasy did more than predict the truth about the Nixon
White House, however, it also described the media's response to
Nixon's resignation—and nowhere is the confluence of the fan-
tastic and the real more striking than in the similarities between
Roth's description of the coverage of Dixon's assassination in *Our
Gang* and the actual coverage of the president's resignation on
August 8, 1974.

Both events occurred after repeated official denials from the
White House press secretary, denials faithfully relayed by the press
to the American people. In both cases the television coverage included stationing reporters in selected cities across the United
States to gather "man on the street" response. And in both cases
the reporters, undaunted by the indifference or hostility of many of
the people whom they interviewed, tried their best to maintain an
air of portentousness. "A hushed hush pervades the corridors of
power. Great men whisper whispers while a stunned capital waits,"
intones *Our Gang*'s television anchorman, Erect Severehead; the
crowds in Lafayette Park on August 8, according to CBS's Walter

Cronkite, who rushed back from vacation to cover the momentous events, were full of anticipation, "like the crowds before the chanceries of Europe when governments are about to fall or war about to be declared." In death, Dixon is eulogized by *Our Gang*'s reporters; similarly, when he refused to join the stampede of commendation for President Nixon's resignation speech led by his colleagues Dan Rather and Eric Sevareid, Roger Mudd was subjected to an outpouring of vitriol which flooded the CBS mails.

Our Gang's street reporter Brad Bathos is an hilarious figure: confronted by hundreds of jubilant people who have flocked to Pennsylvania Avenue to claim credit for Dixon's assassination, he closes his report with the prescribed tone of gravity, saying, "This is Brad Bathos, from the streets of Washington, where the mourners have come to gather, to pray, to weep, to lament, and to hope" (OG, p. 165). But he is only slightly more hilarious than CBS's Bob Schieffer was. Schieffer reacted to the obviously festive atmosphere of the crowd which gathered in Lafayette Park between the hours of seven and nine o'clock on August 8—the same crowd Cronkite had compared to the hushed crowds before European chanceries—in similarly grave tones. As they chanted "Nixon's the One" and "Jail to the Chief," and burst into peals of laughter when a Mayflower moving van symbolically stalled in traffic before the White House, he was finally forced to observe solemnly, with extraordinary understatement, that "I must say there doesn't appear to be a very somber mood here. I would be less than honest if I didn't say that."[4]

All of this is not meant to suggest that *Our Gang* is actually the "wittiest and wickedest political satire since Dryden," as one of its reviewers claimed.[5] In spite of its comic strengths and its distinguished (or infamous) American lineage, the book is clearly one of Roth's least significant. While its emphasis on the reality/fantasy dichotomy so central to all of his fiction makes it anything but an artistic aberration, and though it can claim some semblance of novelistic coherence, *Our Gang* was written hurriedly and must ultimately be judged an uneven, slapdash affair. Although it is funny—in parts immensely funny—it is a failure. And it is a failure on its own terms—as *literature.* Though different in kind, *When She Was Good* is also one of Roth's most "political" works; and the earlier book's strengths point up the source of *Our Gang*'s weakness. Both were designed as works that would alter their readers' perceptions. *When She Was Good* succeeds in that task be-

cause its typical story draws readers who might disagree with
Roth's views about American self-righteousness—draws them into
the life and thoughts of a heroine and *through her story* causes
them to see things in a new way. *Our Gang* does not. The reader
who disagrees with Roth's view of Nixon—and in 1971 that included the voting majority of Americans—will, more likely than
not, cast the book aside as just one more example of unfair "intellectual" attacks on the president. The book's ability to *change* its
readers' perceptions is minimal. The crucial difference is that where
When She Was Good creates a disposition to look at things in a certain way through its artistic power, *Our Gang* depends for its effect
upon its reader being *predisposed* to its biases and perspective. To
begin writing fiction as an attack can, indeed, be a deadly kind of
beginning—and *Our Gang* is proof of the limits of such unsubtle
satire in spite of its success in capturing the fictions at the core of
the Official Version of Reality.

In one of his *Kaddish* poems, "Death to Van Gogh's Ear," Allen
Ginsberg declares that "history will make this poem prophetic and
its awful silliness a hideous spiritual music."[6] The events of the past
few years have conferred a similar status on *Our Gang,* for what it
lacks in artistry is more than made up for by its prescience.

CHAPTER 9

The Great American Joke
(The Great American Novel)

*T*he *Great American Novel* may be viewed as the final step in the comic progression which began in earnest with *Portnoy's Complaint*. In *Portnoy's Complaint* Roth allowed his comic sense to shape his treatment of his persistent moral preoccupations in an effort to approach them from a fresh perspective. His struggle for self-expression in that novel was a purgative one. It freed him from the academic bias which equates morality with seriousness, at the same time that it made him more confident of his ability to figure out his narrative situations stylistically. In *Our Gang* his humor was broader and more self-sufficient, but it was still controlled by a strong moral purpose. Though his techniques in both of these books were those of an American redskin, his intentions were still those of a paleface fully conscious of his moral responsibilities. He allowed himself to be a comic Jeremiah; but he remained a Jeremiah nonetheless. In *The Great American Novel* morality and satire are secondary; comedy—for its own sake and as an expression of the artist's consciousness set free—is paramount. It is his funniest, most purely comic novel, a *tour de force* of native American humor's techniques which makes his use of those techniques in his other comic fiction that much clearer.

Recalling the "bull sessions" that he and his friends had as boys in Newark, Roth commented in 1974 that he associated the "amalgam of mimicry, reporting, kibbitzing, disputation, satire, and legendizing from which we drew so much sustenance," with the vocation he now practices (RM, p. 4). Like *The Great American Novel*, the humor of the Old Southwest also had its origins in the art of oral storytelling, "and the oral tale had an important influence upon the matter of most Western tales and upon the manner of many of them."[1] According to Walter Blair, the content of the stories which grew out of oral sources on the frontier made extensive use of the vernacular, seldom indulged in subtle psychologizing, emphasized masculine pastimes, derived much of their humor from physical discomfort, employed exaggeration and popular myth, and dealt chiefly with the lower classes of society. The content of *The Great American Novel* displays each of these characteristics too.

Though the accurate rendition of American vernacular has always been one of Roth's novelistic strengths, in *The Great American Novel* he makes a point of specifically acknowledging his debt to transcriptions of oral sources by noting that: "The tape recorded recollections of professional baseball players that are deposited at the Library of the Hall of Fame in Cooperstown, New York, and are quoted in Lawrence Ritter's *The Glory of Their Times* (Macmillan, 1966), have been a source of inspiration to me while writing this book, and some of the most appealing locutions of these old-time players have been absorbed into the dialogue." Ritter's book is the source of Luke Gofannon's comments on triples, descriptions of Gil Gamesh's fastball and the spitball, and of many of the comments about the Mundys' coach, Ulysses S. Fairsmith; and comparison of any page in his book with the dialogue in Roth's novel will show how accurately Roth has reproduced the vernacular of his ballplayers.[2] Profanity, clichés, racial epithets, and ungrammatical constructions abound in *The Great American Novel,* just as they do in American speech.

In contrast to Roth's earlier novels and his more recent fiction—all of which are dominated by a concern with psychological realism reminiscent of both James and Kafka—*The Great American Novel* consciously eschews in-depth character analysis. Aside from Smitty, who is another of Roth's obsessed narrators, the only characters who are granted even a semblance of motivation are John Baal, Roland Agni, Mister Fairsmith, and Angela Trust. In each case the purpose is not to provide a more profound understanding of their actions but to enhance the novel's comic possibilities. Thus the personal histories of John Baal and Mister Fairsmith, the rogue and gentleman of the archetypal American comic situation, are provided so that Roth can spin yarns of Base Baal, Spit Baal, the Nicaraguan Mosquito League, and Mister Fairsmith's journey into the "heart of darkness." Roland Agni's biography, placed last in the "Visitors' Line-Up," is only elaborated to set the scene for that chapter's comic climax: Agni's rejection by the draft board and subsequent conversation with his father. It also provides Roland with the foundations of his parodic "tragic flaw"—a flaw necessary for the continued movement of the novel's plot once the humor to be derived from the comic defeats of the Ruppert Mundys has been all but thoroughly exhausted in the description of the Asylum game. Similarly, Angela Trust's scarlet past and subsequent reform are included to furnish the opportunity for tales about Babe Ruth and Ty Cobb, and also to pave the way for her zealous anticommunism, which serves as one of the catalysts for the political action in the last chapter.

By choosing baseball as his subject, Roth clearly limited himself to a primarily masculine audience. And just as a men's sporting magazine, the *Spirit of the Times,* published the humor of the Old Southwest, excerpts from *The Great American Novel* appeared in the pages of its contemporary equivalents: *Esquire* (May 1973) and *Sports Illustrated* (March 12, 1973). Roth's humor is no more welcome in the pages of today's *Atlantic* and *Harper's* than George Washington Harris's was a century ago; and Irving Howe is appalled at Roth's vulgarity as Edmund Wilson was at Harris's—and for the same reasons.

Chief among those reasons is the centrality of the humor of physical discomfort and scatology to his comic inventions. Though the tendency to exploit the comic possibilities inherent in the human body is apparent in American literature as far back as the earliest captivity narratives and almanacs, and *The Sot-Weed Factor,* macabre physical humor and grotesquerie have most frequently been associated with the comic writing of the Old Southwest. In the most famous of the early Southwestern tales, Thomas Bang Thorpe's "The Big Bear of Arkansas," Jim Doggett's account of his confrontation with the bear ends with Doggett's pants around his ankles; and *Sut Lovingood's Yarns* is full of similarly tasteless incidents. For Sut, Walter Blair has pointed out, "the procreative and bodily functions, the animal qualities in humans and the human qualities in animals" were the height of humor[3]—as they were for Mark Twain and are for Roth. In fact, both Southwestern humor and Roth's are equally inconceivable *without* physical discomfort, scatology, and obscenity. Midgets, dwarfs, half-wits, cripples, one-armed and one-legged characters swarm through the pages of *The Great American Novel* and typically tasteless—and hilarious—fun is made of their physical maladies. At the same time, prostitution, vaginal odors, sexual perversity of various kinds, urination, flatulence, and various forms of physical pain and punishment are freely and comically treated in ways designed to offend the squeamish and provoke (slightly embarrassed) delight in everyone else.

The exaggeration of Southwest humor took many forms. One of the most frequent was the hyperbolic treatment of the hero's physical prowess. Simon Suggs, Sut Lovingood, Mike Fink, and the legendary Davy Crockett were all larger than life. And often the heroes of the Southwestern tales were mysterious strangers shrouded in an aura of myth and legend. The heroes of Roth's book are also mythic—but in *The Great American Novel* the Ruppert Mundys reach heroic stature because of their almost superhuman *ineptitude* rather than their prowess.[4] Roth also provides a more conventional Southwestern hero in the person of Gil Gamesh: a ring-tailed roarer outfitted with a Tri-City Greenbacks' uniform. "I can beat anybody," is his bombastic motto; and his antics on and off the field echo the traditional boast and challenge: "nineteen years old and he had the courage and confidence of a Walter Johnson, and the competitive spirit of the Georgia Peach himself. The stronger the batter, the better Gil liked it. Rubbing the ball around in those enormous paws that hung down practically to his knees, he would glare defiantly at the man striding up to the plate (some of them stars when he was still in the cradle) and announce out loud his own personal opinion of the fellow's abilities. 'You couldn't lick a stamp. You couldn't beat a drum. Get your belly button in there, bud, you're what I call duck soup.' Then sneering away, he would lean way back, kick that right leg up sky-high like a chorus girl, and that long left arm would start coming around by way of Biloxi—and the next thing you knew it was strike one. He would burn them in just as beautiful and nonchalant as that, three in a row, and then exactly like a barber, call out 'Next!' He did not waste a pitch, unless it was to throw the ball at the batter's head, and he did not consider that a waste" (p. 56). The homely images, animal metaphors, vernacular speech, and descriptive exaggeration here are all in the Southwestern tradition.

After he throws seventy-seven consecutive strikes, Gil's seventy-eight pitch is declared a ball by his nemesis, umpire Mike the Mouth. As the fans explode in bloodthirsty anger at the temerity of the ump,

Gamesh spat high and far and watched the tobacco juice raise the white dust on the first-base foul line. He could hit anything with anything that boy. "Was a ball."

"*Was?*" Pineapple cried.

"Yep. Low by the hair off a little girl's slit, but low." And spat again, this time raising chalk along third. "Done it on purpose, Pineapple. Done it deliberate."

"Holy aloha!" the mystified catcher groaned—and fired the ball back to Gil. "How-why-ee?"

"So's to make sure," said Gil, his voice rising to a piercing pitch, "so's to make sure the old geezer behind you hadn't fell asleep at the switch! JUST TO KEEP THE OLD SON OF A BITCH HONEST! ... JUST SO AS TO MAKE CLEAR ALL THE REST WAS EARNED!... BECAUSE I DON'T WANT NOTHIN' FOR NOTHIN' FROM YOUSE! I DON'T NEED IT! I'M GIL GAMESH! I'M AN IMMORTAL, WHETHER YOU LIKE IT OR NOT!" (pp. 66-67).

The inept Ruppert Mundys are the central characters of *The Great American Novel,* and the reminiscences of the players in Ritter's book make it quite clear that in the early days baseball players were viewed as members of one of the lower classes of society. When members of the upper classes do appear in the novel, they are clearly aliens who serve as sources of awe or disdain for the Mundys, or as straight men for the comedy—as sophisticated Yankees do in the humor of the Old Southwest.

The *form* of *The Great American Novel* also resembles that of the Southwestern tales. It is characterized, as they were, by a "zest, a gusto, a sheer exuberance" in the telling that is distinctive.[5] Oral sources tend to foster stories made up of "episodes and anecdotes rather than thoroughly integrated plots."[6] And though the exile and destruction of the Ruppert Mundys and the dissolution of the Patriot League give Roth's novel more of a plot line than Southwestern tales characteristically possess, it is still essentially a "picaresque novel in the form of anecdotes within a framework," like *Sut Lovingood.*[7] Instead of using a single picaro whose presence provides a thread of unity to the anecdotes, however, Roth uses the Ruppert Mundys and their individual and/or collective involvement in each incident as a principle of unity within the framework established in his prologue.

Though *The Great American Novel* does not claim to be a mock oral tale as most of the Southwestern stories did, it exhibits many of the qualities associated with that form—vivid phrases from the vernacular, striking figures of speech, well-chosen active verbs, thumbnail sketches of characters, elaborate comic detail, a lot of direct quotation—and one of its most interesting stylistic aspects is its use of a modified frame technique.

The frame tale, characteristic of the best of Southwestern humor: "effectively characterized the storyteller, through direct description, through indirect description (i.e., the depiction of the effect he had upon his listeners), and through a long and highly characteristic dramatic monologue in which, revealingly, the imagination of the yarn-spinner was displayed...."[8]

Smitty's prologue to his tale performs exactly the same functions. Though it is obviously written, not transcribed from speech, it maintains an oral tone from its first sentence ("Call me Smitty") to its last ("HIT THE ROAD YA BUMS"). Smitty's direct address of the reader as "you" and "fans" contributes to this conversational quality. The prologue's purpose is to characterize Smitty in just the ways Blair describes above. To compensate for the absence of the usual third-person introduction of the storyteller, Smitty gives us a long description of himself *written* in the third person: "And just who is Word Smith? Fair enough. Short-winded, short-tempered, short-sighted as he may be, stiff-jointed, soft-bellied, weak-bladdered, and so on down to his slippers, anemic, arthritic, diabetic, dyspeptic, sclerotic, in dire need of a laxative, as he will admit to the first doctor or nurse who passes his pillow, and in *perpetual pain* (that's the last you'll hear about that), he's not cracked quite yet ..." (p. 3).

Indirect descriptions of Smitty form a prominent part of the prologue and are unanimous in their judgment of him and the current state of his sanity. After he has indulged in an opening "orgy of alliteration," for example, his doctor describes his performance as "outright ridiculous in a man of your age—it is tantamount to suicide. Frankly, I have to tell you that the feeling I come away with after reading the first few thousand words here is of a man making a spectacle of himself. It strikes me as wildly excessive, Smitty, and just a little bit desperate" (p. 11). (Here, as in the epilogue, Roth is also having some fun at the expense of his critics who, predictably, made the same charges against him and his book.)

To the other patients at the old age home, Valhalla, he is a "crazy old coot." When he tries to tell little boys in the park about the Patriot League, their fathers tend to put a finger to their temples to indicate that the cute old man is cracked. And the staff of the Hall of Fame tells Commissioner Bowie Kuhn that Smitty has "Bats in the belfry ... too deep to operate." Though Smitty tells us all of this with self-righteous sarcasm, we are prepared to read his fiction as the work of an obsessed narrator—the "paranoid fantasist" Roth described him as in an interview (RM, p. 90).

One of the strengths of the Southwestern frame tales was that they revealed a "splendidly realized character—a character who is memorable because the reader learns not only how he looked, how he talked, how others reacted to him, but also how his mind worked, and, more important, how his imagination worked."[9] And *The Great American Novel*'s prologue demonstrates this same strength. The literary allusions, the mythological foundations, the mixture of real and imagined characters, the juxtaposition of refined language and gutter slang, the penchant for alliteration and the paranoia which characterize Smitty's imagination in the prologue all reappear in his tale as well.

While the prologue is a modified frame tale in itself, it also serves as a frame for the larger tale of the Patriot League. And Roth's adaptation of the form is designed to emphasize the same incongruities that the Southwestern tales highlighted. The contrast between the narrative voice and the speech of the story's characters is developed for comic effect. So Gamesh's earthy vernacular is juxtaposed with the narrator's comment that "the boy would be rough when the call didn't go his way, and games have been held up for five and ten minutes at a time while Gamesh told the ump in question what he thought of his probity, eyesight, physiognomy, parentage, and place of national origin" (p. 58). And only the narrator has a vocabulary which includes words like "physiognomy," "probity," "patois," "ensconced," "felicitous," and "impeccably."

Like the authors of the Southwestern frame tales, Roth uses the incongruity between the situation at the time the tale is being told (1971) and the situation described in the yarn itself to remove the story of the Mundys and the Patriot League "from the realm of harassing reality into the realm of comedy,"[10] thereby rendering it less disturbing and more comic. According to Blair, the frame tale's effectiveness lies in the fact that "side by side with the realistic depiction of a commonplace scene ... there is told a tale colored by details which belong not in realism but in fantasy. Here the world of fact is a revealing background for a wildly imagined world.... This fantastic world is one of mythical splendors and poetic mysteries...."[11] This description of the tall tale's mechanics is, as we noted earlier, the key to Roth's method in *Portnoy's Complaint, Our Gang,* and *The Breast,* as well as in *The Great American Novel.* It characterizes both the overall pattern of his baseball book and the pattern of its individual scenes and chapters. *The Great American Novel*'s first chapter, "Home Sweet Home," illustrates Roth's use of the techniques.

During wartime, sacrifices are required and all ablebodied men are expected to serve in some capacity; Roth's story begins with that premise and opens with a sacrifice resulting from World War II. The Ruppert Mundys of the Patriot League are forced to relinquish their stadium to the government because of its strategic value as an embarkation point for soldiers headed overseas. As a result, the Mundys—their talents already decimated by the money-hungry sons of the late, great owner, Glorious Mundy, and by the war draft—are sentenced to play their whole season on the road. (The situation is analogous to that of the major leagues during World War I after Secretary of War Newton Baker issued his "work or fight" order.) Though General Oakhart, the Patriot League's president, objects to this violation of the rules of fair play upon which the national pastime is founded, he is in no position to protest the decision because of the near-fatal blow his league's prestige had suffered at the hands of the pitcher, Gil Gamesh, in 1933. Gamesh's story fills the bulk of the chapter. It begins firmly grounded in verifiable historical reality: "General Oakhart became President of the Patriot League in 1933, though as early as the winter of 1919–1920 he was being plugged for the commissionership of baseball, along with his friend and colleague General John "Blackjack" Pershing and the former President of the United States William Howard Taft" (p. 53).

The use of specific dates and the mention of recognizable historical personages lull us into accepting the reality of both Oakhart and the Patriot League. After all, numerous third leagues have vied with the American and National Leagues at various times throughout the history of baseball—most notably the Federal League—and the names of their presidents are hardly household words today. The aura of historical accuracy is maintained in the paragraphs which follow and mention Coolidge, Harding, Teapot Dome, and Commissioner Landis as factors in Oakhart's decision to accept the job as a stepping-stone to the presidency of the United States.

During his first year as commissioner, one of those immediate sensations who are annually heralded in the sporting press arrived

in the league: a pitcher named Gamesh, "first name 'a Gil."
Gamesh's gruff personality and heroic rages are perfectly acceptable to any reader who is even slightly familiar with the on- and
off-field exploits of Grover Cleveland Alexander, Babe Ruth, and
Ty Cobb—or of Richie Allen, Billy Martin, and numerous other
modern ballplayers. In fact the integration of such antisocial
"superstars" into the mores and values of the team is one of the
traditional plots of juvenile sports fiction.[12] The rapid public
mythologizing of Gamesh is credibly explained because his exploits, like those of Hank Aaron during the depths of the recession
of 1974, "constituted just about the only news that didn't make
you want to slit your throat over the barren dinner table. Men out
of work—and there were fifteen million of them across the land,
men sick and tired of defeat and dying for a taste of victory, rich
men who had become paupers overnight—would somehow scrape
two bits together to come out and watch from the bleachers as a big
unbeatable boy named Gil Gamesh did his stuff on the mound"
(p. 57).

Gamesh's heroic record soon totals six shutouts in his first six
starts, and a claim that if his seventh game had not been rained out
he would have extended his shutout streak through those nine
innings, *"and on to the very end of the season.* An outrageous
claim on the face of it, and yet there were those in the newsrooms,
living rooms and barrooms around this nation who believed him.
As it was, even lacking his 'fine edge,' as he called it, he gave up
only one run the next day, and never more than two in any game
that year" (p. 56). Against this realistic background, the
"stretchers" increase gradually. At first Gil's pitches are delivered
"by way of Biloxi," and then "by way of the tropical equator."
The conflict between Gamesh and Mike the Mouth develops, simultaneously, on a realistic plane (where it resembles Babe Ruth's repeated clashes with his umpiring antagonist, Brick Owens) and on
the level of a mythic confrontation.

Then Gamesh throws seventy-seven *consecutive* strikes—four
short of a literally perfect game—and the reader is forced to recognize that what is being described has become incredible. And Gil
aims at a batter "just above the nasal bone, [and] the fastball
clipped the bill of his blue and gray Aceldama cap and spun it
completely around on his head" (p. 69)—a feat only possible in a
cartoon or slapstick film comedy.

The same tall-tale pattern is repeated again and again in each of the book's chapters; but each time the line between reality and fantasy becomes more difficult to discern, and the casual reader is increasingly hard put to keep track of just where each tale crosses the line. Some of the *most* apparently fantastic elements in the book—the Ruppert Mundys decimated by the war, one-armed ballplayers, players dressed as women, midget ballplayers, Bob Yamm's farewell speech, *Bob Yamm,* Isaac Ellis's elaborate graphs and charts, the congressional hearings, the Nicaraguan Mosquito League—are actually the ones most firmly grounded in history.[13]

The characteristic content and form of the Southwestern tales grew out of a world-view which *The Great American Novel*—alone among Roth's books—also reflects. In that world capriciousness, coincidence, brute force, greed, viciousness, and duplicity are the universal human laws, and morality, altruism, and high purpose are treated as merely futile dreams of mankind. A character like Sut Lovingood, in "all his prejudice, brutality, cowardice, sensuality, coarseness, and vulgarity—coupled with his basic respect for veracity and freedom and hatred of hypocrisy," is the best we can expect to find in such a world.[14] Southwestern humor savages sacred cows and demolishes shibboleths to show the world as it is, rather than as it ought to be. Unlike Yankee humor, which usually took the form of satire as *Our Gang* did, it deprecates humanity as essentially retrograde and incapable of meaningful reform.

Roth's objections to description of *The Great American Novel* as "satiric"—which sharply contrast with his efforts to redefine that mode in an effort to include *Our Gang* within it—express a fundamentally Southwestern viewpoint:

The comedy in *The Great American Novel* exists for the sake of no "higher" value than the comedy itself; the "redeeming" value is not social or cultural reform, or moral instruction, but *comic inventiveness.* Destructive, or lawless, playfulness—and for the fun of it.

Now there is an art to this sort of thing that distinguishes it from sadism, nonsense, or even nihilism for the fun of it; however, the sadistic, the nonsensical, and the nihilistic are strong ingredients in the making of such comedy, and in the enjoyment of it. I don't like the word "satiric" because the suggestion of crude means employed for a higher purpose doesn't square with what I felt myself to be doing; it's too uplifting. "Satyric," suggesting the pure pleasure of exploring the anarchic and the unsocialized, is more like it (RM, p. 76).

"Southwestern" is even more like it.

Not purely Southwestern, however. For although the form, content, and vision of *The Great American Novel* are clearly in the Southwestern tradition, it would be an oversimplification to view the book as a contemporary example of Southwestern humor in purely undiluted form. Like *Portnoy's Complaint* and *Our Gang, The Great American Novel* combines the techniques of the humor of the Old Southwest with those of other native American comic strains. *Portnoy's Complaint* employs its Jewish context in a manner reminiscent of the Local Colorists; its satiric bite recalls the didacticism of Yankee humor. *Our Gang's* political satire is also in the Yankee tradition, while its emphasis on verbal distortions ties it to the humor of the Literary Comedians. And *The Great American Novel* also uses the techniques of the Literary Comedians to broaden its base and appeal.

Their humor was characterized by its use of amusing verbal devices of all kinds. It stressed deformity—"of sentences, words, quotations, grammar and logic" according to Walter Blair[15]—and was characterized by its use of anticlimax, incongruous lists, juxtapositions of incongruous proper names, euphemisms, puns, misquotations, parody, and burlesque.

Roth uses anticlimax consistently; for example, in his description of Hothead Ptah's opportunity to play for the Ruppert Mundys. Hothead is the Mundys' one-legged catcher, and, the narrator comments, "it is one of life's grisly ironies that what is a catastrophe for most of mankind, invariably works to the advantage of the few who live on the fringes of the human community. On the other hand, it is a grisly irony to live on the fringes of the human community" (p. 113). Incongruous lists appear throughout the book, beginning with Smitty's opening spate of alliterations. Juxtaposition of incongruous names is employed on the reviewing stand for a parade honoring the Mundys included "Secretary of War Stimson, Governor Edison [and] the Mayor of Port Ruppert, Boss Stuvwxyz" (p. 50)—as in s-t-u-v-w-x-y-z; or that the conversation in 1933 centered on Adolph Hitler, Franklin Roosevelt, *and* Gil Gamesh. Then there are the names of the Mundys themselves, each of which combines the banal and the mythic (or mythic-sounding): Wayne Heket, John Baal, Roland Agni, Frenchy Astarte, Jolly Cholly Tuminikar, Deacon Demeter, Howie Pollux, Red Kronos, etc.

The Asylum game—played against the members of a mental institution—is as hilarious and effective a use of understatement as

Edgar Derby's nineteenth-century classic, "Interview Between the Editor and the Phoenix." And euphemism combines with the use of incongruous language in the description of a series of Gamesh's pitches, aimed successively at the batter's "mandible," "occipital," "zygomatic arch" and "nasal bone" (pp. 68–69). Puns appear throughout the book. Bob Yamm, the midget pinch-hitter for the Kakoola Reapers, is such a favorite of the fans that they bellow "YAMM! "YAMM!" like "starving savages invoking their potato god" (p. 210). And Yamm, who is small potatoes in the big leagues, was certainly named with this final pun in mind. When Mike Rama caught a ball, and then proceeded to run into the outfield wall, the "umpire who rushed to the outfield to call the play (before calling the hospital) invariably found the baseball lodged snugly in the pocket of the unconscious left-fielder's glove. 'Out!' he would shout. . . ." (p. 113).

Two of the funnier "one-liners" in the book combine deformity of logic, incongruity, and anticlimax. Each time Mike Rama was released from the hospital following one of his collisions with the left-field wall, we are told, his coach, Mr. Fairsmith, would try to impress the wall's physical reality upon him:

"Michael," Mr. Fairsmith would say, "can you tell me what is going on in your mind when you act like this? Do you have any idea?"

"Sure. Nothin'. I'm thankin' about catchin' the ball, that's all. I ain't havin' no sex thoughts or nothin', Mister Fairsmith, I swear."

"Michael, I am cognizant of the fact that there are no walls surrounding the ball fields in the part of the world where you grew up, but surely, lad, you had walls in your house when you were a boy down there. Or am I mistaken?"

"Oh, sure, we had walls. We wuz poor, but we wuzn't that poor" (p. 114).

When Kid Heket ponders the antics of the inmates of the asylum on the field during the exhibition game, he finally comments judiciously: "You know somethin' . . . those fellas ain't thinkin'. No sir, they just ain't usin' their heads" (p. 174). Roland Agni's draft physical, and his conversation with his father afterward, work on the same comic principles.

Like the humor of the Literary Comedians, *The Great American Novel* makes extensive use of parody and burlesque. The prologue parodies the style of sportswriters, and the style and image of Ernest Hemingway (". . . he turned and went out the door.

Through the window I watched him pass under an arc-light and across the street'' (p. 35) echoes the ending of "The Killers"). It also pokes fun at criticism of *The Canterbury Tales, The Scarlet Letter, Huckleberry Finn,* and *Moby Dick.* Smitty's tale is a mock epic—complete with chapter headnotes like those of the eighteenth-century novels—which burlesques all the conventions of the national epic which "The Great American Novel" supposedly should have, and the very concept of "The Great American Novel" as well. The last section of "Home Sweet Home" burlesques Jewish history as it is related in the Bible and used by contemporary Jewish writers. The Mundys have been chosen to wander, according to Mister Fairsmith, their coach and religious leader, until they are restored to their former greatness. The themes of suffering and salvation in the Diaspora, as they appear in the fiction of Jewish writers like Bellow and Malamud, are implicitly burlesqued too, as the chapter moves to its final punch line: "General Oakhart, let my players go." Mister Fairsmith's trip into the "heart of darkness" to bring baseball to the jungles—jungles where the natives murmur "Typee" and "Omoo"—ends with a native boy saying of him, "Mistah Baseball, he dead" (p. 305) in a parody of Conrad's line. And the epilogue burlesques the reviews of *The Great American Novel*—before they appeared.

There is much more that might be said of the book—of its status as a fan's burlesque history of baseball, of its use of sport as a metaphor for American society and its linking of religion and sports, of its conscious parody of the contemporary writer's fondness for imposing mythological structures on his fictions (as Malamud did in his baseball book, *The Natural*). But its primary importance to the present discussion lies in the fact that it is a casebook display of the comic techniques Roth employed in his two previous novels. It is an example of a "writer's hijinks" which its author decided to publish as the result of a quite conscious choice to see if the redskin could accomplish things the paleface could not. And, having carried the possibilities of "pure" comedy as a means to his ends to its outer limits in *The Great American Novel,* Roth turned in the works he wrote next to different techniques.

In one sense, both *Our Gang* and *The Great American Novel* can be seen as false steps—in spite of their comic inventiveness and their exploration of the fantastic nature of the authorized versions of reality in the American "asylum." For by choosing to focus on the public sphere in both of them, Roth sacrificed much of the "felt life" which has given his best fictions their intensity and power. Both books are vulnerable to charges of unevenness and superficiality; and *The Great American Novel* skirts the "crudest forms of frontier psychology" which Rahv remarked in the worst of the writing of the redskins. Both suffer because they place a priority on the public life which does not allow Roth to exercise his most outstanding talent: his ability to project the private confusions and domestic crises of heroes grappling with unmanageable realities we all must face in one form or another.

In another, more important sense, however, both books were necessary and worthwhile experiments. When he found that humor had helped him to capture the tenor of contemporary experience in *Portnoy's Complaint*—and had allowed him to express the latent impulses of the redskin that he had always felt at the same time—Roth, quite logically, pursued that aesthetic strategy in *Our Gang* and *The Great American Novel,* as a part of his search for a fuller range of expression than his earlier realism permitted. In the process of writing these two books, however, he learned once again the lesson of the four drafts which evolved into *Portnoy's Complaint:* that *for him* neither Jamesian decorum nor Southwestern "satyrs" are satisfactory means to express adequately the incongruities and absurdities of contemporary life. The former cannot deal with the inexplicable; the latter tends to degenerate into meaningless frivolity. For Roth to express his talents most fully a synthesis is required which will admit realistic detail, inexplicability, *and* comedy—the kind of synthesis he had achieved in *Portnoy's Complaint.* The kind that he found in the work of Franz Kafka.

CHAPTER 10

Looking at Kafka

A SKED to pick the story he considered his best for inclusion in a 1974 anthology, Roth chose " 'I Always Wanted You to Admire My Fasting'; or Looking at Kafka," which was first published in *American Review 17* in 1973.[1] The choice was both appropriate and revealing—not only because the story is most certainly one of his most mature, but also because literally and figuratively looking at Kafka has played a central part in the composition of his most significant recent fictions. The story blends reality and fantasy with carefully controlled comedy, and the result is an outstanding example of the Kafkan synthesis Roth also achieved in *Portnoy's Complaint, The Breast, My Life as a Man,* and *The Professor of Desire.*

Since one of the primary concerns of Roth's work has always been the incredibility of the quotidian, the horrors lurking just beneath the surface of our mundane lives, it is hardly surprising that his fiction has reflected an increasing affinity with Kafka's. And this common thematic element has been reinforced by a crucial technical affinity as well. According to Edwin Muir, "the form which Kafka's imagination takes most often is that of comedy; but the originality of this comedy lies in its union with the deepest seriousness."[2] After eight books, Roth told Joyce Carol Oates that "Sheer Playfulness and Deadly Seriousness" were his "closest friends" (RM, p. 111). The Kafkan yoking of these extremes is what Roth achieved in *Portnoy's Complaint* and, in spite of its manic surface, it is in that novel, not *The Breast,* that Kafka's influence on Roth's recent work first became apparent.

A half-century before thirty-three-year-old Alexander Portnoy began his uncensored monologue in a New York psychoanalyst's plush Manhattan office, thirty-six-year-old Franz Kafka sat at his writing desk in a small Prague apartment putting the final touches on a soul-baring letter that would never be delivered. Like Alexander Portnoy's *Complaint,* Kafka's *Letter to His Father* is a filial confession and an indictment, a storyteller's apologia which attempts to come to emotional and intellectual terms with the parent its author holds responsible for the neurotic nightmare that is his life. Though it may not seem especially noteworthy that two Jewish sons' complaints about their parents' detrimental influence on their lives and characters should share some common elements, Portnoy's monologue echoes *so many* of the words and phrases in Kafka's letter that the parallels between the two—and what they imply about Roth's changing literary allegiances—demand fuller investigation than they have yet had.

Roth has been more than willing to acknowledge his debt. In 1969 when George Plimpton asked him if the humor in *Portnoy's Complaint* had been influenced by the routines of stand-up comic Lenny Bruce, Roth replied that, while he admired Bruce's mimicry and his combination of fantasy and social observation, he had been more strongly influenced when writing the book by a "sit-down comic named Franz Kafka and a very funny bit he does called 'The Metamorphosis' " (RM, p. 21). He elaborated, saying that "I don't mean I modeled my book after any work of his, or tried to write a Kafka-*like* novel." But, "at the time I was beginning to play with the ideas for what turned out to be *Portnoy's Complaint,* I was teaching a lot of Kafka in a course I gave once a week at the University of Pennsylvania. When I look back now on the reading I assigned that year, I realize that the course might have been called 'Studies in Guilt and Persecution'—'The Metamorphosis,' *The Castle,* 'In the Penal Colony,' *Crime and Punishment,* 'Notes from Underground,' *Death in Venice, Anna Karenina* . . . my own previous two novels, *Letting Go* and *When She Was Good.* . . . I had read somewhere that [Kafka] used to giggle to himself while he worked. Of course! It was all so *funny,* this morbid preoccupation with punishment and guilt. Hideous, but funny" (RM, pp. 21-22).

Though Kafka's enigmatic, allegorical style is, in many ways, the antithesis of Roth's own—thus he says he did not aspire to write a Kafka-*like* novel—Kafka's humor, his preoccupation with moral action and boundless guilt, and his ability to merge fantasy and realistic detail into a "magic realism" were all elements Roth admired and related to as he struggled to write about the same subjects in his own idiom. Reading and teaching Kafka, as he had earlier read and taught James and Twain, he apparently came to appreciate just how deeply the Prague writer's concerns and techniques were rooted in the soil that nourished his own. "I began reading Kafka seriously in my early thirties," he tells us, "at a time when I was enormously dismayed to find myself drifting away, rather than towards, what I had taken to be my goals as a writer and a man—at a time, in other words, when I was unusually sensitized to Kafka's tales of spiritual disorientation and obstructed energies." And he found that "the ways in which Kafka allowed an obsession to fill every corner of every paragraph, and the strange grave comedy he was able to make of the tedious, enervating rituals of accusation and defense, furnished me with a number of clues as to how to give imaginative expression to preoccupations of my own."[3]

Many contemporary writers have had a similar experience, and, according to Helen Weinberg, they have "transformed the Kafkan vision by using it in a way that coincides with American consciousness and with their own native perceptions."[4] This is certainly true of Roth and *Portnoy's Complaint.* For while Roth's novel grew out of Newark memories and traditional American concerns and conflicts—out of life, not literature—Roth's immersion in Kafka's writing at the time he began it helped to shape his narrative. Roth had his students read the *Letter,* and then "sometimes asked them to take Kafka as their model and try to write letters as candid and self-scrutinizing to their own mothers or fathers." Eventually, he acknowledges now, "I took the assignment upon myself, in a manner of speaking, and wrote a novel about yet another family-obsessed Jewish bachelor in his thirties. . . ."[5]

Kafka's letter to his father was delivered to an intermediary, his mother; Portnoy's complaint is delivered to another intermediary, Dr. Spielvogel, who (purportedly) passes it on to us. Both messages begin by acknowledging the overpowering parent's hold over the child's imagination. "You asked me recently why I maintain that I am afraid of you," Kafka's letter opens;[6] "You ask me why I maintain that I am obsessed with you" is the unstated premise underlying the actual premise of Portnoy's complaint—"She was so deeply imbedded in my consciousness that for the first year of school I seem to have believed that each of my teachers was my mother in disguise" (PC, p. 3).

Kafka's explanation of the impulse which led him to write his fictions also explains the forces which prompt Portnoy's monologue. "My writing was all about you," Franz writes to the parent he sees as both godlike figure and object of contempt, "all I did, after all, was to bemoan what I could not bemoan upon your breast. It was an intentionally long-drawn-out leave-taking from you, yet, although it was enforced by you, it did take its course in a direction determined by me" (L, p. 87).

The direction both complaints take begins by cataloguing remarkably similar childhood memories and proceeds to show how the experiences of that childhood produced a child-man. Both sons recall their parents as oppressors, tyrannical judges who issued harsh, irrational edicts and demanded complete subservience. Franz dredges up the memory of a night when he annoyed Hermann Kafka by whimpering for a glass of water: "After several vigorous threats had failed to have any effect, you took me out of bed, carried me out onto the *pavlatche* [balcony], and left me there alone for a while outside the shut door.... Even years afterwards I suffered from the tormenting fantasy that the huge man, my father, the ultimate authority, would come almost for no reason at all and take me out of bed in the night and carry me out onto the *pavlatche,* and that meant I was a mere nothing to him" (L, p. 17). Portnoy has equally vivid memories of being exiled for comparably minor offenses: "When I am bad I am locked out of the apartment. I stand at the door hammering until I swear I will turn over a new leaf. But what is it I have done? ... Will someone with the answer to that question please stand up! I am so awful she will not have me in her house *a minute longer.* When I once called my sister a cockydoody, my mouth was immediately washed with a cake of brown laundry soap; this I understand. But banishment? What can I possibly have done! ..." (PC, pp. 13–15).

Sophie's highly effective rhetorical methods are the same ones Kafka says "never failed to work with me ... abuse, threats, irony, spiteful laughter, and—oddly enough—self-pity" (L, p. 35). When little Alex refuses to eat his dinner, she sits down next to him with a breadknife in her hand and asks menacingly, "Which do I want to be, weak or strong, a man or a mouse?" And the memory prompts Portnoy to cry, "Doctor, why, why oh why oh why oh why does a mother pull a breadknife on her own son? I am six, seven years old, how do I know she really wouldn't use it?" (PC, p. 16). Franz recalls the trauma caused by similar threats from his father which are fraught with similar Freudian implications of castration: "how terrible for me was, for instance, that 'I'll tear you apart like a fish,' although I knew, of course, that nothing worse was to follow (admittedly, as a child I didn't know that), but it was almost exactly in accord with my notions of your power, and I saw you as being capable of doing this too" (L, p. 37). In retrospect, both sons cannot help but feel that in incidents like these "the expenditure of anger and malice seemed to be in no proper relation to the subject itself" (L, p. 39).

Of course, not all of their childhood memories of their parents are bad ones. Alex fondly recounts loving scenes with his mother and affectionately recalls his exhausted father coming to Bradley Beach to visit his vacationing family on summer weekends; Franz remembers that "you joined us in the country, in the summer holidays, on Sundays, worn out from work" (L, p. 43). Alex wishes for the natural habitat and masculine companionship he and his father shared in the Turkish baths, where he took pride in the manly proportions of his father's *schlong;* Kafka recalls undressing in the same bathing hut with Hermann, "proud of my father's body" (L, pp. 20–21).

Though such wondrously happy moments are not forgotten, both sons cannot help but feel that these incidents had the effect of rendering their suffering more vivid, their guilt more powerful, and of making their world, as Kafka puts it, "still more incomprehensible." And these pleasant memories are heavily outweighed by memories which intensify their resentment of their parents' persistent authoritarianism and unceasing reproaches. Faced with his overbearing father, the Prague son lost the capacity to talk: "I became completely dumb, cringed away from you, and only dared to stir when I was so far away from you that your power could no longer reach me—at least directly" (L, p. 35). The Newark son cannot *stop* talking. Where Franz reacted to his predicament with aphasia and sullen docility, Alex responds with obstreperous rebellion. Where Kafka did not dare to stir, Portnoy practices his own brand of rebellious "stirring" anywhere and anytime.

In spite of these differences in the style their responses take, however, the fundamental nature of those reactions is identical. Portnoy rejects Judaism and chases *shiksas* because he, like Kafka, is determined to "flee everything that even remotely reminded me of you" (L, p. 53). Neither son succeeds very well in his determination to be free of his parent's dominion. In their parents' homes, according to Kafka, "one became a glum, inattentive, disobedient child, always intent on escape, mainly within one's self" (L, p. 41)—and remained, like Portnoy, "locked-up in self" even in adulthood.

"I was so unsure of everything," Kafka writes in a central statement which ironically suggests more clearly than any other his kinship with Portnoy, *"that, in fact I possessed only what I actually had in my hands or in my mouth or what was at least on its way there"* (L, p. 63, my emphasis). Portnoy's selfishness and masturbatory sexuality grow out of the same sense of alienation from his environment, the same sense of dispossession: he calls his penis his adolescent "battering ram to freedom," and echoes Kafka, lamenting, "Doctor, do you understand what I was up against? My wang was really all I had that I could call my own" (PC, p. 33). Both son's insecurities are exacerbated by hypochondria and actual physical ailments—Kafka's generally poor health and eventual tuberculosis, Portnoy's undescended testicle. Both sons see their difficulties as a direct result of their family's Judaism. "Jewish schoolboys in our country often tend to be odd; among them one finds the most unlikely things," Kafka notes cryptically (L, p. 89). Portnoy is typically less restrained and more specific about some of the varieties of that oddness—when he tells the story of Ronald Nimkin, and then delivers his diatribe about all the nice Jewish sons who are flouncing about Fire Island.

Both Franz and Alex are appalled by their parents' prejudices and apparent lack of feeling for the plight of the less fortunate, and both voice liberal sentiments which gall their elders' sense of proprieties. Portnoy insists on having his meals with the black housekeeper, berates his parents for their racial prejudice, and becomes a champion of the downtrodden of Manhattan; to compensate for his father's insensitivity to his business employees—whom Hermann Kafka called "paid enemies"—Franz becomes subservient to them. And both defend themselves against their parents with the weapons of the impotent: jokes and ridicule.

The neuroses of the grown sons, which they attribute to the treatment they received as children, are also similar. Alex and Franz have a common predilection for fantasies of adverse judgment and retribution which are the products of their pent-up guilt. Since they are more dependent on their parents' opinions than their own for their evaluations of themselves—and more dependent on their parents than on anything else, such as external success—and since their parents have already judged them inadequate, both as sons and men, they cannot gain any lasting satisfaction from any of their public triumphs. Kafka imagines his gymnasium teachers as a jury that will one day judge him unworthy, in spite of his excellent grades, and "spew him out"; Portnoy imagines himself exposed as a moral degenerate and a hypocrite before the synagogue's congregation, in banner headlines, and before the "Coppers" in his mind.

As a result of their upbringing, both Franz and Alex are psychologically incapable of marriage—either to another Jew or to a Gentile. Portnoy dreams, at the end of his monologue, of an idyllic life as a Newark husband and father who plays softball with the men on Sundays, visits his parents, and gathers with his wife and family at the end of the day to listen to Jack Benny on the radio. But Jack Benny is no longer on the radio, and Portnoy's dream, like Kafka's abortive engagements, is simply one more of his "grandiose and hopeful attempts at escape" from the unalterable reality of his condition and character. Kafka's letter and Portnoy's psychoanalysis both occur after the failure of a love affair to develop into a permanent relationship, and Kafka's explanation of his failure to make his plans for marriage become reality speaks for both of them. He feels that "marrying, founding a family, accepting all the children that come, supporting them in this insecure world and perhaps even guiding them a little, is, I am convinced, the utmost a human being can succeed in doing" (L, p. 99). But though there was nothing that Kafka admired more than ordinary everyday happiness, like Portnoy he could not find it for himself through marriage because "we being what we are, marrying is barred to me because it is your very own domain. Sometimes I imagine the map of the world spread out and you stretched diagonally across it. And I feel as if I could consider living in only those regions that either are not covered by you or are not within your reach. And in keeping with the conception I have of your magnitude, these are not many and not very comforting regions—and marriage is not among them" (L, p. 115).

"I'm not going to say, of course, that I have become what I am only as a result of your influence," Kafka writes at the beginning of his letter. "That would be very much exaggerated (and I am indeed inclined to that exaggeration)" (L, p. 11). So is Portnoy. And the essential difference between their two complaints lies in their narrators' responses to that exaggerative inclination. Where Kafka resists it, closes his letter with the acknowledgment that "things cannot in reality fit together the way the evidence does in my letter; life is more than a Chinese puzzle" (L, p. 125), Portnoy eagerly embraces a reductionism which explains his life as part of a Jewish joke or a Freudian case study. This difference results in the contrasting tone of the two works, which is more a function of their differing audiences and intentions than of their narrators' actual viewpoints and perspectives.

Kafka, who is writing a letter *to* his adversary, and is therefore restrained in an effort to convince rather than alienate, never addresses his father in a tone of hatred, scorn, or even cold indifference. Portnoy, who is delivering his complaint to his psychoanalyst in the privacy of the doctor's office, has no reason for restraint, and he exhibits none of Kafka's fair-mindedness. Another major difference between the two works is, of course, the gender of the sons' chief antagonists. In part, this is a result of their authors' differing personal demons; in part, it is a natural result of a shift in location from a patriarchal to a matriarchal culture.[7] But these differences do not obviate the fact that the two works are alike in so many respects.

This is not to say that Roth simply imitated Kafka's letter. His description of the five-year genesis of *Portnoy's Complaint,* which spans the period when he was still influenced by the styles of Henry James and the American humorists, militates against such a facile conclusion. But his comments about the book, and about Kafka, suggest that while he was already writing the novel out of his own experience and fictional concerns he discovered—or at least fully realized for the first time—just how much that experience and those concerns had in common with Kafka's. "On a recent trip to Prague," he wrote, "I found it reminded me of nothing so much as the Newark in which I'd grown up in the thirties and forties, a shabby, impoverished provincial capital under the cloud of war...."[8]

And so, having set out to write a Freudian novel about parent-child relations in the Jewish families he had known in that Newark, he could hardly have escaped echoing some of the themes and primal experiences so central to Kafka's imagination and letter. Once he discovered this coincidence of concern and technique while writing *Portnoy's Complaint,* Roth apparently made a conscious decision to pursue that relationship in the fiction he wrote next. Kafka managed to combine surface detail and fantasy into a realism which achieved the effects Roth has sought to produce in his own work. When he turned from the humor of *Our Gang* and

The Great American Novel to the more substantive fictions of *The Breast, My Life as a Man,* and *The Professor of Desire* Roth continued to look to Kafka for models of the technical synthesis he first explored in *Portnoy's Complaint*—and continued to look *at* Kafka's picture, which he hung in both of the rooms where he normally works.[9]

CHAPTER 11

The Credible Incredible and the Incredible Credible (The Breast)

I N *The Breast* Roth created a sexual variation on "The Metamorphosis" which reveals his own artistic preoccupations. Though published before *The Great American Novel*, it was *written after* the baseball novel and before *My Life as a Man*,[1] and it is best approached as a transitional work which bridges the wide technical and thematic gap which separates those two, highly disparate books. *The Breast* bridges that gap by employing an inversion of the tall-tale pattern used in *The Great American Novel* to highlight the existential and aesthetic questions which dominate *My Life as a Man*. Its language is a combination of the obscenity which marks his comic fiction and the more moderate and restrained diction of his other work. Though the story contains humorous passages, they are chiefly made up of Kepesh's puns and jokes ("a little bitter and quite lame," as he admits) and, after the comic extravagance of *The Great American Novel*, indicate a significant shift in emphasis. Frederick Crews captured the essence of the change, when he observed that Roth "having chosen a story line that looks ideally suited to his taste for outrageous sexual farce, has side-stepped the opportunity and instead written a work of high seriousness."[2] The story focuses, as all of his best work has, on the social being's private life—but in this case that private life belongs to a man turned into a creature as fantastic as the Big Bear of Arkansas.

The book is novella length—seventy-eight pages in the cloth edition—and the fact that Roth chose to publish it *as a book*, instead of as a story, may be interpreted as an indication of his own evaluation of its significance to the evolution of his *oeuvre*; an evaluation with which many of the book's reviewers were inclined to disagree. Used as an opportunity for punning headlines ("Clean

132

Breast," "Uplift," "A Suitable Case for Mastectomy," "Falsie," "Literary Titillations," "Braless in Gaza," "a tempest in a D-cup," etc.), scorned as a popular author's money-making scheme which should have been relegated to publication in *Playboy*, attacked for its brevity and allusiveness, dismissed as final proof of the essential vulgarity of its author's imagination, *The Breast* has probably aroused more critical hostility toward Roth than anything else he has written.

It has also been subjected to less substantive comment. Yet understanding his intentions in it, and recognizing its relationship to the works which precede and follow it, is crucial to any thorough appreciation of the coherence and conscious direction that Roth's fiction has taken since *Goodbye, Columbus.*

Peter S. Prescott of *Newsweek*, consistently one of Roth's most perceptive reviewers, suggested some of that coherence in his review of *The Breast* when he commented that "most of Roth's best work is at least partly aimed at some arrested area of our development. Excess, obsession, perversion (in the broadest sense of vectors deflected from their proper courses), the self-enclosed universes that we build around ourselves and our efforts to escape them: these are Roth's themes. Humor, teetering on hysteria, the shriek deflated by self-conscious irony, the narcissistic maundering of the analysand; these are his tones of voice."[3] From the beginning of his career, as we have seen, Roth's fiction has focused on precisely these themes, used these tones of voice, in an effort to convey the interpenetration of reality and fantasy in the private and public spheres. His constant aim has been, as he said in "Reading Myself," to "establish a passageway from the imaginary that seems real to the real that seems imaginary, a continuum between the credible incredible and the incredible credible." And it has always seemed to Roth that that was "an activity something like what many deranged countrymen must engage in every morning, reading the newspaper on the one hand and swooming over the prophetic ingenuity of their paranoia on the other" (RM, pp. 91–92).

In the process of trying to establish that passageway, Roth, like Kafka before him, has been an artist of neurosis. As he told Alan Lelchuk in a conversation on *The Breast*, "it seems to me that I've frequently written about what Bruno Bettelheim calls 'behavior in extreme situations.' Or perhaps until *The Breast* what I've written about most has been extreme behavior in ordinary situations. From the beginning, at any rate, I seem to have concerned myself with men and women whose moorings have been cut, and who are swept away from their native shores and out to sea, sometimes on a tide of their own righteousness and resentment ... Lucy Nelson in *When She Was Good*, Gabe Wallach and Paul Herz in *Letting Go*, Alex Portnoy in *Portnoy's Complaint*—all are people living beyond their psychological and moral means; it isn't a matter of sinking and swimming—they have, as it were, to invent the crawl" (RM, pp. 65–66). "Frustration in reality," Freud called it. In Roth's fiction, that frustration *in* reality is projected as a direct result of the frustrating nature *of* reality—as it is experienced by his obsessed but somehow representative heroes and heroines. And none of his protagonists faces a more frustrating reality than David Alan Kepesh.

In *Portnoy's Complaint, Our Gang,* and *The Great American Novel*, Roth began with real people and events and then fantastically exaggerated them for comic effect in an effort to convey the texture of the reality that he sees around him. In *The Breast* he reverses that process, begins with a patently unreal event, a fantastic and comic transformation, and then explores its implications with restraint and rigorous realism. The approach is a cross between Kafka's and the Southwestern humorist's.

Though it was inspired by Kafka's tale of Gregor Samsa's metamorphosis, however, Roth's story is marked by a critical difference in intention. Where his predecessor's third-person narrative insists on the reality of its situation through its use of point of view, Roth's first-person tale tries to make its readers accept "the fantastic situation as taking place in what we call the real world," at the same time that it works to make "the reality of the horror one of the issues of the story." Kafka chose to deny his story some of its potential ramifications by asserting on the first page that Gregor's transformation into a gigantic beetle "was no dream"; Roth makes explanation—and the impulse toward explanation—a central element in his tale. Kepesh cannot be absolutely sure of where the reality of his predicament lies, and so neither can we. Whether his transformation is or isn't a "dream, or a hallucination, or a psychotic delusion" is the question which determines both the form and the meaning of *The Breast* (RM, p. 67).

Through his use of this perspective, Roth manages to create a provocative fable: of a rational man forced to acknowledge the irrationality of experience, of the artist struggling to make the incredibility of reality credible in his fiction and thereby create ordered art out of chaotic and disordered experience. The vehicle for his fable is the story of a moral humanist absurdly confronted with the ultimate in dehumanizing reification: metamorphosis into a 155-pound erogenous zone.

Before this fantastic transformation, Kepesh is a professor of comparative literature, a survivor of a "Grand Guignol marriage" and a lacerating divorce, a product of five years of psychoanalysis (i.e., self-dramatization), a self-confessed hypochondriac, a devotee of aesthetic and ethical satisfactions and of the virtues of punctuality, courtesy, honesty, and "good grades in all subjects"—in other words, a typical Roth hero. As Theodore Solotaroff has noted, "Kepesh might be Portnoy five years later—Dr. Spielvogel's work being done, the inner tumult reduced to manageable nervousness, the vanity to a certain finickiness; the wild joking replaced by a cool wit; the depressive ties to Jewishness, family and especially women all loosened and made manageable by a little gap that has been opened between impulse and act known as reason; and the swamps of the id, at least the more malarial of them, reclaimed by solidified ego. The terms of the reality principle having been clarified, accepted, and internalized, Kepesh is all set for a well-adjusted life and then reality turns him into the grotesque image of his deepest fear (and desire): six feet ... of blind, immobile, and maddeningly tactile flesh in which all this newly found 'strength of character' and 'will to live,' to quote his analyst, are buried intact and put to the ultimate test."[4]

So after the transformation he is still the same "man," retains all of his premetamorphosis personality characteristics. But physically he has become an (un)reasonable facsimile of a female breast: "an organism with the general shape of a football, or a dirigible ... of a spongy consistency ... [with] a nipple, cylindrical in shape, projecting five inches from my 'body,' and perforated at the tip with seventeen openings ... [which] provide me with something remotely like a mouth and ears" (pp. 12–14). His condition, one of the book's reviewers noted, is not covered by Blue Cross.

"Ridiculous!" we say. "Unbelievable! Incredible!"—and David Alan Kepesh, professor and rational humanist, cannot help but agree: "A man cannot turn into a breast other than in his own imagination," he protests to his analyst at one point, "it is a physiological and biological and anatomical impossibility" (pp. 49–50). To which Dr. Klinger placidly replies, "How then do you explain your predicament?" How Kepesh explains it—or tries to—is the subject of his narrative.

Like his readers, Kepesh is a reasonable man who expects the events of his life to be, if not pleasant or completely under his control, at least *explicable*. Thus he is compelled to search for explanations. But his search is ultimately futile because his predicament defies absolute explanation; his unmooring "can't be traced (much to his dismay, too) to psychological, social or historical causes," as the plights of Roth's other heroes can be (RM, p. 66).

His metamorphosis is even more radical than Gregor Samsa's because it deprives him of sight, smell, taste, and movement, as well as human form. He is not just reduced to a lower rung on the chain of being, but to a normally inanimate *part* of a being—and a sexual part at that. Left with nothing but sensation, speculation, and faulty expression, he is more literally "locked up in self" than any of Roth's other heroes. But not only is he the Roth hero *in extremis*, he is more alienated, more solipsistic, than any other hero in recent American fiction. He is pure self-consciousness and can do nothing *but* think about his condition and its possible causes.

His narrative actually begins after he has come to an uneasy and ironic acceptance of the inexplicability of his condition; and its form is essentially that of a disputation which "proceeds by attempting to answer the objections and reservations that might be raised in a skeptical reader by its own fantastic premise" (RM, p. 68). Roth intended that it have the design of a rebuttal or a rejoinder—and it does. Kepesh recounts all of the alternatives that he grasped at and finally had to discard in favor of the final supposition that his metamorphosis is real, and, in the process, he answers the objections that his readers also have, thereby forcing them to accept his supposition themselves.

His tale inverts the strategy of the tall-tale pattern Roth employed in his three previous novels. The tall tale, like Kepesh's story (and Kafka's), mingles real and fantastic creatures and events. But where the tall tale is designed to distance the reader from its action so that its comic events can be removed from the realm of harassing reality, *The Breast*'s approach is specifically designed to eliminate that distance. The tall tale begins with realistic detail—names, dates, places, recognizable situations—and then gradually shades into fantasy in an effort to dupe the reader into accepting the fantastic as real. Kepesh's tale also begins in realistic detail, but it presents the fantastic *as* fantastic—he admits that he has become a mammary gland "such as could only appear, one would have thought, in a dream or a Dali painting'' (p. 12)—and then demands that his reader accept the fantastic as real, the incredible as credible, *in spite of* what ''one would have thought.'' Where the tall tale coerces a willing *suspension of disbelief, The Breast* attempts to coerce *belief* by meeting its readers' objections to its believability head-on. ''This is a true story, if not for you, reader, for me,'' Kepesh insists (p. 34)—and he tries to make his readers accept its truth by using the same kind of careful documentation we find in both the tall tale and in Kafka's fiction.[5]

He begins with a precise and realistic description of the symptoms which preceded his metamorphosis. This description of the ''incubation period'' of his illness is full of vivid detail—detail which is absolutely necessary to establish Kepesh's authenticity and candor as a person and a narrator. ''It began oddly,'' he writes (or dictates, or whatever), ''with a mild, sporadic tingling in the groin'' which he attributed to his inveterate hypochondria and chose to ignore. But a week later he noticed a faint ''pinkening of the skin just barely perceptible beneath my corkscrewed black pubic curls''; and a week after that, ''making, for the record, an incubation period of twenty-one days,'' he discovered that his penis had turned a ''soft reddish shade'' (pp.3–5). In addition to the tingling sensation and the penile discoloration, he also describes the progress of a third symptom during the same three week period: a dramatic increase in local sensation which he had experienced when he made love to his mistress, Claire. Before he can get to his doctor, however, ''a phenomenon that has been variously described to me as a 'massive hormonal influx,' and 'endocrinopathic catastrophe,' and/or 'a hermaphroditic explosion of chromosomes' took place in my body between midnight and four A.M. on February 18, 1971, and converted me into a mammary gland...'' (p. 12).

The cause of his symptoms is still unknown, as is their relationship to the biological mutation they apparently signaled, although there are those ''who claim to be on the brink of some conclusive scientific explanation.'' (All of this exposition of the events preceding the complication is, of course, pure Roth, since Kafka's story begins with its climax in the first sentence and makes no attempt to account for Gregor's transformation except metaphorically.)

Once the reader has granted Roth his metamorphic premise—and through this preliminary section of the novella Roth attempts to make that acceptance a bit easier—*The Breast*, like ''The Metamorphosis,'' pursues the implications of its situation with logical rigor. It moves from Kepesh's identity crisis, through his "crisis of faith," to his final ironic comment on the overpowering force of reality.

Both Kepesh and Samsa reverse the normal process, awake *into* a nightmare, and through their experiences their creators try to focus our attention on the nightmare world of absurdity that is just below the surface of our own everyday experience. "WHAT DOES IT MEAN? HOW HAS IT COME TO PASS? AND WHY? IN THE ENTIRE HISTORY OF THE HUMAN RACE, WHY DAVID ALAN KEPESH?" Roth's hero moans (p. 23). And his cries for reasonable explanation reflect those each of us have made in the face of our own confrontations with irrational grief and disappointment. Like Kepesh, when such incidents occur in our lives we are counseled to cling to our "will to live," to exercise our "strength of character." And most of the time most of us *do* cling to them—for the same reason that Kepesh does. These banal phrases, he tells us, "are the therapeutic equivalent to my lame jokes. In these, my preposterous times, we must keep to what is ordinary and familiar; better the banal than the apocalyptic—for after all is said and done, citadel of sanity though I may be, we both recognize that there is just so much that even I can take" (p. 24). So, faced with the overpowering circumstances of his condition, he spends his time clinging to habits and searching for rational explanation.

Like Samsa, he begins by believing that his predicament is some kind of temporary indisposition, and so he tries to continue to think and act as he had in his former state. He listens to recordings of Shakespearean productions, imagines ways for him to continue in his capacity of professor of literature, is devastated when a colleague laughs at him, and continues to think of himself—even though he is now a mammary gland—as the possessor of a male member. In fact, his crisis of identity is most intense, appropriately enough, in this sexual sphere.

It was difficult enough for Neil Klugman and Alex Portnoy to cope with the conflicting claims of the disapproving moralist and the libidinous slob within them, but in Kepesh the intensity and importance of the conflict is increased a hundredfold. Portnoy explained the crux of his situation by quoting a Yiddish saying: "*Ven der putz shteht, ligt der sechel in drerd*" ("When the *putz* stands up, the brains get buried in the ground"). Kepesh's brain is literally buried in his sexual organs: "what now passes for his head has become one libidinal powerhouse which his superego struggles to contain, and a crisis ensues that is a far more intense version of Portnoy's perpetual debate between how much he wants sexually, and, after all, has coming to him, and how little he can afford [to allow] himself.''[6]

Having defined himself as a civilized man in terms of his repressions and discontents, Kepesh cannot now afford to give them up if he wants to retain his human identity. Besides, he may be on television! And increasing his sexual demands on his girl friend, Claire, might drive her away, and eliminate one more link to his former self. It is not, Kepesh tells us, just "a matter of doing what is right or seemly; I am not concerned, I can assure you, with the etiquette of being a breast. It is rather doing what I would do if I would continue to be me. And I would, for if not me, who? what? Either I will continue to be myself, or I will go mad, and then I will surely die" (pp. 20–21). In spite of his metamorphosis, in other words—and here he differs totally from Gregor Samsa, whose consciousness does change—Kepesh's "mode of apprehending and valuing" himself has not "appreciably altered" (p. 29).

And so, in the name of reason and humanity and civilization, we are treated to the spectacle of a man-turned-breast—of a man-turned-gigantic-erogenous-zone capable of infinite stimulation but incapable of orgasmic release—who denies himself sexual pleasure at the same time that his condition denies him most of the pleasures of the human state. Ironically, of all Roth's heroes and heroines Kepesh is the only one who *clings* to his past and his internal conflicts instead of trying to escape them.

Faced with the inexplicable, Kepesh feels compelled to discover an explanation, and his various efforts to do so comprise the bulk of his narrative, as he moves from explanation to explanation. Perhaps he is actually a quadruple amputee . . . the victim of punitive wish-fulfillment . . . is suffering from a postanalytic collapse . . . has succumbed to the impulse to revert to the safety and security of the womb . . . is trying to escape a trauma through self-delusion . . . has read too much Kafka, Gogol, and Swift . . . is trying to out-Kafka Kafka by making the metamorphic word flesh . . . is dreaming . . . etc. But in one of the novella's most inventive twists, his analyst dismisses each of these alternatives in the name of the Freudian deity, Mr. Reality. "It happened," Klinger insists.

Roth pointed out in a recent comment on the use of psychoanalysis in his fiction that Dr. Klinger is simply doing what any competent analyst would do in a similar situation. In his view, Klinger speaks "more or less in the voice of enlightened common sense," and "favors the cadences and vocabulary of psychotherapeutic demystification. The only difficulty is that the affliction he is confronted with in *The Breast*—Kepesh's transformation into a human-sized mammary gland—is bottomlessly mysterious and horrifying. But to the suffering patient, what affliction isn't? Then too, in the course of a single day, a doctor in Klinger's line of work dutifully hears out half a dozen patients who, if they do not consider themselves to be breasts, imagine with some degree of conviction that they are testicles, or vaginas, or bellies, or brains, or buttocks, or noses, or two left feet, or all thumbs, or all heart, or all eyes or what-have-you. 'I'm a p----! She's a c---! My partner is an a------!' Granted, say the doctors Klinger—but nonetheless what shall you do out in the great world where you are obliged to call yourself (and may even wish others to refer to you) by another name?" (RM, p. 95). In other words, though he may indeed be the boob one reviewer saw him as, though he may also be a nebbish, he is also David Alan Kepesh—and must try to deal with his situation accordingly.

He must face the fact—and for him, at least, it *is* a fact—that this grotesquerie is his reality, in spite of its fantastic absurdity. Pretending that it is not absurd, retreating into simple explanations, escaping into dreams, or art, or madness, or seclusion will not do. Kepesh's tale recounts the process by which he came to the realization that he must learn to deal with the grotesque and fantastic nature of his reality as best he can.

In the same way, the artist who would write American fiction must learn to deal with the grotesque and fantastic because they are a prominent part of our contemporary social reality. As much as Kepesh and Roth might wish that this were not so—might wish that they could "change" the nature of that life and that reality—they cannot. Like Kafka and Rilke before them, all they can do is seek to understand and convey—with admittedly faulty means of expression and visions colored by their own personal obsessions—just what *is* real. Their task is a difficult one. And it is not made easier by the fact that to accomplish it they must find the passageway from the credible incredible to the incredible credible which threads its way through the corridors of experience to the inner sanctum of Mr. Reality.

CHAPTER 12

Such Things Simply Do Not Happen (My Life as a Man)

My Life as a Man, begun after *Portnoy's Complaint* and completed after *The Breast,* also deals with the incredible credible, the real that seems imaginary—with *its* hero's efforts to come to grips with the unmanageability of *his* reality. Supposedly "drawn from the writings of Peter Tarnopol," it tells the story of Tarnopol's struggle to tell the story of his horrendous marriage to one Maureen Johnson Tarnopol—a marriage that was responsible for a metamorphosis that is just as inexplicable and fantastic to him as Kepesh's was in more objective terms. Once the twenty-seven-year-old "golden boy of American literature," with a future bright before him, Tarnopol was transformed by his marriage into a thirty-four-year-old man, spent and obsessed, whimpering about yesterday and afraid of tomorrow. Like Kepesh he wants his readers to accept the veracity of his narrative and the authenticity of his humanity: "I am not a character in a book . . . I am real. And my humiliation is equally *real,"* he insists (p. 86); "You must believe what I've been through—I am not exaggerating! To the contrary, I'm leaving things out!" he tells his analyst, Dr. Spielvogel (p. 212). Like Kepesh he clings to habit, continues to write—even though his writing seems to be getting him nowhere. And, again like Kepesh, he feels compelled to attempt to explain the nature and sources of his altered condition: "HOW COULD SHE? TO ME!" he cries (p. 212).

Thus the novel's epigraph, "I could be his Muse, if only he'd let me"—taken not from the works of the great writers but from Maureen's diary—is the first of many painful ironies. Just as Kepesh cannot help but contemplate the central fact of his reality, his life as a breast, Tarnopol cannot help but think and write about

141

the central fact of his—his life with Maureen. She *is* his Muse, the inspiration for all he writes, and he cannot *help* but let her be. Had Tarnopol picked a more literary epigraph for his story of an artist's struggle to deal with his obsessions, he might well have chosen the lines from Delmore Schwartz's *Genesis* which Roth quoted in an interview on *My Life as a Man:* "Why must I tell, hysterical, this story/And must, compelled, speak of such secrecies?/ . . . Where is my freedom, if I cannot resist/So much speech blurted out . . . ?/How long must I endure this show and sight/Of all I lived through, all I lived in: Why?" (RM, p. 107).

The writer "sheds his sickness in books—repeats and presents again his emotions to be master of them," D. H. Lawrence wrote;[1] that Lawrentian aesthetic is at the heart of *My Life as a Man.* If he can just *explain* his obsession, Tarnopol thinks, he will finally be able to exorcise it; but in order to explain it he must find the right narrative voice. He recognizes that "to give up the obsession would surely have made more sense." But "obsessed, I was as incapable of not writing about what was killing me as I was of altering" it (p. 105). Instead, he writes, "all I can do with my story is tell it. And tell it. And tell it. And *that's* the truth" (p. 231). So he tries to assimilate and transcend his experiences through his art, tries to "write it all out": first, through two "useful fictions" about an alter ego, and then through a long autobiographical essay.

"Tarnopol's attempt to realize himself with the right words—as earlier in his life he attempted realizing himself through the right deeds," is, according to Roth, the subject of *My Life as a Man* (RM, pp. 96–97). His best novel to date, it can be read on at least four levels: as deeply moving confession of the intimate details of a destructive marriage, as a coda to the persistent concerns of all his previous work, as an exemplary tale on the process of creating art out of the emotional welter of personal experience, and as the most fully realized of Roth's recent variations on Kafkan themes and techniques. A complex and multi-faceted work, it is the kind of book which compels its readers to reconsider all that its author has written before, and provides a standard of excellence by which to measure all that may follow.

"Salad Days," the first of Tarnopol's useful fictions, is a comic narrative which catalogues the scholastic and sexual triumphs of an adolescent named Nathan Zuckerman. Narrated in the third person, it may be viewed as a "comic idyll honoring a Pannish (and as yet unpunished) id" (MLM, p. 113). It describes Zuckerman's "puppyish, protected upbringing above his father's shoe store in Camden" (p. 3); his undergraduate rebellion against his parents and his background; his preeminence (as cofounder of the college literary magazine) as an intellectual leader and *summa cum laude* English major at predominantly Gentile Bass College; his sexual conquest of the beautiful Jewish Princess, Sharon Shatsky (daughter of Al "the Zipper King"); and his first encounter, in the army, with a larger world where he was no longer the master of all he surveyed. The events of these prelapsarian salad days are all described in an appropriately exuberant tone—until, in the story's last paragraphs, the tone becomes more ominous and prepares the way for the second of Tarnopol's useful fictions:

> pain would come to Zuckerman in time—in the form of estrangement, mortification, fierce and unremitting opposition, antagonists who were not respectable deans or loving fathers or dim-witted officers in the Army Quartermaster Corps; oh yes, pain would enter his life soon enough, and not entirely without invitation. As the loving father warned him, looking for trouble, he would find it—and what a surprise that would be. For in severity and duration, in sheer *painfulness,* it would be like nothing he had known at home, in school, or in the service, nor would it be like anything he had imagined while contemplating the harrowed, soulful face of Virginia Woolf, or while writing his A + honors paper on the undercurrent of agony in her novels.... He would begin to pay ... for the vanity and the ignorance, to be sure, but above all for the contradictions: the stinging tongue and the tender hide, the spiritual aspirations and the lewd desires, the softy boyish needs and the manly, magisterial ambitions.
>
> But that is another story, and one whose ... suffering calls for an approach far more serious than that which seems appropriate to the tale of his easeful salad days. To narrate with fidelity the misfortunes of Zuckerman's twenties would require deeper dredging, a darker sense of irony, a grave and pensive voice to replace the amused, Olympian point of view ... or maybe what the story requires is neither gravity nor complexity, but just another author, someone who would see it for the simple five-thousand word comedy that it may very well have been (pp. 30–31).

Tarnopol's second story, "Courting Disaster (or Serious in the Fifties," tries to match the gravity and complexity of the events it recounts with exactly that kind of restrained and serious narrative voice. It is a mature (and biographically slightly different) Nathan Zuckerman's self-conscious rumination on the particular disaster he courted while serious in the Fifties: his relationship with Lydia Jorgenson Ketterer—a relationship which results in her suicide and the destruction of his promising career as a writer and teacher at the University of Chicago.

The subject here is marriage. The question to be answered is why did Nathan Zuckerman feel called upon to insist that Lydia marry him and thereby destroy both their lives? When he first meets her, he is a young man on his way up the ladder to the higher reaches of academia and the literary world. She is a plainly neurotic divorcée, five years his senior, with a daughter and a nightmarish past that includes incest, a violent and degrading marriage, and a "flirtation" with madness. She is also a student in one of the adult extension courses he teaches. As he reads her autobiographical class assignments, he is struck by the contrast between her brutal experiences and his own sheltered salad days. As a student of literature, he is enamored of the moral and intellectual virtues of the Fifties—ambiguity, *angst,* seriousness, responsibility, maturity, commitment—and of the era's literary masters like Flaubert, Mann, Dostoevsky, Conrad, James, and Kafka. He cannot help but admire Lydia because, like the heroes and heroines of the novels he devours, "she had suffered so." And "not only that she had survived, but *what* she had survived, gave her enormous moral stature, or glamor" in his eyes (p. 70). That moral glamor is heightened by her narrative style in the papers he reads, for "who could call 'crazy' a woman who spoke with such detachment of her history of craziness? Who could find evidence of impulses toward suicide and homicide in a rhetorical style so untainted by rage or vengeful wrath? No, no, this was someone who had *experienced* her experience, who had been deepened by all that misery" (p. 46).

Though she has had little formal education, Lydia has had plenty of practical education—in this, she is exactly the opposite of Nathan—and she realizes from the start how mismatched they are. She tries, at first, to make him leave her alone. But he is determined to *redeem* them both: to redeem her by offering the sacrifice of his promising future as her salvation; to redeem himself by placing a constant strain on his spirit, as Paul Herz did before him—and thereby achieve manhood through responsibility. He rushes headlong into marriage, seeking maturity and a life full of moral content. He winds up an exile in Italy with his Lolita, Lydia's daughter Moonie. Lydia winds up dead.

Zuckerman is aware that there is an element of incredibility in his narrative's unrelieved gloom; and he interrupts himself midway through his story to say so: "To the reader who has not just 'gotten the drift,' but begun to balk at the uniformly dismal situation that I have presented here, to the reader who finds himself unable to suspend his disbelief in a protagonist who voluntarily sustains an affair with a woman sexless to him and so disaster-ridden, I should say that in retrospect I find him nearly impossible to believe in myself. Why should a young man ... pursue ... a course so *defiantly* not in his interest? For the sake of defiance? Does that convince you? ... To make some sort of accounting, the writer emphasizes Lydia's 'moral glamor' and develops, probably with more thoroughness than is engrossing, the idea of Zuckerman's 'seriousness,' even going so far, in the subtitle, as to describe that seriousness as something of a social phenomenon; but, to be frank, it does not seem, even to the author, that he has, suggestive subtitle and all, answered the objection of implausibility" (pp. 79–80). "Impossible," "preposterous," "implausible," "inconceivable"— these words recurr like punctuation throughout both *My Life as a Man* and *The Breast.*

And *narrator* Zuckerman also recognizes the reader's temptation to refuse to take *character* Zuckerman seriously, whether that reader is convinced of his predicament or not. As a matter of fact, he repeatedly acknowledges that he is tempted to make fun of his earlier self himself: "To treat this story as comedy would not require more than a slight alteration in tone and attitude," he says. Not only can he see how foolish Zuckerman may appear, but he also realizes that, "to some, the funniest thing of all, or perhaps the strangest, may not be how I conducted myself back then, but the literary mode in which I have chosen to narrate my story today; the decorousness, the orderliness, the underlying sobriety, that 'responsible' manner I continue to affect" (pp. 80–81). Just as the narrator of "Salad Days" was incapable of the seriousness this tale of woe seemed to require, this Zuckerman is incapable of the comic, absurdist perspective that might give the events he describes a greater sense of credibility. He is forced to conclude his story "in a traditional narrative mode," saying, "I leave it to those writers who live in the flamboyant American present, and whose extravagant fictions I sample from afar, to treat the implausible, the preposterous, and the bizarre in something other than a straightforward and recognizable manner" (p. 87).

The frantic grasping at straws of adequate explanation in "Courting Disaster"'s last paragraph is an expression of his recognition of that straightforward manner's inadequacy. His careful, serious, realistic analysis is stymied by the inexhaustible and the inexplicable: "She saw the way out of her life's misery, and I, in the service of Perversity or Chivalry or Morality or Misogyny or Saintliness or Folly or Pent-up Rage or Psychic Illness or Sheer Lunacy or Innocence or Ignorance or Experience or Heroism or Judaism or Masochism or Self-Hatred or Defiance or Soap Opera or Romantic Opera or the Art of Fiction perhaps, or none of the above, or maybe all of the above and more—I found the way into mine" (p. 95).

In "My True Story," the long autobiographical essay which makes up most of the book, Tarnopol—writing in the flamboyant American present—sets aside the mask of fiction and the guise of Zuckerman to present his version of the real events which formed the basis of his stories. His tone combines the comedy of "Salad Days" and the moral seriousness of "Courting Disaster" to deal with his experience more effectively than either of the Zuckermans could.

The personalities of the Tarnopols are by now familiar to the reader of Tarnopol's fiction (and Roth's). Maureen Johnson Mezik Tarnopol is a *shiksa* extraordinaire—exactly the kind of woman the nice Jewish boy was warned against by his doting parents and siblings, "Thereal McCoy." Like most of the women in Roth's fiction, she has intellectual and artistic aspirations which her background has kept her from realizing. Her relationship with her Jewish lover begins casually, but soon turns into a life-or-death struggle for survival and sanity in which both parties become prey and predators. Driven by her own character and by social mores, she tries to live vicariously through her man and soon becomes both his Muse and his Bartleby. Peter's background—Jewish home, protective parents, educational precocity, emotional immaturity, moral aspirations, and literary ambitions—is one he shares with his own hero, Nathan Zuckerman, and with most of Roth's. For Tarnopol and Roth's other heroes, the problem is not that women mean too little, but that they mean too much, "the testing ground, not for potency, but for *virtue!*" (MLM, p. 243). And his essay, like his two fictions, tries to explain how he came to marry Maureen "entirely against my inclinations but in accordance with my principles" (p. 128).

Like Paul Herz and David Alan Kepesh before him, Tarnopol's "model of reality, deduced from reading the masters, had at its

heart *intractability."* And "stuffed to the gills with great fiction
... I now expected to find in everyday experience that same sense
of the difficult and the deadly earnest that informed the novels I
admired most.... And here it was, a reality as obdurate and recalcitrant and (in addition) as awful as any I could have wished for in
my bookish dreams. You might even say that the ordeal that my
daily life was shortly to become was only Dame Fortune ... dishing
out to her precocious favorite whatever literary sensibility required.
Want Complexity? Difficulty? Intractability? Want the deadly
earnest? Yours!" (p. 194). However, "I also wanted my intractable
existence [to] take place at an appropriately moral altitude, an
elevation somewhere, say, between *The Brothers Karamazov* and
The Wings of the Dove. But then not even the golden can expect to
have everything: instead of the intractability of serious fiction, I
got the intractability of soap opera. Resistant enough, but the
wrong genre" (pp. 194–95).

Maureen knows nothing about genres; and she was never under
the illusion that life would be as subtle and controlled as fiction.
"You want subtlety, read The Golden Bowl," Tarnopol imagines
her saying. *"This is life, bozo, not high art"* (p. 309). And life—at
least their life—is not composed of the witty *badinage* of James's
characters, but of another order of conversation entirely, of which
the following exchange is a representative sample:

"Peter, I caught you red-handed with that girl with the braids!" *"That is
not left and right, Maureen!* And you are the one who turned me against
you with your crazy ... paranoia!" "When? When did I do that. I'd like
to know?" "From the *beginning!* Before we were even married!" "Then
why on earth did you marry me, if I was so hateful to you even then? Just
to punish me like this?" "I married you because you *tricked* me into marrying you! Why else!" "But that didn't mean you *had* to—you still could
decide on your own! And you did, you liar! Don't you ever remember
what *happened?* You *asked* me to be your wife. You *proposed."* "Because
among other things you *threatened to kill yourself if I didn't!"* "And you
believed me?" *"What?"* "You actually believed that I would kill myself
over *you?* You actually do think that you are the be-all and end-all of
human existence!" "No, no, it's *you* who think I am! Why else won't you
leave me alone!" "Oh, Jesus," she moaned, "oh, Jesus—haven't you ever
heard of *love?"* (pp. 127–28).

Their confrontation on the matrimonial battleground (which lasts
for three years) and in the divorce courts of the State of New York

(which lasts for four) is so painstakingly revealed that, next to it, Strindberg's bitter plays and stories of marriage seem almost idyllic. The major difference between the central characters in "My True Story" and those in "Courting Disaster" is that where Lydia is presented as a pathetic victim, more sinned against than sinning, Maureen is cast as a villain—a pathetic villain, but a villain nonetheless. But in spite of his overwhelming impulses toward self-dramatization and self-justification, Tarnopol's portrait of their relationship somehow manages to evoke sympathy for both the harried combatants. We finish reading it with a profound sense of two lives mutually destroyed by their own fictions, illusions, and pathologies.

Though these characters may not be completely new, Roth has never envisioned them more completely or conveyed the misery of their predicament with more intense effect. What is relatively new, in a body of fiction whose persistent flaw has been a tendency toward diffusiveness, is a clear structural principle which molds the action into a coherent whole and offers another level of meaning beyond that of the surface conflict. *Goodbye, Columbus, Portnoy's Complaint,* and *The Professor of Desire* are the only other full-length works in which Roth has displayed such complete control of his materials; and *My Life as a Man* sheds light on all of the work which separates these three milestones. Rereading his major fiction with it as a guide, shows more clearly than any critical argument can that, though Roth's *techniques* have varied as widely as Tarnopol's do, his central preoccupations have remained just as constant.

Graham Greene once remarked that "every creative writer worth our consideration, every writer who can be called in the wide sense of the term, a poet, is a victim: a man given over to an obsession."[2] Like Kafka and Peter Tarnopol, Philip Roth is a writer thus obsessed. Above and beyond any private obsessions which have played a part in his writing, Roth's long-standing *artistic* obsession has been the same as Tarnopol's: finding the means to express the incredibility of reality, the feel of this cockeyed world. "The struggle to achieve a description" (RM, p. 97). Though their Muses differ—Mr. Reality has been Roth's Maureen—their difficulties have been the same.

When Peter learns Maureen's secret—that she paid a pregnant Negro woman for a urine sample so that her own pregnancy test would be positive and Peter would feel morally obligated to marry her—he is as awed by the revelation as Roth has always been by his society's news reports. "I didn't do anything," Tarnopol tells his analyst, "just stood there for awhile. I couldn't right off get over the *ingenuity* of it. The *relentlessness*. That she had thought of such a thing and then gone ahead and done it. I actually felt *admiration*. And pity, *pity!*" (p. 209). Contemplating contemporary social reality in "Writing American Fiction," Roth, too, reacted with both pity and admiration for *its* relentlessness and ingenuity. And just as Roth questioned the capacity of traditional realism to deal with the daily life he saw around him, Tarnopol questions its capacity to deal with his personal experience.

Informed that Maureen has died in an auto accident, he is again awed: " 'She's dead,' I remind myself, 'and it is over.' But how can that be? Defies credulity. If in a work of realistic fiction the hero was saved by something as fortuitous as the sudden death of his worst enemy, what intelligent reader would suspend his disbelief? Facile, he would grumble, and fantastic. Fictional wish fulfillment, fiction in the service of one's dreams. Not True to Life. And I would agree. Maureen's death is Not True to Life. Such things simply do not happen, except when they do. (And as time passes and I get older, I find that they do with increasing frequency)" (pp. 112–13).

Like Tarnopol, Roth has sought the right narrative voice, the right techniques; and the imaginative recapitulation of that search and its attendant difficulties serves as the underlying structural principle of *My Life as a Man*. How does one express the incredibility of the private and public quotidian? How does one turn the personal frustration and impotence that incredibility inspires into art? These are the questions Roth and Tarnopol try to answer in their writing.

Each of *My Life as a Man*'s sections may be viewed as a stylistic experiment on Tarnopol's part which mirrors a similar experiment in Roth's fiction. "Courting Disaster" exhibits the same moral seriousness of tone and theme, the same realistic detail and narrative punctiliousness which mark *Goodbye, Columbus, Letting Go,* and *When She Was Good*. "Salad Days" presents a subdued version of the exuberant humor and comic perspective which characterize *Portnoy's Complaint, Our Gang,* and *The Great American Novel*. And Tarnopol recognizes what Roth discovered during the composition of *Portnoy's Complaint:* that neither approach is completely sufficient by itself. In spite of its moral force, the first

technique tends to be inadequate because it takes itself too seriously
and has difficulty dealing with the inexplicable and outrageous in
everyday life. In spite of its appealing iconoclasm and invention,
the second approach can suffer from a loss of moral weight and
dissipate into giggles. A synthesis combining the best of both
approaches—which Roth has used in *Portnoy's Complaint, The
Breast, My Life as a Man,* and *The Professor of Desire*—is what
Tarnopol achieves in "My True Story."

Roth takes pains to identify his intentions and difficulties with
Tarnopol's through obvious and oblique references to the characters and themes of his own fiction which are carefully woven into
the novel's complex fabric. Tarnopol's first novel, *A Jewish
Father,* bears the same epigraph from Thomas Mann as Roth's
first, *Letting Go. My Life as a Man* as a whole, and "Courting Disaster" in particular, can be seen as a kind of *Letting Go Redux,*
written with all the added skill and insight Roth has acquired in the
dozen years which separate the earlier work from the more recent
one. One of Tarnopol's correspondents describes "Courting Disaster" as a "disguised critical essay by Tarnopol on his overrated first
book, a commentary and a judgment on all that principledness that
is *A Jewish Father's* subject and downfall" (p. 117)—a rather accurate description of its relationship to *Letting Go* as well. Like Paul
Herz and Gabe Wallach in the earlier novel, Zuckerman and
Tarnopol are victims of a "Prince Charming phenomenon" which
casts them as saviors in their own eyes and the eyes of the women
they plan to save. Maureen may be viewed as a composite figure
combining Martha Reganhart's earthy toughness and worldly
wisdom, Libby Herz's neuroticism, Theresa Haug's abused vulner-
ability, and Marge Howell's intellectual pretensions. (Or *they* may
be viewed as imaginative portrayals of the different aspects of *her*
personality.) Tarnopol's older brother, Morris, shares Paul's Uncle
Asher's curious combination of idealism, cynicism, and brutal
frankness. Alfred Kazin imagined in his review of *Letting Go* that
one of Roth's characters had asked, "Why should such an
intellectual-type boy make such a mess? It's not possible!"[3] In *My
Life as a Man* Roth tries to explain just how it was not only possible
but virtually inevitable.

The novel also makes allusions to Roth's other works.
Tarnopol's descriptions of the day World War II ended echoes passages in both *Portnoy's Complaint* and the early essay "Recollections from Beyond the Last Rope." Zuckerman and Tarnopol

share physical ailments like the one suffered by the protagonist in Roth's prize-winning story "Novotny's Pain." Sharon Shatsky and Dina Dorsbach are variations on the character of Brenda Patimkin. Dr. Spielvogel reappears as Tarnopol's analyst. And a novel based on his article reducing Tarnopol's neuroses to a casebook Oedipal explanation would look very much like *Portnoy's Complaint.* "Many things are conceivable that may have little basis in reality," he tells his patient, echoing Dr. Klinger (MLM, p. 166). Tarnopol's withdrawal and self-imposed sexual quarantine at Quashay could easily be transformed imaginatively into Kepesh's predicament in *The Breast*—a novel written at a writers' colony, Yaddo. The diametrically opposed critical reactions to Tarnopol's short stories, which are quoted in the book, accurately reflect the range of critical response to Roth's own changing modes, and to *My Life as a Man* itself. (This technique of criticizing his own fictions before his critics have an opportunity to is, along with "foregrounding" of other kinds, becoming a standard one in Roth's fiction.)

Reading *My Life as a Man* also reinforces the central observations we have already made about Roth's heroes and heroines. Like Tarnopol, each of them is obsessed. Each of them reacts to the feel of his or her cockeyed world by constructing fictions—more often use*less* than use*ful*—designed to cope with that reality. The narrative voice in Roth's major fiction has gradually assumed the characteristic form of a self-contained monologue narrated by an artist-figure; and that progress is repeated in the movement of the narrative voices of the sections of *My Life as a Man*—from third person, to first person, to autobiographical monologue. Portnoy, Kepesh, Word Smith—and all of Roth's protagonists, to greater and lesser extents—tell their own stories. Again and again we learn what reality feels like *to them,* and, in the process, the thin line between reality and fantasy blurs. We are constantly forced to ask, as we read both Roth's fiction and Tarnopol's, just how much of the narrator's obsession is grounded in reality, and how much is a projection of his or her own paranoia. The uncomfortable sense of ambiguity this point of view produces in the reader is exactly the effect Roth is trying to create.

In *My Life as a Man* Roth intensifies this sense of ambiguity by using details from his own biography. In his acceptance speech at the National Book Awards ceremonies in 1960, Roth inveighed against the tendency of writers to become public figures. Unlike Norman Mailer, Truman Capote, or Gore Vidal, in the period since he made that speech he has shunned personal publicity and has tried to keep his private life private. However, "it's in the nature of being a novelist to make private life public" *in* his fiction, as Peter Tarnopol tells Dr. Spielvogel (p. 250). And in this novel Roth uses his personal experiences—and his awareness of his audience's tendency to interpret confessional fiction as autobiography—with maximal effectiveness. He makes the line between fact and fiction, the real and the imaginary, even more difficult to find than it usually is in his fiction by making many of the details or Tarnopol's life correspond to the publicly known details of his own. The reader infers that Tarnopol is an alter ego of Roth's in the same way that Zuckerman is Tarnopol's; but while we learn through Tarnopol's "True Story" how much of Zuckerman's history is his own and how much is not, we cannot be equally sure of the extent of the identity between Tarnopol and Roth.

Both writers had similar childhoods. As young, beginning writers, both were dedicated to art of the "earnest moral variety." In 1959, at the age of twenty-seven, both published highly praised first books, and both married divorcées. Both received Guggenheim grants, spent time in Rome, gave a public lecture in California in 1960, and taught during the same years at large Midwestern state universities. Both were separated from their wives and underwent psychoanalysis between 1962 and 1967; and both of their estranged wives died violent deaths in auto accidents in Central Park.

By making these, and the other, kinds of overt connections, Roth runs the risk that his fiction will be read by some as unadulterated autobiography, instead of as the "legend of the self" that he intended it to be. On the other hand, by having the courage to run that risk he is able to discomfit his readers and to keep them constantly wondering about just how much of Tarnopol's story is "true" to Roth's experience, and how much is imaginary. He keeps the nature of the interpenetration of reality and fantasy before us constantly, and thereby conveys it with an intensity none of his other works can quite match.

Roth's use of biographical references has several other functions as well. While many of the details of Tarnopol's biography parallel those in Roth's, they *also* reflect those of many other contemporary American writers. In a sense, the book is not just Tarnopol's story but a kind of "Everybody's Autobiography." It is not accidental or incidental from this point of view, that Roth has his contemporary writer retreat to Quashay, where he finds that, "with only five exceptions, *all those in residence* right now happen to be in flight, or in hiding, or in recovery—from bad marriages, divorces, affairs" (p. 111, my emphasis). Nor is it accidental that Roth has Tarnopol's brother, Morris, the voice of common sense in the novel, comment on the typicality of Peter's situation: "What is it with you Jewish writers? Madeline Herzog, Deborah Rojak, the cutie-pie castrator in *After the Fall,* and isn't the desirable shiksa of *A New Life* a kvetch and titless in the bargain? And now for the further delight of the rabbis and the reading public, Lydia Zuckerman, that Gentile tomato. Chicken soup in every pot, and a Grushenka in every garage. With all the Dark Ladies to choose from, you Luftmenschen can really pick 'em" (p. 118). His story, Tarnopol points out, is "only an instance" (p. 173).

In an even broader sense, Roth makes Tarnopol an exemplar of the contemporary fictionist he profiled in "Writing American Fiction" years ago: the author who turns his back on social reality to create fictions of the self. Tarnopol notes, for example, that while his mind was totally occupied with his own marital problems, "the most vivid and momentous history since World War Two was being made in the streets around me," but it "did nothing whatsoever to mitigate my obsession" to recognize that (pp. 268–69). Though Tarnopol does not presume to argue that his story furnishes "anything like an explanation or a paradigm"—in much the same way that Roth once disavowed making Lucy Nelson a representative figure—Roth seems to intend that his story do just that. But Tarnopol's marital melodrama is not just a paradigm for many of the marriages of the Fifties, or for the impact on the personal level of what Roth has described as the "demythologizing decade" of the Sixties: it is also a paradigm of the difficulties that every artist faces when he tries to create structured, controlled, meaningful art out of incredible and disordered public and private experience. In this sense, Tarnopol is an alter ego for that part of Roth which feels so overwhelmed by reality that he feels he can no longer adequately handle it in his art. But where Roth has published eight novels since his first, highly praised book—and has, in each of them, grappled with Mr. Reality—Tarnopol has published only a few stories before *My Life as a Man.*

In its emphasis on the biographical sources of art, *My Life as a Man* also suggests its connection with Kafka's fiction. In the interview on *Portnoy's Complaint* in 1969, Roth told George Plimpton that he had considered writing a story about Kafka writing a story at one time (RM, p. 22)—and *My Life as a Man* may be viewed as the story of a modern Kafka doing just that. Both Kafka and Tarnopol were driven to write their fiction by their own personal demons; both see themselves as perpetual defendants before a court which has already judged them guilty. In spite of the parallels between Roth and Tarnopol or Kafka and K. or Joseph K., both writers' heroes should be viewed as Ronald Gray viewed Kafka's, as no more than possible worlds, potential developments from their authors' personal situations at a given time. At the same time we are forced to recognize that both men's fictions are, in essence, spiritual autobiographies.

If *Portnoy's Complaint* bears comparison to Kafka's *Letter to His Father,* and *The Breast* is clearly indebted to "The Metamorphosis," reading *My Life as a Man* is analogous to reading *The Trial* or *The Castle,* and then reading an artistically ordered version of Kafka's *Diaries* or his *Letters to Milena.* In both Tarnopol's fiction and Kafka's we note common characteristics which reflect their author's obsessive concerns. In *The Castle,* for example, Friedrich Beissner has noted that nothing happens without K., "nothing happens that has not some relationship to him, and nothing happens in his absence. Everything that happens, happens to him. And everything is told as clearly and as unclearly, as distortedly and as precisely as he himself perceives it in his disappointment his vexation, and his weariness."[4] The same is true of Tarnopol's "useful fictions."

The form and content of Tarnopol's fiction is explained by an observation Ronald Gray made about Kafka's: "Just as the neurotic will spin on and on with the exploration of his motives, explaining one by another, and that by another, so Kafka's compulsive need drives him to these ramified constructions, both in the individual parts and in the wholes of his works. This was his nature; he had to be true to this if he was to be a writer, and if the result is often oppressive, it also exerts a fascination simply because it is so ruthlessly faithful to Kafka's experience as it came to him."[5] Just as reading *Letters to Milena* provides fresh insights into *The Castle,* and reading the *Letter to His Father* illuminates *The Trial* or "The Metamorphosis," reading "My True Story" opens up new meanings in the ramified constructions of "Salad Days" and "Courting Disaster." Like Kafka's fictions, Tarnopol's reflect on both their author's biography and the act of writing itself.

In addition to these general similarities of approach, and to the Kafkan technical synthesis already commented upon, *My Life as a Man* also makes repeated allusions to Kafka's works and the details of his life which suggest the importance of Kafka's model to Roth's work. Like Kafka's affair with Dora Dymant, for example, Nathan Zuckerman's affair with Sharon Shatsky in "Courting Disaster" (she becomes *D*ina *D*orsbach in "My True Story") is terminated by the girl's father because of the suitor's ill health. And the character of Maureen Johnson Tarnopol is very much like that of Kafka's Gentile divorcée, Milena Jesenka-Pollak. "Impetuous, frenetic, indifferent to conventional restraints, a woman of appetite and anger," Milena aroused "more elemental yearnings and more elemental fears" in her author-lover than he had ever experienced in any of his other affairs, according to Roth in "Looking at Kafka." To some, he reports, Milena was psychopathic; to others, she was "powerfully sane, extraordinarily humane and courageous" (RM, pp. 250–51)—and these are the same contradictory views expressed about Maureen in Roth's novel.

"Looking at Kafka" was published while Roth was completing *My Life as a Man,* and it suggests another reason for his being attracted to Kafkan models in his own writing. In the story, Roth recounts the events of the last year of Kafka's life and points out how incredible the happiness he found with Dora in his last days seems. That the last year of Kafka's *real* life should be so incredible, leads Roth to fantasize another end for him, an *imaginary* life that *seems* real. Kafka becomes Dr. Kafka, nine-year-old Philip Roth's Hebrew teacher in Newark—an escapee from both early death from tuberculosis and the Holocaust, and a suitor of Roth's maiden aunt, Rhoda. Having left his overpowering father, Hermann, behind in Prague, Kafka is confronted in Newark by another overpowering father, Herman Roth—who expresses familiar sentiments and issues familiar warnings. " 'Alone,' says my father," quotes Roth, " 'alone, Dr. Kafka, is a stone.' Dr. Kafka ... allows with a nod how that is so" (RM, p. 262).

After a weekend in Atlantic City with Dr. Kafka, however, Aunt Rhoda terminates their affair in an atmosphere of sexual mystery. As the story ends, Roth is a junior in college beginning to write his own fiction. In a letter, his mother encloses an obituary notice from the Essex County *Jewish News* which announces that Dr. Kafka has died at the age of seventy ... leaving no books: "no *Trial,* no *Castle,* no 'Diaries.' " For one of the points of this story is that

Kafka leaves no books in Newark because only out of the life he actually lived, only out of his illness and the personal obsessions which haunted him in Prague, could he have created his highly individual fictions. Only out of the experience and art of "This me who is me being me and none other!" as Peter Tarnopol says (MLM, p. 330). In that, Kafka is like Tarnopol—and like Philip Roth.

CHAPTER 13

Some Terrible Mechanism
(The Professor of Desire)

O F the twenty books judged the most important of 1977 by the
editors of the *New York Times Book Review,* only five were
novels: John Cheever's *Falconer,* Robert Coover's *The Public
Burning,* Joan Didion's *A Book of Common Prayer,* Toni
Morrison's *Song of Solomon*—and Philip Roth's *The Professor of
Desire.* Though Roth's fiction has never elicited unanimously enthusiastic reviews, the initial responses to his tenth book, which
were reflected in the *Time*'s choice, were genuinely staggering in
their use of superlatives. Calling it everything from "the year's best
novel" to "one of the most distinguished books of the decade" and
"among the major achievements of the literature of our time," reviewers praised it as brilliantly moving, stylistically elegant, and
more mature than anything he had written before.[1]

The reception of *The Professor of Desire* was all the more noteworthy because it so sharply contrasted with that of *The Breast,*
whose hero, Professor David Alan Kepesh, it reconstructed. But
Kepesh's second monologue deserves the testimonials it garnered,
for in it Roth does, indeed, display a new maturity—a maturity
born of his continuing preoccupation with Franz Kafka, nurtured
by his exploration of the characters and themes of his previous
work, and tempered by the influence of his reading Anton
Chekhov's fiction.

My Life as a Man clearly posed the question of what Roth would
write next, since, as we have seen, it was a technical and thematic
summation of all he had written before. The mood of middle-aged
self-assessment which its title and content implied was underlined
when he told Joyce Carol Oates that he felt he had reached a "natural break of sorts" in his work with its completion (RM, p. 112).
And with the publication of his collected essays and interviews in

Reading Myself and Others (1975) he provided a nonfictive comple-
ment to *My Life as a Man's* fictive recapitulation of his career
which seemed to clear the decks for a fresh start.

All that was apparent about the next step he would take from
what he published between *My Life as a Man* and *The Professor of
Desire* was that it would be taken with Kafka's spirit nearby. *Reading Myself and Others* began with Roth's comparing his view of his
role as an artist shuttling back and forth between the written and
unwritten worlds to that of Barnabas, the ambiguous messenger in
The Castle. It included a previously unpublished rumination on the
Nixon pardon titled "Our Castle," and concluded with the book
publication of "Looking at Kafka." In "In Search of Kafka and
Other Answers" (1976) he recounted how his fascination with
Kafka led him to visit Prague and Kafka's gravesite in the spring of
1972, shortly before *The Breast* appeared; and how his trip to
Prague led him to meet Kafka's direct literary heirs—the contem-
porary writers of Eastern Europe—and to make subsequent visits
each year since.

After returning from a trip to Prague and Budapest in early
1975, Roth approached Penguin Books with a proposal for a paperback reprint series designed to introduce the work of these writers
to an American readership by publishing several of their books annually. Penguin's "Writers from the Other Europe" series, with
Roth serving as general editor, was thus inaugurated in late 1975.
So far, the series includes six books: Milan Kundera's *Laughable
Loves* (stories, with an introduction by Roth) and *The Farewell
Party,* which treat personal and political illusions through a comedy
of erotic possibilities much like Roth's own; Ludvík Vaculík's *The
Guinea Pigs,* the story of a bank clerk caught in a web of mysteri-
ous bureaucratic intrigue; Tadeusz Borowski's *This Way for the
Gas, Ladies and Gentlemen,* a group of chilling concentration-
camp stories by a Polish survivor of Dachau and Auschwitz;
Tadeusz Konwicki's nightmarish *A Dreambook of Our Time,* and
Bruno Schulz's mythopoetic *The Street of Crocodiles.* In connection with the series Roth also conducted an interview with Isaac
Bashevis Singer on Bruno Schulz and published an introduction to
the first English translation of two stories about Nazis and Jews by
the Czech writer Jiri Weil, a contemporary of Isaac Babel's.

With *The Professor of Desire* it became clear that Roth's own
writing during this period had also continued to draw on the
Kafkan legacy. For after the publication of *My Life as a Man* he be-

gan a sequel to *The Breast*—eighty pages of Dave "The Breast" Kepesh traveling to his country home on weekends in a specially outfitted padded van, Kepesh on the Johnny Carson show, Kepesh the subject of various scientific studies—which he finally abandoned when he recognized that he could continue to invent "social humiliations" for Kepesh indefinitely to no real purpose. But this exercise led him to consider who Kepesh really was and, as a result, "the details that had formed the realistic underpinnings of a very surreal story" then seemed to be "begging to be brought to life, only this time on their own terms." The novel this process produced, Roth has said, "is a book that doesn't bear a necessary relationship to *The Breast,*" although it certainly repeats "a number of motifs from" its predecessor.[2]

That the two Kepesh books were not begun simultaneously is obvious; that the latter is superior is just as clear. And the reader of *The Professor of Desire* who returns to *The Breast* in hot pursuit of relationships will find as many discrepancies as connections. *The Breast* does introduce the names and characters of most of the major figures whose histories are developed more fully in the more recent novel—Abe Kepesh, Dr. Klinger, Helen Kepesh, Claire Ovington, Arthur and Debbie Schonbrun—and it alludes, as well, to a young poet-professor (Baumgarten) and to a London interlude with two Swedish girls. *The Breast* also has as part of its subject the paradoxes of "desire" and the constant struggle within Kepesh to suppress his need for "MORE" satisfaction. And like the Kepesh of *The Breast* and the heroes of *My Life as a Man*, the hero of *The Professor of Desire's* frustration in reality springs from incompatible conceptions of himself. But where one of the crucial elements in *The Professor of Desire* is Kepesh's impotence (like Portnoy's, it is the proximate cause of his seeing a psychiatrist), *The Breast's* Kepesh boats of his "dependable sexual potency." Where *The Breast's* Helen's second husband proved a lush, *The Professor of Desire's* Les Lowery is clearly no such thing; and since Helen disillusions Kepesh about Arthur Schonbrunn's apparently unshakeable reserve in *The Professor,* Schonbrunn's failure of composure in *The Breast* should not shock Kepesh as it does. The "enraged wife" who provided *The Breast's* "Grand Guignol" marriage would appear to have more in common with Maureen Johnson Tarnopol than she does with the Helen Kepesh we meet in *The Professor of Desire*. On the whole, of course, the facts and characterizations of the two novels do coincide closely enough for the later book to be viewed as an "antecedent" of *The Breast*—and we are certainly fortunate that Roth did not feel too tightly bound by the sketchy character conceptions of the earlier, slighter book. But it is probably best simply to note the obvious connections and then move on to consider *The Professor of Desire* on its own terms, rather than to read it for hints of the absurd metamorphosis we know a character named Kepesh will alter undergo. (That Roth did not do as much in the source of one of the book's few flaws—the last several paragraphs, which distort the natural ending's Chekhovian mood to provide suggestions to the impending *physical* transformation.)

On its own terms, *The Professor of Desire* introduces a series of important new notes to Roth's repertoire, while its underlying themes and movement echo those of "Goodbye, Columbus," *Letting Go, Portnoy's Complaint, The Breast,* and *My Life as a Man.* The central conflict is, once again, between the disapproving moralist and the libidinous slob, the lawful and anarchic selves, the ego/superego and the id. The battlefield is again sexual. Stylistically, the book refines the Kafkan synthesis of Roth's two previous novels and modifies the voices of *The Breast* and "My True Story." Here the synthesis provides a framework that permits both the dream of Kafka's whore and the tender realism of the last third of the novel. The voice is, as one reviewer observed, "the most supple and accomplished Roth has yet found."[3] Less exuberant, less hysterical, more measured than any of its recent predecessors, it allows Kepesh to be, by turns, thoughtful and flippant, sympathetic and self-conscious, nostalgic and ironic. Through it, he can speak convincingly of lust and longing, loneliness and joy, great books and great *borscht.*

Next to this voice, one of the first things that strikes the reader of *The Professor of Desire* is its formal ingenuity. "After great pain," Emily Dickinson wrote, "a formal feeling comes"; and after the painful exorcism of *My Life as a Man* comes *The Professor of Desire,* one of the most formal of Roth's fictions. This formality is not imposed from without, however, but integral to the novel's contents. For the entire book may be viewed as a monologue in the present tense that is the introductory lecture on "the professor's desire" which Kepesh prepares during the last half of the book for his comparative literature seminar, "Desire 341." "Indiscreet, unprofessional, unsavory as portions of these disclosures will surely strike some of you," he writes in the preface to this lecture, "I nonetheless would like, with your permission, to go ahead now and give an open account to you of the life I formerly led as a human being" (p. 185). The form of that account is that of a debate between the two sides of his nature, with each side scoring points and the final decision no more available than knowledge of the future. Appropriately, then, this account ends with the Labor Day weekend immediately preceding the first class in which it is delivered. Every incident, every character, every detail, every nuance and shift in tone of voice is carefully chosen to elaborate this conflict in this context.

Kepesh's character and the nature of the struggle within it are implied in the many connotations of the novel's title. He *professes*—lays claim to, frankly admits, affirms allegiance to, at times claims proficiency in, and seems to have dedicated himself as to a religious order to—desire. He is *a professor* of—a university teacher of, an instructor in the skilled art of, and one who professes his sentiments and beliefs about—desire. And the crux of his problem is that he lives up to a final meaning of the word "professor": he is a man who in the words of the *Random House Dictionary of the English Language* "makes a business of an occupation or hobby in which amateurs often engage." What he professes and is dedicated to is not love or lust, not sex or sensuality, but *desire*—perpetual and undiminished longing.

In an introduction to Frederica Wagman's novel *Playing House* (1974), Roth touched on the source of Kepesh's unhappiness when he observed that "it is the lost *corruption* of childhood that is elegized and the passing of a little girl's erotic frenzy that is wretchedly mourned" by Wagman's heroine. For "against the memory of that exquisite hellishness [she] measures the decency of the husband who would rescue her if only she were willing." But she isn't willing because for her *"everything* is 'just' something else that will not satisfy ... it is all as nothing to 'the way it can be,'* which is to say, the way it once was and never can be again" (RM, p. 211). Kepesh also mourns the lost "corruption" of his Fulbright year abroad with Birgitta and the "exquisite hellishness" of both that year and his years with Helen. Though Claire would rescue him if only he could let her, he, too, cannot totally rid himself of the feeling that everything she offers is "just" something that will not satisfy his desire for what was but "never can be again." Kepesh's progress is, as Allen Lacy has noted, "an inversion of the old theme of lost innocence." For Kepesh's journey leads him *to* an

Edenic garden in the Catskills—one surrounded by an apple orchard and presided over by "apple-cheeked" Claire. But having reached that garden, he cannot rest satisfied. Instead, Helen appears like the serpent to tempt him again with knowledge of his condition.

"Temptation" is the lecture/book's first word—"temptation ... in the conspicuous personage of Herbie Bratasky, social director, bandleader, crooner, comic, m.c. of my family's mountainside resort hotel" (p. 3), whose appeal to the young Kepesh stands in direct opposition to the self-sacrificing moral dignity of his "Mosaic dad," Abe. The conflict they represent is developed and explored on every page of the novel, and the heart of Roth's narrative is that for Kepesh its two camps are both omnipresent and forever irreconcilable. Herbie, like Jake the Snake and Arnold G., an exemplar of the adventurous and the unsocialized, is succeeded by the other characters in Kepesh's "rogues gallery": Louis Jelinek, Birgitta, Helen, and Baumgarten. Abe, exemplar of the lawful and dutiful, is followed by Elizabeth, Arthur Schonbrunn, Dr. Klinger, and Claire. From the outset it seems to Kepesh that "whichever I want I can have.... Either the furnace or the hearth" (p. 47)—*but,* since he is "a young absolutist" (p. 12), *not both.* His desire, of course, is always for the one he doesn't have.

At college he took as one of his mottoes Macaulay's description of Richard Steele: "a rake among scholars, a scholar among rakes." It seemed at the time to reconcile the two sides of the conflict he felt. In fact, the motto is a perfect one for Kepesh, but not because it implies reconciliation. It fits him because it suggests a man never at home, never at rest, never satisfied, always a stranger.

Whenever the battle appears to have been won by one side or the other, whenever the debate seems finally decided, Mr. Reality inevitably appears to show him that he is "sadly deluded and mistaken" (p. 52). As always in Roth's fiction, Mr. Reality takes many forms. The erotic paradise of a sixteen-day *ménage à trois* with two Swedish girls is destroyed by one's attempted suicide and the consequent guilt Kepesh feels. Sexual abandon with the remaining girl, Birgitta, is undermined by his realization that the temptations she inspired were "inimical to my overall best interests" (p. 53). But the scholarly calm and literary high-mindedness that he attempts to achieve when he leaves her for graduate studies at Stanford are, in turn, shattered "just when the battle appears to have been won" by the appearance of Helen (p. 52). Helen, whose exotic adventures make his seem like child's play, understands him best. "You're mis-using yourself, David," she says. "You're hopelessly intent on being what you're not" (p. 60). Their marriage brings pain; but its dissolution brings even greater misery, loneliness, and impotence. Alone in New York after his divorce, he meets the young Jewish-American poet Baumgarten. Baumgarten's appeal, like Helen's, is due to the fact that, unlike Kepesh, he is someone "on the friendli-est of terms with the sources of his excitement, and confidently op-posed to—in fact, rather amused by—all that stands in opposition" (p. 135). But Baumgarten, like Birgitta, unleashes the libidinous slob in Kepesh and is, therefore, finally rejected as dangerous.

"And then," the second half of the novel begins, "I meet a young woman altogether unlike this small band of consolers, coun-selors, tempters, and provacateurs ... off whom my benumbed and unsexed carcass has been careening since I've been a woman-less, pleasureless, passionless man on his own" (p. 149). The rest of the book sensitively traces the course of his affair with Claire—of his joyously embracing her simplicity, orderliness, and youthful passion, only to realize that it all will eventually end.

His love of Claire has undertones of dissatisfaction and incom-patibility from the beginning. If, at first, her orderliness is exactly what he needs, it isn't long before he acknowledges that "I see how very easily I could have no use for her. The snapshots. The lists.... Everything" (p. 162). If he feels as if he is being "sealed up into something wonderful" (p. 164), he, nonetheless, senses that he *is* being sealed up. If her common-sense response to learning that Kafka thought the only fit food for a man was half a lemon—she says, "Poor dope"—momentarily makes Kepesh feel "de-Kafkafied," it also suggests their temperamental incompatibility (p. 178). And if she makes him feel stunned with "the awesome fact of my great good luck" as they visit Vienna and Prague (p. 165), his dream of Kafka's whore makes it clear that the struggle within him has been repressed, not ended.

During the last third of the novel, Kepesh's rising dissatisfaction is counterpoised against his idyllic summer in the country with Claire. Its first clear sign is a diminution of desire: "Leveling off. Overheated frenzy subsiding into quiet physical affection.... And I for one will not quarrel, or sulk, or yearn, or despair. I will not make a religion of what is fading away" (p. 199). (But as a *profes-sor* of *desire* he is doomed by his character to do precisely that.) "I am willing to settle on these terms," he thinks. "This will suffice.

No more *more*. . . . And before whom am I on my knees trying to strike such a bargain? Who is to decide how far from Claire I am going to slide? Honored members of Literature 341, you would think, as I do, that it would, it should, it must, be me'' (p. 200).

When their pastoral retreat is finally invaded by the outside world—first by Helen and her new husband, then by Abe Kepesh and his friend, the concentration-camp survivor Barbatnik—these intimations of the mortality of their relationship begin to dominate his consciousness. ''Now I take what I can get, and I'm grateful to have it,'' Helen tells Kepesh (p. 213); ''I don't care anymore about being happy. I've given that up. All I care about is not being tortured (p. 216). ''Doesn't she drive you even a little crazy,'' she asks, ''being so bright and pretty and good?'' (p. 217). Each of her statements is like an electric shock, disturbing Kepesh's peace and elevating the voltage of his discontent until it eventually explodes.

The explosion finally occurs over the Labor Day weekend while his father is visiting. Kepesh is discomfited by the satisfaction with which his father foresees his future with Claire, at the same time that he wishes he could do what would make his father happy. When he overhears Claire describing her parents' marriage to Abe—''they probably never belonged together in the first place'' (p. 249)—he senses that the same is true of them, but thinks, ''Why should I feel as though I have lost a bloody battle when clearly I have won?'' (p. 250). Then, as the ripe apples begin dropping, symbolically forecasting the end of both love and a season, he feels like a helpless apple himself, pulled away from Claire with the force of gravity.

When he touches the ground, the impact is devastating. ''Why continue to cast this spell over myself wherein nothing is permitted to sift through except what pleases me? . . . How much longer before I've had a bellyful of wholesome innocence—how long before the lovely blandness of life with Claire begins to cloy, to pall, and I am out there once again, mourning what I've lost and looking for my way!'' It will be, he thinks, ''only a matter of time—that's all it seems to take, just time—[before] what we have together will gradually disappear, and the man now holding in his hand a spoonful of her orange custard will give way to Herbie's pupil, Birgitta's accomplice, Helen's suitor, yes, to Baumgarten's sidekick and defender, to the would-be wayward son and all he hungers for. Or, if not that, the would-be *what?* When this too is gone in its turn, what then?'' (pp. 251–52).

Kepesh's sense of frustration in reality, his inability to solve the struggle within or to marry Claire, his psychological impotence in the force of "some terrible mechanism" that prevents him from achieving the goals he seeks, his view of himself as a "would-be wayward son"—all link him to Kafka and Kafka's heroes and suggest the importance of the Kafkan episode to the novel. When Kepesh travels to Prague with Claire, on his way to deliver a lecture on Kafka titled "Hunger Art" at Bruges, his visit is a fictionalized version of Roth's own. Like Roth, Kepesh assigns his classes the task of writing their own versions of Kafka's *Letter to His Father;* like Roth, he is impressed by the realistic basis for Kafka's tales when he sees the Gymnasium and Cathedral and hears of xenophobic Czech villages; like Roth, Kepesh meets and converses at length with a post-Dubcek Prague writer; like Roth, he visits Kafka's grave. Most importantly, Kepesh's explanation of his preoccupation with Kafka paraphrases Roth's own and helps to explain the significance Kafka has gained for Roth in his most recent fictions. "While it lasted," Kepesh says, "while I couldn't be what I had always just assumed I was, well, it wasn't like anything I had ever known before . . . stories of obstructed, thwarted K.'s banging their heads against invisible walls. . . suddenly had a disturbing new resonance for me. . . . In my own way, you see, I had come to know that sense of having been summoned—to a calling that turns out to be beyond you, yet in the face of every compromising or farcical consequence, being unable to wise up and relinquish the goal" (pp. 171–72). The words might just as well be Zuckerman's or Tarnopol's.

What Kepesh doesn't realize as he speaks of his problems in the past tense is that his Kafkan days are far from over. Though he is happy with Claire in Prague, though he feels confident enough that he has "come through" to begin describing the experience in his introductory lecture to his class—a lecture about the "life I formerly led"—by the end of the novel he has again become a blood brother to the Czech professor who tells him that "the way we live now is not what we had in mind" (p. 170).

The professor confesses to Kepesh that "many of us survive almost solely on Kafka" (p. 169), and, in a sense, the statement seems to be a fair description of Roth's art, as well, in the years when "looking at Kafka" helped him to write *Portnoy's Complaint, The Breast,* and *My Life as a Man.* In *The Professor of Desire,* however, the emphasis is on "almost." For, in terms of Roth's artistic development, one of the most significant aspects of *The Professor of Desire* is that, in it, Kafka's spirit is joined—and, for much of the novel, superseded—by Anton Chekhov's. Where "the life I formerly led" at first reminds Kepesh of Kafka's "Report to the Academy," at the end of the novel the same phrase seems the title of a Chekhov story. Where Kepesh's lecture, "Hunger Art," focused on the theme of "spiritual starvation" in Kafka (p. 165), his studies of Chekhov focus on "the varieties of pain engendered by spiritual imprisonment" (p. 156). But what is most interesting about Roth's novel is the way that this new influence modifies the Kafkan tone of his two previous novels, producing a tenderness, a compassion, and an extension of authorial sympathy beyond the protagonist that add yet another dimension to his work.

Chekhov is as important to *The Professor of Desire* as Henry James was to *Letting Go,* as the Southwestern humorists were to *The Great American Novel,* as Kafka was to *The Breast.* Kepesh's doctoral thesis was on "romantic disillusionment in the stories of Anton Chekhov"—"a subject," he notes, "I'd chosen even before meeting my wife" (p. 70). And since romantic disillusionment is at the very core of *The Professor of Desire,* we should not be surprised to find Kepesh commenting early on that, as he taught Chekhov's stories, "each and every sentence seems to me to allude to my own plight above all" (p. 72). Every reference to Chekhov in the novel, all of Kepesh's analyses of Chekhov's fiction, relate to his own predicament and lead to the novel's last pages where, instead of seeing himself as one of Kafka's characters, he sees himself as a character in Chekhov.

After his divorce, when life with Claire brings some peace of mind, Kepesh returns to his thesis and begins rereading Chekhov and making notes for a book. He starts with "Man in a Shell," "Gooseberries," and "About Love," the stories of "spiritual imprisonment." He returns to Chekhov nightly, "listening for the anguished cry of the trapped and miserable socialized being." Simultaneously, he is "watching how Chekhov, simply and clearly, . . . reveals the humiliations and failures—worst of all, the destructive power—of those who seek a way *out* of the shell of restrictions and convention, out of the pervasive boredom and the stifling despair, out of the painful marital situations . . . into what they take to be a vibrant and desirable life" (p. 156).

What Kepesh notes in Chekhov here, of course, is Chekhov's

descriptions of the situation he and so many of Roth's heroes from Neil Klugman through Peter Tarnopol face. Like the man in a shell, Belikov, Kepesh and Roth's other heroes and heroines are "irritated...frightened...kept in a state of continual agitation" by reality. One of the characteristics of Kepesh, Zuckerman, and Tarnopol is that, like Belikov, they "laud the past and things that never existed" and turn to books as "concealment from real life." Aloyin, in "About Love," touches Kepesh's condition just as directly, when he observes that "when we are in love, we never stop asking ourselves whether it is honorable or dishonorable, sensible or stupid, what this love will lead to, and so on. If that is a good thing or not I don't know, but that it is a hindrance and a source of dissatisfaction, of that I am certain."[4] Kepesh's own comments on several other Chekhov stories can also be read as allusions to the action in Roth's novel. Kepesh speaks, for example, of "the agitated young wife in 'Misfortune' who looks for 'a bit of excitement' against the grain of her own respectability"—and we are reminded of Kepesh himself. He speaks of "the lovesick landowner in 'Ariadne' confessing with Herzogian helplessness to a romantic misadventure with a vulgar trampy tigress who gradually transforms him into a hopeless misogynist, but whom he nonetheless waits on hand and foot"—and we are reminded of Kepesh and Helen. He contemplates "the young actress in 'A Boring Story,' whose bright, hopeful enthusiasm for a life on the stage, and a life with men, turns bitter with her first experiences of the stage and men, and of her own lack of talent" (pp. 156–57)—and we recall Helen, sitting in the airport terminal waiting for men to be attracted to her beauty because she feels it is all she has to offer, and then crying out to Kepesh, "why must they always be either brutes or choirboys" (p. 91).

Kepesh's studies of Chekhov produce two results: his first book and the tone of *The Professor of Desire*. His book, titled *Man in a Shell,* is "an essay on license and restraint in Chekhov's world—longings fulfilled, pleasures denied, and the pain occasioned by both; a study, at bottom, of what makes for Chekhov's pervasive pessimism about the methods—scrupulous, odious, noble, dubious—by which the men and women of his time try in vain to achieve 'that sense of personal freedom' to which Chekhov himself is so devoted" (pp. 158–59). Certainly no one is better equipped to investigate the subject than Kepesh—except Philip Roth.

The thematic connection between Chekhov's fiction and *The Professor of Desire* is manifest, then. But the voice we have noted in Roth's novel is more difficult to define without extensive quotation. It is heard, however, in the difference between Tarnopol's obsessive attempts at explaining the causes and consequences of his marriage and Kepesh's relatively laconic description of his decision to marry: "Doubting and hoping, then, wanting and fearing (anticipating the pleasantest sort of lively future one moment, the worst in the next), I marry Helen Baird" (p. 66). Or in the difference between the elaborate, blow-by-blow and word-by-word descriptions of the Tarnopols' arguments and Kepesh's touchingly mature summary: "At our best we make resolutions, we make apologies, we make amends, we make love. But at our worst ... well, our worst is just about as bad as anybody's, I would think" (p. 68).

Kindness and humanity, a sense of the unexplainable mystery of life, a blend of comedy and pathos, a sympathy for the human condition and a hard-won understanding—these are the qualities, present sporadically in all of Roth's work, which are developed most fully through this voice. Kepesh convinces us that he genuinely loves his parents, Helen, and Claire—and his love is masterfully conveyed through dozens of understated details and descriptions. Consider David's longing to sneak into his parents' bed, as he did when he was a child, on the night he learns of his mother's cancer; or his description of his mother teaching him to type in their deserted, snow-covered Catskill hotel—"No one, before or since, has ever taught me anything with so much innocence and conviction"—and the impact it adds to her leaving him a package of food, with "DAVID" typed neatly in the center of the card. There is also the touching description of his father's arrival for the Labor Day weekend; Abe's love and thoughtfulness, suggested by his gifts of a silver paperweight embossed with a rose for Claire and the Shakespeare medallions for David (collected one-a-month for thirty-six months), and his insistence that Claire then read the inscription on the *Romeo and Juliet* medallion, "A rose by any other name would smell as sweet"; David's longing to embrace his father as he thinks, "Is there a man alive... who had led a more exemplary life" (p. 246). The same sensitivity and compassion is evident in David's description of his visit to Kafka's grave, when, after adding a pebble to the pile on Kafka's gravesite, "for the first time I notice the plaques affixed to the length of the cemetery wall, inscribed to the memory of the Jewish citizens of Prague exterminated in Terezin, Auschwitz, Belsen and Dachau. There are not pebbles enough to go around" (p. 176).

"If that kid sang serious he could be in the Metropolitan Opera," one of the guests at Kepesh's Hungarian Royale says of Herbie at the beginning of the novel. "If he sang serious he could be a cantor, for Christ sakes, with no problem," another responds. "He could break your heart" (p. 5). If these comments about Herbie remind us of comments by the Roth critics who argue that his work has steadily declined as its comedy has increased, they're probably meant to. In *The Professor of Desire* Roth does "sing serious," with Chekhov's help, and the result is indeed heartrending—especially in the closing pages where Kepesh and Chekhov come together for the last time. The sound of apples falling to the ground in his apple orchard replaces the sound of axes in Chekhov's cherry orchard, as Kepesh realizes that his life with Claire has been *"only an interim,"* that he is destined "never to know anything durable. Nothing except...unrelinquishable memories of the discontinuous and provisional; nothing except this ever-lengthening saga of all that did not work" (pp. 251–52).

"It's a simple Chekhov story," he tells her. "This. Today. The summer. Some nine or ten pages, that's all. Called 'The Life I Formerly Led' " (p. 259). And *The Professor of Desire* does seem most Chekhovian as it ends. "Chekhovian," because it displays the same qualities Kepesh admired in "Lady with a Lap Dog"—a movingly transparent ending, "no false mysteries, only the harsh facts directly stated"; "ridicule and irony" gradually giving way to "sorrow and pathos"; a "feel for the disillusioning moment and for the processes wherein actuality pounces upon even our most harmless illusions, not to mention the grand dreams of fulfillment and adventure" (p. 74). And "Chekhovian" in the same way that Roth applied the label to one of Kundera's stories: "not merely because of its tone, or its concern with the painful and touching consequences of time passing and old selves dying, but because it is so very good" (RM, p. 207).

CHAPTER 14

Man with a Hammer

R OTH has said that book ideas come to him with all the appearance of pure accident or chance, though "by the time I am
done I can see that what has taken shape was actually spawned . . .
by the interplay between my previous fiction, recent undigested
personal history, the circumstances of my immediate everyday life,
and the books I've been reading and teaching" (RM, pp. 112–13).
The purpose of this study has been to explore the elements of that
creative interplay as they have manifested themselves in the books
Roth has written since 1959.

Literary criticism isn't prophecy, and to attempt to predict what
an artist as imaginative and surprising as Roth will write next would
be nothing less than foolhardy. Who could have predicted, after
all, that *When She Was Good* would be followed by *Portnoy's
Complaint*, or that *My Life as a Man* would be followed by a novel
heavily influenced by Chekhov? As we await his next books, all
that can be said with some degree of surety is that—if my sense of
the evolution of his fiction is right—Roth will continue to stalk Mr.
Reality, and continue to explore the social being's private life and
the feel of our cockeyed world, continue to express his vision of the
interpenetration of reality and fantasy in contemporary American
culture. and that vision will inevitably grow out of his personal experiences and obsessions. It also seems clear that he will continue to
undertake technical experiments in order to combine moral seriousness and comic insight in his expression of all these concerns.

To date, Roth's fiction has been an accurate barometer of the
trends and tensions in American life. *Goodbye, Columbus, Letting
Go* and *When She Was Good* explored the conflict between alienation and accomodation/assimilation which dominated the personal and social life of the Fifties; the experimentation and liberation of *Portnoy's Complaint, Our Gang, The Great American*

Novel and *The Breast* reflected the strengths and pitfalls of the de-mythologizing Sixties; *My Life as a Man* and *The Professor of Desire* speak with the softer, more reflective voice of the self-assessing, weary Seventies. Such relationships between books and their times are never simple, of course. Roth is no longer a twenty-six-year-old golden boy, and the changes in his fiction are intimately bound up with the maturing of the man who has created it.

It is inconceivable to me that the young author of *Goodbye, Columbus* could have ended an interview, as Roth did in 1977, by referring to this quotation from Virginia Woolf—"Life has to be sloughed; has to be faced; has to be rejected; then accepted on new terms with rapture. And so on, and so on; till you are 40, when the only problem is how to grasp it tighter and tighter to you, so quick it seems to slip, and so infinitely desirable is it."[1] Yet we are not at all surprised to hear the creator of *The Professor of Desire*—now forty-five years old—thinking such thoughts out loud.

On the other hand, Lionel Trilling's comments in an essay on reality in America seem as pertinent to an understanding of Roth's latest book as to his first. "A culture is not a flow, not even a confluence," Trilling wrote; "the form of its existence is struggle, or at least debate—it is nothing if not dialectic. And in any culture there are likely to be certain artists who contain a large part of the dialectic within themselves, their meaning and their power lying in their contradictions." These artists," he went on to say, "contain within themselves ... the very essence of the culture, and the sign of this is that they do not submit to serve the ends of any one ideological group or tendency." Finally, he observed that "it is a significant circumstance of American culture ... that an unusually large proportion of its notable writers of the nineteenth century were such repositories of the dialectic of their times—they contained both the yes and no of their culture, and by that token they were prophetic of the future."[2]

Only time will tell whether the most notable writers of the *twentieth* century will also turn out to be those who are the "repositories of the dialectic of their times," but should that be the judgment, Roth will be high on the list of those artists. For he has, from the beginning, said both yes and no to his culture in its many manifestations. And as he continues to write, he will certainly continue to play the indispensable role Trilling described and Chekhov alluded to when he wrote in "Gooseberries" that "behind the door of every contented, happy man there ought to be someone standing with a little hammer and continually reminding him with a knock that there are unhappy people, that however happy he may be, life will sooner or later show him its claws, and trouble will come to him."[3]

That the man with a hammer can make us think and laugh and wince all at the same time is something that Henry James, Mark Twain, Franz Kafka, and Chekhov would have appreciated.

Notes and References

Preface

1. "Second Dialogue in Israel," *Congress Bi-Weekly* 30 (September 16, 1963): 35. All subsequent references to this symposium will be included parenthetically in the text as SD.

Chapter One

1. Quoted in Robert Gutwillig, "Dim Views through Fog," *New York Times Book Review*, November 13, p. 68.
2. Philip Roth, *Reading Myself and Others* (New York, 1975), p. 128.
3. "Good and Short," *Hudson Review* 12 (Autumn 1959): 358–59.
4. *Commentary*, March 1961, p. 229. All subsequent references to this and Roth's other collected essays and interviews will be to their publication in *Reading Myself and Others*, and will be included parenthetically in the text as RM.
5. "American Fiction," *Commentary*, September 1961, pp. 250–51.
6. "Realism and the Contemporary Novel," *Partisan Review* 26 (Spring 1959): 203.

Chapter Two

1. Urjo Kareda makes this observation about the film adaptation of Mordecai Richler's 1959 novel *The Apprenticeship of Duddy Kravitz* in "Is There Any Future for Bad Taste," *New York Times*, August 18, 1974, p. 11D.
2. The chronological order of the stories according to their first publication is: "You Can't Tell a Man by the Song He Sings" (*Commentary*, November 1957), "The Conversion of the Jews" (*Paris Review*, Spring 1958), "Epstein" (*Paris Review*, Summer 1958), "Defender of the Faith" (*New Yorker*, March 14, 1959), and "Eli, the Fanatic" (*Commentary*, April 1959).
3. In 1952 and 1953, Roth published topical satire and stories in the Bucknell University literary magazine, *Et Cetera*. Copies of each of the *Et Cetera* issues in which Roth's work appeared are included in the Roth Collection housed at the Library of Congress.
4. Quoted in Martha McGregor, "The NBA Winner Talks Back," *New York Post*, April 3, 1960, p. 11.

5. Boston, 1973, p. 145.

6. *The New Novel in America: The Kafkan Mode in Contemporary American Fiction* (Ithaca, 1970), p. 60.

7. John J. Clayton makes this observation about *The Victim* in his *Saul Bellow: In Defense of Man* (Bloomington, 1971), p. 161.

8. This statement appears in the original version of the story published in *Commentary* (pp. 301–302), and in the Literary Guild edition of *GC* (p. 292). Though it was eliminated from the Houghton Mifflin edition of *GC*, the same sentiments are expressed in all versions of the story in Eli's letter to Tzuref.

9. The phrase comes from one of Roth's early autobiographical essays, "Recollections from Beyond the Last Rope" (*Harper's*, July 1959, pp. 42–48). John N. McDaniel uses this image as an extremely effective paradigm in *The Fiction of Philip Roth* (Haddonfield, N.J., 1974), pp. 19–21.

Chapter Three

1. "In Defense of Philip Roth," *Chicago Review* 17 (Nos. 2 & 3, 1964): 89.

2. *The Great Gatsby* (New York, 1925), p. 99.

3. *The Fiction of Philip Roth*, p. 74.

4. "The Sadness of Philip Roth: An Interim Report," *Massachusetts Review* 3 (Winter 1962): 260.

5. New York, 1953, p. 536.

Chapter Four

1. "A Late Look at *Letting Go*," January 12, 1963, p. 22.

2. Philip Roth to the author in conversation, December 28, 1973.

3. This title is mentioned in "Philip Roth Papers," *Quarterly Journal of the Library of Congress* (October 1970): 343–44.

4. *The American Novel and Its Tradition* (New York, 1957), p. 129.

5. "The Vanity of Human Wishes," *The Reporter*, August 16, 1962, p. 54.

6. "Is Life a Spectator Sport?" *Cosmopolitan*, July 1952, p. 18.

7. "The Journey of Philip Roth," *Atlantic*, April 1969, pp. 64–65.

8. New York, 1967, p. 9.

9. *The American Novel and Its Tradition*, pp. 132, 134.

10. Marion Montgomery makes this point about James's characters in "The Flaw in the Portrait," in Peter Buitenhuis, ed., *The Portrait of a Lady: A Collection of Critical Essays* (Twentieth Century Interpretations, Englewood Cliffs, N.J., 1968), p. 61.

11. Quoted in Joe David Bellamy, ed., *The New Fiction: Interviews with Innovative Writers* (Bloomington, 1974), p. 29.

12. "The Vanity of Human Wishes," p. 55.

13. "The Meanings of *Letting Go*," *Contemporary Literature* 11 (Winter 1970): 24.

Chapter Five

1. "On the dissemination of realism," *TriQuarterly* 11 (Winter 1968): 166.
2. "Novels: Recognition and Deception," *Critical Inquiry* 1 (September 1974): 111–12.
3. *Adventure, Mystery and Romance* (Chicago, 1976), p. 315.
4. Mark Shechner, "Philip Roth," *Partisan Review* 41 (Fall 1974): 427.
5. Quoted in "An American Storyteller," *Time*, December 13, 1954, p. 72.
6. "The War in the Back Seat," *Atlantic*, July 1972, p. 54.
7. *Studies in European Realism* (New York, 1964), p. 6.
8. Philip Roth, "Iowa: A Very Far Country Indeed," *Esquire*, December 1962, pp. 102–103.
9. See "Philip Roth Papers," pp. 343–44, for other titles Roth considered.
10. "*Playboy* Interview with David Halberstam," *Playboy*, August 1973, pp. 58, 59, 66, 69.
11. Eliot Fremont-Smith, "Looking Back: Two Good Novels Reconsidered," *New York Times*, June 16, 1967, p. 41.

Chapter Six

1. *The Comic Imagination in American Literature* (New Brunswick, 1973), p. 9.
2. Philip Roth to the author in conversation, December 28, 1973.
3. The inscription in Blair's copy of *The Great American Novel* is quoted with his permission.

Chapter Seven

1. See Guerard, "Notes on the rhetoric of anti-realist fiction," *TriQuarterly* 30 (Spring 1974): 12, and Dickstein, "Black Humor and History: Fiction in the Sixties," *Partisan Review* 43 (Spring 1976): 191–94 (reprinted in his *Gates of Eden: American Culture in the Sixties*). The book's impact on the cultural scene is suggested by the fact that, in a survey of prominent intellectuals who were asked to name those who had influenced their opinions on cultural matters—a survey conducted in 1970, one year after *Portnoy's Complaint* appeared—Roth and Saul Bellow were the only fictionists listed among the "top" choices. See Charles Kadushin, *The American Intellectual Elite* (Boston, 1974), pp. 28–32.
2. "The Poet," in Brooks Atkinson, eds., *The Complete Essays of Ralph Waldo Emerson* (New York, 1940), p. 397.
3. "American Fiction," p. 248.

4. For a discussion of Roth's frustrations with *When She Was Good*, see Albert Goldman, "Wild Blue Shocker: *Portnoy's Complaint*," *Life*, February 7, 1969, pp. 62–63.

5. "The Journey of Philip Roth," p. 70.

6. Richard Poirier, *A World Elsewhere* (New York, 1966), p. 5.

7. Ibid., p. 6.

8. Ibid., p. 15.

9. Ibid., p. 7.

10. Ibid., p. 27.

11. Ibid., p. 35.

12. Ibid., p. 29.

13. Ibid., p. 7.

14. "*Portnoy's Complaint* and the Sociology of Literature," (September 1971): 260, 267.

15. "Mark Twain: The Height of Humor," in Rubin, ed., *The Comic Imagination in American Literature*, p. 144.

16. Walter Blair, *Native American Humor*, rev. ed. (San Francisco, 1960), p. 64.

17. "A Man's Voice, Speaking," in Harry Levin, ed., *Veins of Humor*, Harvard English Studies 3 (Cambridge, 1972), p. 197.

18. "Wild Blue Shocker," p. 58F.

Chapter Eight

1. Philip Roth to Walter Clemons, quoted in "Joking in the Square," *Newsweek*, November 8, 1971, p. 111.

2. "Ishmael Reed on Ishmael Reed," *Black World*, June 1974, p. 20.

3. "A Short Course in Nixon's Rhetoric," *Village Voice*, January 13, 1972, pp. 1, 70–71.

4. This statement, and those of the other CBS newsmen, is quoted from notes taken by the author on the evening of August 8, 1974.

5. Phoebe Adams, *Atlantic*, January 1972, p. 97.

6. *Kaddish and Other Poems 1958–1960* (San Francisco, 1961), p. 63.

Chapter Nine

1. Blair, *Native American Humor*, p. 70.

2. *The Glory of Their Times* (New York, 1966), pp. 33, 57, 113–15, and *passim*.

3. Blair, *Native American Humor*, p. 97.

4. For some explanation of Roth's choice of baseball players as his mythic heroes, see Leslie A. Fiedler, "The Jew in the American Novel," in *To the Gentiles* (New York, 1972), p. 112, where he says that the baseball player was "the last symbol for the city-dweller of the heroic." Also see Roth's comments about the genesis of *The Great American Novel* (RM,

pp. 89–90), and about the mythic quality baseball had for him when he was a boy(RM, pp. 179–84).

5. Blair, *Native American Humor*, p. 69.

6. Ibid., p. 88.

7. Ibid., p. 96.

8. Ibid., pp. 89–92.

9. Ibid., p. 220.

10. Ibid., p. 94.

11. Ibid.

12. Walter Evans, "The All-American Boys: A Study of Boys' Sports Fiction," *Journal of Popular Culture* 6 (Summer 1972): 104–21. This article is especially interesting because it outlines many of the conventions which Roth is undercutting throughout *The Great American Novel*.

13. For some of the actual parallels, see Richard Gilman's review, "Ball Five," *Partisan Review* 40 (Summer 1973): 467–71. Also see Joe Wood's story in *The Glory of Their Times* (p. 149), in which he tells of dressing as a girl to play in minor-league exhibition games. Ellis's charts and graphs, as Roth points out in his acknowledgments, are taken almost verbatim from a book called *Percentage Baseball*. The rhetoric of Yamm's speech is an amalgam of Richard Nixon's Checkers Speech and Edward Kennedy's Chappaquidick address; and Yamm's treatment at the hands of organized baseball and the fans is modeled on the treatment accorded Jackie Robinson.

14. M. Thomas Inge, "Introduction" to *Sut Lovingood's Yarns* by George Washington Harris (New Haven, 1966), p. 21.

15. Blair, *Native American Humor*, p. 21.

Chapter Ten

1. Rust Hills, ed., *Writer's Choice* (New York, 1974), p. 351.

2. "Franz Kafka," in Ronald Gray, ed., *Kafka: A Collection of Critical Essays* (Twentieth Century Views, Englewood Cliffs, N.J., 1962), p. 40.

3. "In Search of Kafka," *New York Times Book Review*, February 15, 1976, p. 2.

4. *The New Novel in America*, p. 13.

5. "In Search of Kafka," p. 2.

6. Franz Kafka, *Letter to His Father*, translated by Ernst Kaiser and Eithe Wilkins (New York, 1953), p. 7. Subsequent references to this edition, designated L, will be included parenthetically in the text.

7. For a discussion of this shift within the Jewish family structure after immigration to America, see Harold Fisch, "Fathers, Mothers, Sons and Lovers: Jewish and Gentile Patterns in Literature," *Midstream* 18 (March 1972): 48–51.

8. *Writer's Choice*, p. 351.

9. Joyce Carol Oates noted that a photograph of Kafka like the one Roth describes in "Looking at Kafka" (RM, p. 247) hung on the wall of his study when she interviewed him in Manhattan in May 1974 ("A Conversation with Philip Roth," *Ontario Review* 1, Fall 1974: 20). A poster-size portrait of Kafka also dominated one wall of the cabin at his home in New England when I visited him in December 1973.

Chapter Eleven

1. Roth to the author, December 28, 1973.
2. "Uplift," *New York Review of Books*, November 16, 1972, p. 18.
3. "Off His Chest," *Newsweek*, September 25, 1972, p. 118.
4. "Fiction," *Esquire*, October 1972, p. 84.
5. This paragraph is developed from ideas in an unpublished paper by Judith Yaross Lee, entitled "Philip Roth's Cockeyed Humor."
6. Solotaroff, *Esquire*, October 1972, p. 84.

Chapter Twelve

1. Quoted in Leo Hamalian, ed., *Franz Kafka: A Collection of Criticism* New York, 1974), p. 2.
2. Quoted in Philip Rahv's introduction to *The Selected Short Stories of Franz Kafka*, translated by Willa and Edwin Muir (New York, 1952), p. x.
3. "The Vanity of Human Wishes," p. 55.
4. "Kafka the Artist," in *Kafka: A Collection of Critical Essays*, p. 26.
5. "Kafka the Writer," Ibid., p. 67.

Chapter Thirteen

1. *Chicago Tribune Book World*, October 23, 1977, p. 2, and Allen Lacy, "A Hint of Nightmare Amid Innocence," *Chronicle of Higher Education*, October 25, 1977, p. 16.
2. Sara Davidson, "Talk with Philip Roth," *New York Times Book Review*, September 18, 1977, p. 51.
3. Robert Towers, "One-Man Band," *New York Review of Books*, October 27, 1977, p. 12.
4. Quotations are from Avrahm Yarmolinsky, ed., *The Portable Chekhov* (New York, 1977), pp. 355–56, 385.

Chapter Fourteen

1. Stephen E. Rubin, "Dialog: Philip Roth," *Chicago Tribune Magazine*, September 25, 1977, p. 75.

2. *The Liberal Imagination* (New York, 1950), p. 9.

3. *The Portable Chekhov*, p. 381.

Selected Bibliography

PRIMARY SOURCES

1. Books:

The Breast. New York: Holt, Rinehart and Winston, 1972; Bantam Books (pa.), 1973.

Goodbye, Columbus. Boston: Houghton Mifflin Co., 1959; World Publishing Company, Meridian Books (pa.), 1960; Bantam Books (pa.), 1963; Random House, Modern Library, 1966.

The Great American Novel. New York: Holt, Rinehart and Winston, 1973; Bantam Books (pa.), 1974.

Letting Go. New York: Random House, 1962; Bantam Books (pa.), 1963.

My Life as a Man. New York: Holt, Rinehart and Winston, 1974; Bantam Books (pa.), 1975.

Our Gang. New York: Random House, 1971; Bantam Books (pa.), 1972; Bantam "Watergate Edition," 1973; Bantam "Pre-Impeachment Edition," 1974.

Portnoy's Complaint. New York: Random House, 1969; Bantam Books (pa.), 1970.

The Professor of Desire. New York: Farrar, Straus and Giroux, 1977; Bantam Books (pa.), 1978.

Reading Myself and Others. New York: Farrar, Straus and Giroux, 1975; Noonday (pa.), 1976; Bantam Books (pa.), 1977. This collects all of Roth's important essays and interviews except for those listed below.

When She Was Good. New York: Random House, 1967; Bantam Books (pa.), 1968.

2. Uncollected Fiction and a Screenplay

"Armando and the Fraud." *Et Cetera*, October 1953, pp. 21–32.

"The Box of Truths." *Et Cetera*, October 1952, pp. 10–12.

"The Contest for Aaron Gold." *Epoch* 5–6 (Fall 1955): 37–51.

"The Day It Snowed." *Chicago Review* 8 (Fall 1954): 34–45.

"Expect the Vandals." *Esquire*, December 1958, pp. 208–28.

"The Fence." *Et Cetera*, May 1953, pp. 18–23.

"The Final Delivery of Mr. Thorn." *Et Cetera*, May 1954, pp. 20–28.

"Good Girl." *Cosmopolitan*, May 1960, pp. 98–103.

"The Great American Pastime" (A Screenplay). In Bob Booker, ed., *Pardon Me, Sir But Is My Eye Hurting Your Elbow?* New York: Bernard Geis Associates, 1968, pp. 134–55.

"Heard Melodies Are Sweeter." *Esquire*, August 1958, p. 58.

"The Love Vessel." *Dial 1* 1 (Fall 1959): 41–68.

"The Mistaken." *American Judaism* 10 (Fall 1960): 10.

"Novotny's Pain." *New Yorker*, October 27, 1962, pp. 46–56.

"On the Air." *New American Review* 10 (August 1970): 7–49.

"Philosophy, Or Something Like That." *Et Cetera*, May 1952, pp. 5, 16.

"Psychoanalytic Special." *Esquire*, November 1963, pp. 106–109, 172–76.

3. Uncollected Essays

"American Fiction." *Commentary*, September 1961, pp. 248–52. Letters about "Writing American Fiction" and Roth's response.

"An Actor's Life for Me." *Playboy*, January 1964, pp. 84–86, 228–35.

"In Search of Kafka and Other Answers." *New York Times Book Review*, February 15, 1976, pp. 6–7.

"Introduction: Juri Weil—Two Stories About Nazis and Jews." *American Poetry Review*, September/October 1974, p. 22.

"Iowa: A Very Far Country Indeed." *Esquire*, December 1962, pp. 132 + .

"The Kind of Person I Am." *New Yorker*, November 29, 1958, pp. 173–78.

"Mrs. Lindbergh, Mr. Ciardi, and the Teeth and Claws of the Civilized World." *Chicago Review* 11 (Summer 1957): 72–76.

"Philip Roth Talks to Teens." *Seventeen*, April 1963, p. 170.

"Philip Roth Tells About *When She Was Good.*" *Literary Guild Magazine*, July 1967, unpaginated.

"Positive Thinking on Pennsylvania Avenue." *Chicago Review* 11 (Spring 1957): 21–24.

"Recollections from Beyond the Last Rope." *Harper's*, July 1959, pp. 42–48.

"Roth and Singer on Bruno Schultz." *New York Times Book Review*, February 13, 1977, pp. 5 + .

"Second Dialogue in Israel," *Congress Bi-Weekly* 30 (September 16, 1963): 4–85.

4. Uncollected Interviews

CLEMONS, WALTER. "Joking in the Square." *Newsweek*, November 8, 1971, pp. 110–11. On *Our Gang*.

DAVIDSON, SARA. "Talk with Philip Roth." *New York Times Book Review*, September 18, 1977, pp. 1, 51–53. On *The Professor of Desire*.

RUBIN, STEPHEN E. "Dialog: Philip Roth." *Chicago Tribune Magazine*, September 25, 1977, pp. 74–75. On *The Professor of Desire*.

SECONDARY SOURCES

1. Bibliography

RODGERS, BERNARD F., JR. *Philip Roth: A Bibliography.* Scarecrow
Author Bibliographies #19. Metuchen, N.J.: Scarecrow Press, 1974.
An annotated checklist of writing by and about Roth from 1954 to
1974.

2. Books about Roth

COOPERMAN, STANLEY. *Philip Roth's 'Portnoy's Complaint.'* New York:
Monarch Press, 1973. Not the usual Monarch Notes chapter-by-chap-
ter analysis, but a critical commentary on key ideas in the books
through *Portnoy.*

MCDANIEL, JOHN N. *The Fiction of Philip Roth.* Haddonfield, N.J.:
Haddonfield House, 1974. The first full-length study of Roth's work
applies Helen Weinberg's categories of "victim-hero" and "activist-
hero" to the fiction through *My Life as a Man.* Discussions of the
short stories, and the first and last chapters are especially noteworthy.

————. "Heroes in the Fiction of Philip Roth." Dissertation: Florida
State University, 1972. First chapter, "Philip Roth and the Critics,"
which was cut from the book version, is the fullest discussion of critical comment on Roth's work compiled to date.

MEETER, GLENN. *Philip Roth and Bernard Malamud: A Critical Essay.*
Grand Rapids, Mich.: William B. Eerdmans, 1968. Emphasis on
Roth as a religious writer dates this study of three motifs in the pre-
Portnoy fiction—the Jew as a Man of Faith, the quest, and the
conversion.

PINSKER, SANFORD. *The Comedy That "Hoits": An Essay on the Fiction
of Philip Roth.* Columbia: University of Missouri Press, 1975. An
introductory essay which treats Roth as a confessional writer who
fails to transcend his experience through his art.

2. Articles and Chapters of Books Discussing Roth
(Roth is discussed in almost all commentaries on contemporary Jewish-American literature and his books are widely reviewed—both in the
United States and in Europe. The followng list, which is highly selective,
excludes most reviews and all articles published in foreign journals. For
further bibliographical information on Roth criticism, the reader is referred to *Philip Roth: A Bibliography* and the annual *MLA Bibliography.*)

ALLAN, MARY. "Philip Roth: When She Was Good She Was Horrid."
The Necessary Blankness: Women in Major Fiction of the Sixties.
Urbana: The University of Illinois Press, 1976, pp. 70–96. Discusses
Roth's women characters through *Portnoy's Complaint.*

BETTELHEIM, BRUNO. "Portnoy Psychoanalyzed," *Midstream* 15 (June–July 1969): 3–10. "Therapy notes found in the files of Dr. O. Spielvogel" interpret the six sections of the novel from a psychoanalytic point of view.

CHEUSE, ALAN. "A World Without Realists." *Studies on the Left* 4 (Spring 1964): 68–82. Argues that Roth is guilty in *Letting Go* of the very flight from social reality he complained of in "Writing American Fiction" and contrasts Roth's ability to capture American reality with Thomas Pynchon's in *V.*

COOPERMAN, STANLEY. "Philip Roth: 'Old Jacob's Eye' with a Squint." *Twentieth-Century Literature* 19 (July 1973): 203–16. A survey of Roth's fiction through *Portnoy* which argues that Roth is best when most "Jewish"—i.e., most concerned with conflicting moral imperatives, as in *Letting Go*. Good example of arguments made by those critics who prefer the "early" Roth.

CREWS, FREDERICK. "Uplift," *New York Review of Books*, November 16, 1972, pp. 18–20. One of the most interesting reviews of *The Breast* which characterizes it as a work of "high seriousness."

DEER, IRVING and HARRIET. "Philip Roth and the Crisis in American Fiction." *Minnesota Review* 6 (No. 4, 1966): 353–60. Roth's first two books show him working beyond alienation to an earned affirmation and epitomize the possibilities open to the American writer.

DETWEILER, ROBERT. "Philip Roth and the Test of the Dialogic Life." *Four Spiritual Crises in Mid-Century American Fiction*. Gainesville: University of Florida Monographs #14, 1963, pp. 25–35. *Letting Go* is viewed in the context of Martin Buber's concept of personal and superpersonal encounter.

DICKSTEIN, MORRIS. "Black Humor and History: The Early Sixties." *Gates of Eden—American Culture in the Sixties*. New York: Basic Books, 1977, pp. 91–127. Roth is discussed as an example of the "verbal black humorist."

DONALDSON, SCOTT. "Philip Roth: The Meanings of *Letting Go*." *Contemporary Literature* 11 (Winter 1970): 21–35. The best analysis of *Letting Go* published to date approaches it as an outgrowth of the ideas expressed in "Writing American Fiction."

FRIEDMAN, ALAN WARREN. "The Jew's Complaint in Recent American Fiction: Beyond Exodus and Still in the Wilderness." *Southern Review* 8 (Fall 1972): 41–59. *Portnoy* is central to this discussion of contemporary Jewish fiction and the theme of the ambiguous role of intellect in Jewish culture.

GOLDBERG, MARK F. "Books: The Jew as Lover." *National Jewish Monthly*, November 1969, pp. 64–67. David Levinsky, Moses Herzog, and Portnoy are examined as representative examples of three generations of the Jew as lover.

GOLDMAN, ALBERT. "Wild Blue Shocker: *Portnoy's Complaint*." *Life*,

February 7, 1969, pp. 56B–65. A biographical and critical portrait of Roth and his work through *Portnoy*.

GUTTMAN, ALLEN. "Philip Roth and the Rabbis." *The Jewish Writer in America—Assimilation and the Crisis of Identity.* New York: Oxford University Press, 1973, pp. 64–76. A survey of the fiction through *Portnoy* from the perspective of the conflict between Jewish tradition and assimilation, which sees *Portnoy* as a "joke about Jewish jokes" and a "terminus" to satires of assimilation.

HOCHMAN, BARUCH. "Child and Man in Philip Roth." *Midstream* 13 (December 1967): 68–76. Roth's fiction (through "Whacking Off") focuses on characters bursting with fury and forces us to adopt a child's-eye view of the world.

HOWE, IRVING. "Philip Roth Reconsidered." *Commentary,* December 1972, pp. 69–77. A ferocious attack on Roth's work since *Goodbye, Columbus* for its sense of superiority, its oversimplification, and its fundamental "vulgarity."

ISAAC, DAN. "In Defense of Philip Roth." *Chicago Review* 17 (Fall/Winter 1964): 84–96. A defense by a rabbi against rabbinical charges of self-hatred and anti-Semitism leveled at Roth which praises "Writing About Jews" and suggests that rabbis use Roth's stories as sermon texts.

ISRAEL, CHARLES M. "The Fractured Hero of Roth's *Goodbye, Columbus.*" *Critique: Studies in Modern Fiction* 16 (December 1974): 5–11. The struggle in *Goodbye, Columbus* is to achieve the "coordinated soul," to reconcile the contradictions within so that Neil may perform the "ideal hero-deed" and face his true nature.

KAZIN, ALFRED. "The Earthly City of the Jews." *Bright Book of Life.* Boston: Atlantic, Little, Brown and Company, 1973, pp. 144–49. Discussion of Roth's "toughness" and "moral lucidity."

LANDIS, JOSEPH. "The Sadness of Philip Roth: An Interim Report." *Massachusetts Review* 3 (Winter 1962): 259–68. Study of the stories in *Goodbye, Columbus* as evidence that under the ferocity of Roth's satire there is a terrible sadness at the limitations of "normalcy."

MONAGHAN, DAVID. *"The Great American Novel and My Life as a Man*: An Assessment of Philip Roth's Achievement." *International Fiction Review* 2 (1975): 113–20. Roth's persistent theme is lack of commitment, and his search for an appropriate American literary mode to convey it has led him to popular forms such as pulp fiction and the soap opera.

MUDRICK, MARVIN. "Who Killed Herzog? or Three American Novelists." *University of Denver Quarterly* 1 (1966): 61–97. This study of Bellow, Malamud, and Roth as "the most intelligent and most considerable American novelists since World War II" discusses *Goodbye, Columbus* and *Letting Go*.

NELSON, GERALD B. "Neil Klugman." *Ten Versions of America.* New

York: Alfred A. Knopf, 1972, pp. 147–62. Treats Neil as a modern Gulliver exhibiting "nasty condescension" and views the book's humor as "bitter, not sympathetic."

PODHORETZ, NORMAN. "Laureate of the New Class." *Commentary*, December 1972, p. 4. Companion piece to Howe's essay in the same issue, which argues that Roth's work has deteriorated since *Goodbye, Columbus* and that his popularity is due to the fact that an educated audience shares his view that "Americans are disgusting people."

RABAN, JONATHAN. "The New Philip Roth." *Novel* 2 (Winter 1969): 153–63. One of the best articles on Roth, this surveys his work through "Civilization and Its Discontents" to argue that he has consistently questioned the relationship between formal structures and the disarray of modern life and has created a series of unattainable fictions. In the excerpts from *Portnoy's Complaint*, Raban finds that Roth seems to have knit the strands of his work into a "complete, wholly achieved" fiction.

SABISTON, ELIZABETH. "A New Fable for Critics: Philip Roth's *The Breast*." *International Fiction Review* 2 (1975): 27–34. In *The Breast* Roth deliberately set a trap for critics and we are forced to react to it. Roth uses a metaphor of oral-sexual gratification to remind us that the aim of art is pleasure and creates erogenous zones in his text.

SHECHNER, MARK. "Philip Roth." *Partisan Review* 41 (Fall 1974): 410–27. A fascinating psychological reading of Roth's fiction through *My Life as a Man* focusing on fathers, sons, and manhood.

SHEED, WILFRED. "Howe's Complaint." *New York Times Book Review*, May 6, 1973, p. 2. A defense of Roth against Howe's charges of vulgarity which argues that Roth has tried every way he knows to "get his Panza and Quixote onto the same horse," and describes his career as both "honorable and adventurous."

SIEGEL, BEN. "The Myths of Summer: Philip Roth's *The Great American Novel*." *Contemporary Literature* 17 (Spring 1976): 171–90. This excellent commentary on Roth's comic fiction after *Portnoy* insists that Roth should be viewed as a highly conscious and moralistic satirist, in spite of his disclaimers about satiric intent. It also discusses Roth's baseball mythology and his use of commentary on his fiction within the fiction itself.

SOLOTAROFF, THEODORE. "The Journey of Philip Roth." *Atlantic*, April 1969, pp. 64–72. The most comprehensive biographical sketch of Roth and the persistent themes of his work through *Portnoy's Complaint*, by a friend and editor.

―――. "Philip Roth and the Jewish Moralists." *Chicago Review* 13 (Winter 1959): 87–99. This first article about Roth in a literary quarterly compares and contrasts Roth with Bellow and Malamud and argues that, far from being anti-Semitic or self-hating, Roth's satire in *Goodbye, Columbus* displays the "traditional Jewish banner of sentiment and humaneness and personal responsibility."

TANNER, TONY. "Fictionalized Recall—or 'The Settling of Scores! The Pursuit of Dreams!' " *City of Words: American Fiction 1950-1970.* New York: Harper and Row, 1971, pp. 295-321. Kafka's *Letter to His Father* and "The Judgment," Lenny Bruce's monologues, and *Herzog* are cited as precedents for *Portnoy.* The two impulses in Roth's work are identified as observation of the social scene and the desire to understand the obsessed self.

VANDERBILT, KERMIT. "Writers of the Troubled Sixties." *Nation,* December 17, 1973, pp. 661-65. A survey of "eight serious books of recent years that were also bestsellers" which discusses *Our Gang.*

WISSE, RUTH. "Requiem in Several Voices." *The Schlemiel as Modern Hero.* Chicago: University of Chicago Press, 1971, pp. 118-23. Sees *Portnoy* as a reaction to the genre of schlemiel writings, which reverses the process of the Jewish joke and, instead of turning pain *into* laughter, exposes the pain lurking *beneath* the laughter.

WOLFF, GEOFFREY. "Beyond Portnoy," *Newsweek,* August 3, 1970, pp. 66-67. A brilliant analysis of "On the Air" and its importance to the development of Roth's work.

Index